Mediterranean
Cruising
Handbook

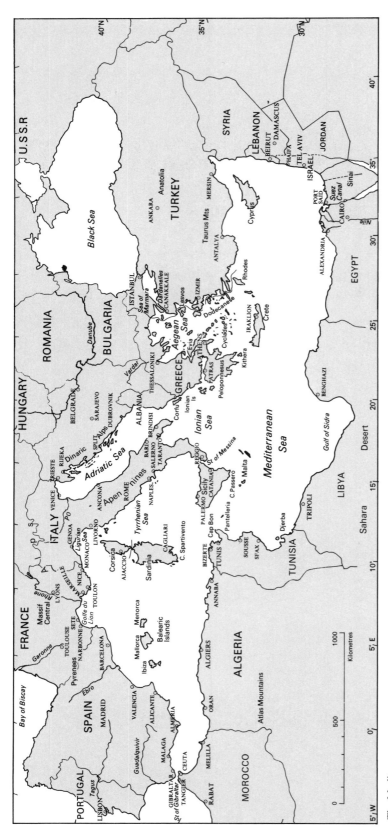

The Mediterranean

Mediterranean Cruising Handbook

ROD HEIKELL

Imray Laurie Norie & Wilson Ltd

Published by
Imray, Laurie, Norie & Wilson Ltd
Wych House, St. Ives, Huntingdon,
Cambridgeshire PE17 4BT. England

© Rod Heikell 1990
  1st edition 1985
  2nd edition 1988
  3rd edition 1990

British Library Cataloguing in Publication Data

Heikell, Rod *1948–*
Mediterranean cruising handbook – 3rd ed.
1. Mediterranean Sea. Coastal waters. Pilots' guides
I. Title
623.89′291638

ISBN 0 85288 148 7

CAUTION

Whilst every care has been taken to ensure accuracy, neither the Publishers nor the Author will
hold themselves responsible for errors, omissions
or alterations in this publication. They will at all
times be grateful to receive information which
tends to the improvement of the work.

Printed at The Bath Press, Avon

Contents

ACKNOWLEDGEMENTS

I would like to thank the following people for their help with this book: Bridgit Marsh, Helen Penney, Richard Wilson, Sharon Ho, Richard Seabrook, Joe and Bonnie, Mike and Diana Harper, Nancy and Andreas Larson, Neville Bulpitt, David and Pat Nesbit, Ion Voyantis and Smiley, Robin and Netia Piercy.

My thanks to the following organisations for information: The tourist offices of Spain, France, Italy, Malta, Yugoslavia, Greece, Turkey, Cyprus, Egypt, Tunisia and Morocco. The Cruising Association, Marina Bay in Gibraltar, Manoel Island boatyard in Malta.

My thanks to all of the staff of Imrays and especially to William Wilson for the many hours he put into reading and checking the manuscript and to Andrea Plum who drew most of the plans.

Fiskardo, Greece

Preface

In 1978 I wrote an article for a yachting magazine which briefly detailed the sort of things to expect in a number of countries around the Mediterranean. It touched on formalities, what kind of harbours and anchorages to expect, the prevailing winds, facilities for repair and maintenance, provisioning: the sort of information you quickly acquire from your own and other's experience once you have arrived in a country, but about which you have little or no idea before that. For several years afterwards I kept encountering people who showed me a sheaf of tatty pages ripped out of the yachting magazine. My article had been invaluable and why didn't I expand on it.

In many ways this book is an expansion of that article. Four years ago I began gathering the information for it not realising it would take this long to acquire and shape into a useful form. The bulk of the information is first hand but any I have obtained second-hand has been checked by friends who do have detailed first-hand experience of the country.

The introductory chapters dealing with the type of yacht best suited to Mediterranean conditions and the equipment to put in or on it are not intended to be an exhaustive treatise on the matter. They are an assorted bag of tips and hints gleaned from my own and other's experience. I forget that what I now take for granted on a yacht in the Mediterranean is not necessarily common knowledge to those preparing to come for the first time. Simple things like the choice of anchor can be difficult to someone who habitually noses into a finger berth in a marina or picks up a mooring. Berthing stern-to a quay in a cross-wind is still a daunting problem to those of us who have done it often.

Every now and again someone will ask me why I still cruise around the Mediterranean. Don't I get sick of the same countries, the same cruising grounds, the hundreds of yachts cluttering up the place? Some of the answers are in this book. The Mediterranean is surrounded by three continents and seventeen countries steeped in nearly three millennia of recorded history. We can only hope to see a tenth part of the sea and the land in a lifetime and most of us will see much less. The regional variations in any one country provide a feast for the senses. And while parts of the Mediterranean are crowded, the other larger part is not. One of the joys of cruising in the Mediterranean is to pull into a marina one day and the next day to find a beautiful deserted anchorage a short distance away.

For me the Mediterranean offers a proximity of different cultures, religions, cuisine, architecture, geography, history — all of the things included in the now much used phrase 'local colour'. It offers cruising grounds of great variety and beauty. For those like myself who are potterers and gunk-holders, whose sailing ambitions do not include being trapped in pack-ice, riding out a hurricane, or breaking yet another record, the Mediterranean is a sea unparalleled elsewhere.

Rod Heikell
Poole 1985

PREFACE TO THE SECOND EDITION

Since the publication of *Mediterranean Cruising Handbook* I have thought of extra bits and pieces that should have gone into the first edition and these I have incorporated into the second edition. Minor corrections to some of the information in the country by country sections have also been made, but basically this is the same book except it is bigger and better with extra added photos and diagrams.

One criticism that has been levelled at the book is that I do not get down to the actual nitty gritty of exactly what it costs to live and keep a boat in the Mediterranean. The reason for this is very simple and I allude to some of the reasons for this in the first section of the book. The cost of living depends to a large extent on your needs and wants – some people can't live without all sorts of expensive items whereas others survive on very little. There are other reasons as well. The strength of the currency of the country you are in can fluctuate dramatically making a country more or less expensive depending on which way it goes. Over the last three years, of three of the common hard currencies, the dollar, deutschmark, and sterling, the deutschmark has kept its value better than the other two and goes further in any of the Mediterranean countries than it did several years ago. Now if you have Japanese yen . . . New taxes in a country can increase the cost of living such as the introduction of value added tax in Turkey and Greece.

In a similar vein the running costs of a boat in the Mediterranean depend on you and your needs and skills. If you keep a boat in a marina most of the time, the cost of cruising is that much more than if you use fishing harbours or anchor in a bay somewhere. If you contract to have maintenance and refit work done by someone else, it costs – do the work or some of it yourself and costs plummet. I put all new standing rigging on *Tetranora* last year and by doing it myself, saved several hundred pounds. Most maintenance and a lot of refit work is within the scope of most of us, no matter how inexpert in the art and science of boat technology we are. Moreover doing your own maintenance gets you closer to the boat and gear and how it works, or doesn't, and it is in that boat and gear that you put your trust in good weather and bad.

Numerous people supplied information, but in particular I would like to thank Austen Whitten and Patricia Sadleir of S.Y. *Discovery II* for information on Monaco and Neville Bulpitt for detective work on radio beacons, and information on boatsharing.

Rod Heikell
London 1987

PREFACE TO THE THIRD EDITION

Like the second edition, this third edition of *Mediterranean Cruising Handbook* has been expanded with extra information and a few new sections, though basically it remains the same book. Part I has been corrected where necessary and small sections added on subjects like the boat's tool kit, Loran C, berthing in marinas, consulate services abroad, seasickness, winterising an engine and the like. Part II on the individual countries has been corrected and amended and I have added some plans where I thought it useful.

For the information on Israel my thanks to Amos Raviv, a local yachtsman who spent some time researching his home coast. For the corrected section on the Maghreb countries, Tunisia, Algeria and Morocco, my thanks to Hans van Rijn who has recently written a pilot on the area for the RCC Pilotage Foundation. My thanks also to John Farrugia and Charles Ellul in Malta, Don Bamford of S.Y. *Foudroyant*, and to Joe Charlton in Levkas for practical boat information learned doing it rather than from books.

Rod Heikell
Martigues, France 1990

For my Mother and for Shirley.

I GENERAL

But do not hurry the journey at all.
Better that it should last many years;
Be quite old when you anchor at the island,
Rich with all you have gained on the way.

Ithaca. Cavafy transl. by John Mavrogordato

The Yacht

There is no such beast as the perfect cruising yacht; the pros and cons of what comes close to the proper little ship could and frequently do fill a good sized book. But then the contents of that book must be measured off against the others on the subject and your own personal experience in order to arrive at some sort of overall conclusion. Fortunately most of us are saved from dwelling too long on the matter by the simple constraints of our wallets and the benevolence or otherwise of the bank manager. Or, it may be that you already have a yacht that must perforce do the job.

The first yacht I sailed down to the Mediterranean was a twenty foot early JOG (Junior Offshore Group) boat that looked all of fifteen foot long. Hard chine plywood construction, moderate fin and a spade rudder, three-quarter rig, powered by a four horsepower Stuart Turner that once ran a water-pump in 1944, sitting headroom only, narrow gutted and hard-mouthed: *Roulette* was aptly named but she delivered me safely to Greece. My

Tetranora: all the virtues and vices of boats of her vintage

second boat was a modern twenty-eight foot fin and skeg glassfibre sloop bought new from the factory where I learned that a new boat can be as much of a problem as a second hand one. *Fiddlers Green* was a tear-drop shape when viewed from above with a high freeboard, wedge-shaped coachroof, numerous berths and boasted luxuries like a permanent chart table, shower, refrigerator, large galley and double berth. I sailed her down to Greece in a rather nasty winter and together we clocked up around 9,000 miles before I sold her in Athens. There I found *Tetranora,* sitting neglected in the marina: a thirty-one foot strip-planked boat designed and built in 1962 by Cheverton in the Isle of Wight, she weighs nearly twice as much as *Fiddlers Green.* By today's standards of narrow beam, long keeled, with a fine entry and a barn-door transom, she is typical of her era with all the vices and virtues of the period.

The general guidelines that follow are no attempt to define that mythical beast, the perfect cruising yacht, but rather the yacht most suited to Mediterranean cruising. A yacht designed as a world-girdling little ship may or may not be suitable for the purpose as there are factors particular to the Mediterranean that in themselves impose design criteria on a vessel. So if you are considering the purchase of a yacht in which to cruise around the Mediterranean the following points should be borne in mind: on the other hand if you already own a yacht do not be deterred from setting out as many, myself included, have done before in quite unsuitable but not unsafe craft.

SIZE

The overall size of your yacht is of course dependent on your financial situation, yet I must say here that it is possible to buy a yacht which is too hefty to sail. In general I believe that a medium displacement yacht of forty-five feet or more can become a liability that forever causes you apprehension. It will for most of the time be sailed without its best spread of canvas in case the wind gets up; the anchor and chain will be too hefty to get up by hand if the electric anchor winch breaks down; above and below decks the gear is out of the realm of the make-shift repair category and above all berthing becomes a complicated affair. With a yacht of this size, once the wind has taken charge when manoeuvring in a confined space, the consequences can be catastrophic. That you can have a seaworthy craft fit to voyage anywhere, as well as a comfortable and gracious home, in a yacht between thirty and forty-five feet cannot be disputed, but whether you can competently and comfortably handle a fifty footer (or bigger) without extra crew is open to question. Labour saving devices may make it easy to hoist sail and haul anchor but the sheer size of the craft has moved beyond the comfortable capabilities of a short-handed crew. If you rely on your family for crew remember that sons and daughters may want to go their own way some of the time and eventually leave for good. Consequently a family yacht should be well within the capabilities of a husband and wife.

Remember this: sailing to and around the Mediterranean is not the same as sailing around the world with a few stop-overs. In the Mediterranean you will spend a large part of your time in a harbour of some sort and that means you must be able to berth your yacht quietly and efficiently if it is not all going to turn into a nightmare. Many large yachts with small crews spend most of their time in one place, it being all too much effort to take the boat out sailing for a day or two. The fun of sailing has been eclipsed by a floating home that can only occasionally go sailing.

A concluding thought, instead of buying the largest yacht you can afford why not buy a slightly smaller more manageable yacht and use the money saved for renting an apartment or small house in whatever country you are in? In most of the Mediterranean countries, during the off-season accommodation can be cheaply obtained (with a bit of haggling) and you can leave the boat free for a refit. In this way you can have the best of both worlds.

SAILERS AND MOTOR-SAILERS

It is common to hear from those who cruise regularly in the Mediterranean that it either blows too much or too little so that ideally you need a motor-sailer. Personally I think the constancy or otherwise of winds in the area does not vary so radically from many other cruising grounds and a comparison of wind strengths from the Admiralty tables

appears to bear this out. In any case the sailer versus motor-sailer argument is a dead one in this age of light and compact marine diesels. A motor-sailer was once defined as a yacht which could motor faster to windward than it could sail; most modern production yachts fitted with light powerful diesels have this attribute and have consequently become, by definition, motor-sailers. The times have long gone when a thirty or forty foot yacht was fitted with a spiteful four or eight horsepower petrol engine that was used, when it could be coaxed into life, to get in and out of harbour. It is not uncommon now for a thirty-five foot yacht to have a twenty to thirty horsepower motor and many have considerably more powerful engines.

The term motor-sailer is also generally accepted to mean that you have a sheltered steering position where you can 'drive' out of the wind, spray and rain. While being all in favour of sheltered steering positions, on every yacht there should be an outside steering position as well. This is not just for visibility when manoeuvring under power (so you don't have to stick your head out of a hatch or door like a train-driver) but also because it can get very stuffy in an enclosed wheel house no matter how many hatches you have. A friend who has a converted Danish fishing boat with a wheelhouse is selling it to get a boat with an outside cockpit; 'Like being in a glasshouse in the Sahara', is his verdict on enclosed steering positions.

Whether the yacht you have is classified as a sailer or a motor-sailer, (the classification is further confused by pilot-house versions of yachts), you will in any case need a reliable diesel with sufficient power to bash into the short choppy seas of the Mediterranean and to power you economically through the calms. Looking back over the passage times for my first yacht which did not have a reliable engine, I find them to be agonisingly slow, as most over 100 miles were done at an average of 1½-2 knots — enough said, unless you are exceptionally patient.

FIN KEEL OR LONG KEEL

I can say at the start that you do not need bilge keels (or twin keels) in the virtually non-tidal waters of the Mediterranean. In fact they can be a positive nuisance if you run aground as getting two keels out of the mud is a good deal more difficult than getting one out when there is no tide to help you.

The advantage of long keeled medium to heavy displacement yachts are well known. A long keeled yacht which is a steady plodder can be kept sailing faster and more comfortably in all weather than can an extreme fin keeled type. A yacht which is skittish and frisky in a sea is tiring to sail for any length of time and in practice passage times for a short-handed crew are no faster than for a heavier more placid boat. I once delivered an extreme IOR derived half-tonner which broached continuously in anything over a Force 5 obliging me to reduce sail to a ludicrously small amount in order to maintain a modicum of control. With a full crew I could have sailed her fast, but short-handed all I prayed for were calms so that I could motor to my destination. Exhaustion in a small crew from the demanding task of sailing some IOR derived yachts can easily lead to errors which inevitably multiply and may lead to disaster. I should add here the rider that many old plodders are as much of a pain to sail as the newer breed of cruiser-racers; they didn't always get it right on older yachts and they never got all of it right.

But in the Mediterranean the less extreme modern fin keel yachts have some significant advantages. For a start your passages are often quite short and so the plodding comfort of a traditional long keeled yacht is not so important. Moreover once you arrive in harbour the ability of a fin keeled yacht to turn on the proverbial sixpence puts it at a decided advantage. In many Mediter-ranean harbours you must manoeuvre into tight spots and going astern with a fin keeled yacht is considerably easier than with long keel yachts which have a mind of their own when going astern.

Probably the best compromise is a long fin keel and skeg so that you have the steadiness and tracking ability of a long keel yacht and one which is not an utter cow when going astern and which is easily manoeuvred in tight corners. Some thought should be given to an anti-snag device so that floating lines, semi-submerged plastic rubbish and the like, do not get caught between the keel and the skeg or worse become entangled with the propeller. A long keel yacht is less likely to pick up warps and other rubbish than the increasingly common sail-drives and 'P'-bracket arrangements on fin and skeg yachts. Some yachts have a solid strap between the keel and skeg to prevent stray rubbish getting to the propeller but of course this sort of anti-snag device cannot be fitted to the more extreme fin and skeg or unsupported rudder configurations. Certainly I have fewer problems with a long keel than I previously experienced with a fin and skeg yacht. And in our plastic orientated world it is a sad fact that more and more plastic rubbish finds its way into the sea and around propellers.

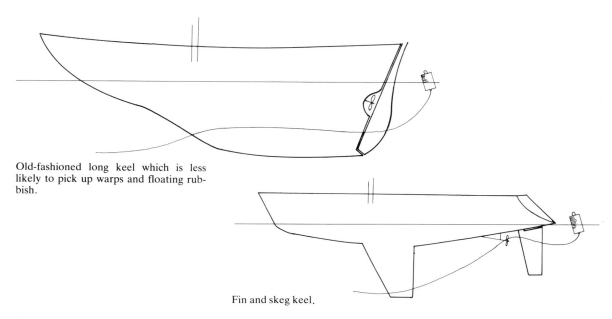

Old-fashioned long keel which is less likely to pick up warps and floating rubbish.

Fin and skeg keel.

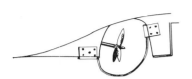

The propeller should be protected against stray lines in the water.

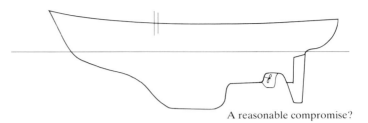

A reasonable compromise?

WEIGHT

On a trip to the Mediterranean you will want to take a considerable amount of stores and a large number of spares for everything. It is astounding just how much can be stowed on a yacht when you see it all sitting on the quay; it seems inconceivable that it will ever fit into the space available but fit it nearly always does. On a light displacement yacht and more spectacularly on multihulls and planing power boats the additional weight of stores and spares can drastically affect performance. A friend who skippers a fifty foot power boat now finds that he is so burdened with additional equipment (air-conditioning, ice-maker, deep freeze, a larger generator to run all the extras, a tender and large outboard) that he must empty one of his water tanks so that he can get the boat planing. The performance of a multihull is critical in this respect and I have yet to meet the owner of a cruising multihull who will not tell me that he has a 'go fast' machine if only he could get rid of half the gear on board. Overloading a small multihull with cruising gear can wipe out any speed advantages it may have.

On monohulls the weight of gear you must take on board makes a nonsense of those production craft where weight has been kept to a minimum in their construction; not only do you negate the weight-saving that has gone on in the building process, but worse, you put the weight back in all the wrong places. For medium-to-heavy displacement yachts the additional weight of stores and spares taken on does not disadvantage the craft to anything like the proportions it does on light displacement craft. It is small wonder that the owner of a new production IOR type yacht is sometimes disappointed in its performance: the construction process adds weight because the manufacturer cannot afford to put the original exotic and expensive materials into the production model. Extra ballast has to be added to counteract the heavier weight atop and to make the yacht stiffer. The new owner invariably adds equipment, sometimes putting a radar scanner half way up what was in the original design a weight-saving multi-spreader mast and if he wants to go cruising then stores and spares come on board to further overload his yacht. It is an interesting thought that a 6 ton 30 foot yacht with 2 tons of gear and stores aboard is only one third as heavy again. Whereas a 2½ ton 30 foot yacht will be nearly twice as heavy once the same amount of equipment is added. It is not difficult to guess which yacht will lose most performance when in cruising trim. I must say I am always impressed with the space in some of these new exceptionally beamy craft where two double quarter berth cabins, galley and chart table, saloon, heads and hanging locker and forward double cabin have been squeezed into thirty-five feet, but it is a mistake to equate load-carrying ability with space in many IOR-derived yachts unless the load is in the form of moving human ballast that can sit along the weather rail to properly trim the yacht.

If you are buying a light displacement monohull or a multihull then it is best to think of these as roomy alternatives to other craft rather than as 'go-fast' machines. With a small crew and the gear you bring aboard you will negate most of the performance advantages you perhaps experienced on a demonstration sail when the boat was in an unloaded condition.

There is another side to the coin. Given that you will be spending up to eighty percent of your time at anchor or in a harbour, then the gain in space in a multihull or beamy IOR derived yacht can be more important than the more limited space in a robust but often cramped world-girdler of a similar length. You must decide where your priorities lie and what your requirements for space and amenities on board are. There is little point in having the ultimate sea-going boat if you hate every minute spent aboard it because the accommodation is cramped and inconvenient. The pros and cons of space and amenities set against the conventional wisdom that you first get a thoroughbred cruising boat and accept whatever accommodation it offers is a matter dictated by the type of cruising you intend to do. Your problem may be that you just do not know (yet) what your plans will be until you get a little experience and if this not uncommon dilemma confronts you then all I can suggest is that you buy a yacht that has a good re-sale value, then you can easily sell it if you don't like the life or if you wish to get another craft more suited to your needs and style of cruising.

CONSTRUCTION MATERIALS

In the Mediterranean the hot summers and long hours of strong sun pose special problems for some types of materials.

GRP This is the most common material and one with few maintenance problems. Dark coloured hulls fade quickly in the sun and even white hulls will discolour after several years. Dark coloured hulls also raise inside temperatures significantly over light coloured hulls. Even well insulated GRP decks with foam sandwich cores and liners drip with condensation in the winter, extra ventilation and good heating being the only solution. While minor repairs to GRP hulls are straightforward they are also tedious and often expensive because of the time involved rubbing down to get a good finish.

Whether by choice or lack of it, most people opt for GRP. Ensure that the hull of the boat you buy is stoutly laid up with adequate longitudinal stringers and stress-breakers between the bulkheads and the hull. If possible the yacht should be hauled out for at least two or three months in the winter so that the hull can dry out. This dramatically lessens the incidence of osmosis – most charter boats in the Mediterranean are hauled out for the winter and few have had to be treated for the 'plastic disease'.

Steel and aluminium Strong but not as maintenance free as some would have you believe. Many steel and aluminium boats have a number of electrodes that can be hung over the side in harbour to overcome electrolysis problems. Insulation in steel and aluminium boats must be the best possible so that condensation problems are minimised, this insulation also helps cut down on outside noises, usually the water lapping on the hull, which are amplified inside the boat. In some yachts the after and quarter-berth cabins are impossible to sleep in being something like the inside of the sound-box of a musical instrument, except that the sounds being amplified are not melodic.

Ferro Cement Like steel is not as maintenance free as some people believe. It should also be remembered that in the eastern Mediterranean you will have problems getting specialist paints for protecting the hull.

Wood Most carvel built boats open up badly for the first two years or so, but after they have acclimatised maintenance is much the same as in more northerly climes. Special attention must be paid to antifouling on wooden boats as teredo and gribble are a problem in warmer waters. Underwater epoxy putty is useful for making good any bare spots where the antifouling has been rubbed off. Varnished hulls,

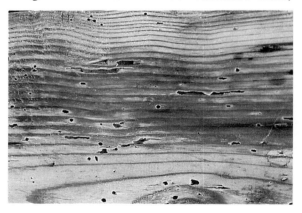

Beware the dreaded teredo with a wooden boat.

indeed varnished anything, do not last well in the sun and the proportion of brightwork on a yacht quickly diminishes in direct proportion to the number of years you spend in the Mediterranean. In a season you will have to do brightwork at least twice and in my experience none of the new ultra-violet-resistant varnishes or oils can really cope with the sunny conditions. My advice is to paint it!

DESIGN FEATURES

Most of the following features relate to all cruising boats but some are specific to a Mediterranean cruising yacht and may indeed be unsuitable in a world-girdler or for cruising in more northerly waters.

Cockpits A large cockpit is desirable because in the summer you will spend a good deal of your time there. It becomes, in effect, another room for reading, writing, eating, entertaining, sleeping or just plain relaxing. A roomy cockpit may not be ideal on a world-girdler but it is necessary in the Mediterranean for the *al fresco* life. Some large charter yachts are built with two cockpits: one for the crew to sail the yacht from and one for the charterers to relax in without the clutter of the wheel, winches, sheets and the like.

A cockpit table is an essential piece of equipment but it does not have to be complicated, in fact it should not be an elaborate affair that is a lot of trouble to put up. A small wood or pressed steel table that folds flat is quite suitable and it can be stowed in a quarter berth or cockpit locker when not in use. Some boats have a fitting in the cockpit floor so that the saloon table can be used in the cockpit which solves the storage problem neatly. Cockpit cushions add greatly to your comfort and are best made with a vinyl or other PVC backed material cover, over which canvas or other cloth can be fitted.

Cockpit stowage Many modern yachts have a single cavernous cockpit locker so that you must rearrange everything to get at the one thing you want in the bottom. Conversely many centre cockpit yachts that utilise the space under the cockpit and side-decks for living accommodation have totally inadequate stowage. Remember that amongst other things you must find a home for diesel cans, water cans, a length of hose-pipe, gas bottles or paraffin cans, engine oil, fishing tackle, not to mention fenders and warps. Good cockpit stowage is essential and two or three cockpit lockers that are not impractically deep will not be too many for the gear you will have to stow.

Access You will need good access not only to the engine but to all the other bits of equipment which may need repairs when in constant use. This includes the generator, batteries, refrigeration unit, water pumps, toilet pump, bilge pumps and the fuel and water tanks. Too many modern yachts are built around equipment so that interior joinery or moulding must be removed to effect repairs.

Modifications and maintenance After being in the Mediterranean for a season or two you will probably decide to make some additions and modifications based on your newly acquired experience and you should reckon on 5% of the

A roomy cockpit is a necessity for the *al fresco* life. Entertaining on *Fiddlers Green* with spillover!

7

value of your yacht as a conservative figure for this. In addition you will need at least 5% of the value of your yacht for maintenance, insurance and on-the-spot repairs. This must all be totted up and included in your budget.

Ventilation   You can't have too much. The galley should be near the main hatch and/or have opening ports or an extractor fan to waft away not only cooking smells but also the heat generated when cooking. Quarter berth cabins are often too stuffy for use in the summer no matter how many opening ports you have and you will be better off in the fore-cabin or an aft cabin where adequate ventilation can be arranged. In the saloon it is a good idea to install an opening hatch in the coach roof.

Alternatives

BOATSHARING

Getting a number of like-minded individuals together to form a syndicate and buy and run a boat makes a lot of sense for someone who wants a part-time boat in the Mediterranean. The initial cost of the boat and the running costs are reduced to a half or a quarter or a sixth depending on the number of people in on the scheme. There is nothing new in boatsharing, but there are some simple rules to be followed for a partnership to work successfully.

The partners   This is the key to the whole business and can make or break a boatsharing syndicate. If the partners are at each others' throats over what is happening to the boat, bickering over where it should be based for the season, and are dissatisfied with the way other partners treat the boat, it would be better to forget the whole thing. Boatsharing has to be an amiable arrangement with a fair amount of tolerance built into the partnership rather than just a business arrangement to get a percentage of time afloat. If it is not there are bound to be hiccups.

The number of people in the partnership depends on how much time you intend to spend on the boat. The ideal arrangement would be two, but four is probably the most practical with six around the maximum you want. Syndicates do exist with ten or twelve partners, but the grumbling from syndicates of this size is alway audible and the boat suffers from a group neglect because no-one feels any real responsibility

for it. All the partners should get on well and be able to afford not only the initial cost, but the running and ancillary costs as well. They should have similar sailing experience and common aims for the use the boat is to be put to. It is no use putting together someone who wants a state of the art racing machine with a retired couple who want a sedate shallow draught cruising boat to potter around creeks and bays. Nor should the partners all have school age children or everyone will want to use the boat during the school holiday period. Indeed some partners should positively prefer to cruise in the early or late season.

It is a tall order getting four or six totally like-minded people together for this sort of scheme and this is where the tolerance bit comes in. The partners in the scheme must be prepared to absorb the foibles of others in the scheme without letting anything rub them up the wrong way. Most partnerships have dissolved not because boatsharing was impractical, but because Joe didn't replace the broken crockery or Fred didn't clean the shower tray properly. Partners in a boatsharing syndicate must understand that they have a share in a common boat and therefore a share in the idiosyncrasies of the other syndicate members. Some syndicates have written rules and instructions on the operation of the yacht and its equipment, but I'm not sure whether rules and regulations are necessary if you have the right mix of partners and good communication between them. It may be that organisation which is too rigid will prevent full utilisation of the boat, and worse, take the fun out of it.

Setting up   One thing that is of the utmost importance is that no boatsharing syndicate should be set up, even between life-long friends, without a formal, written, legal document that all the partners will sign. The RYA publish a suggested form of agreement which although not intended for overseas use, provides a guide to the sort of agreement to be drawn up. The final document should detail the shares of the partners, what expenditure requires prior approval by the syndicate, and what the wider responsibilities of the partners are.

While the document should spell out the whys and wherefores of the syndicate, it should not be overly constricting on matters such as where the boat is to be based or how the boat is to be maintained. It may be that the syndicate decide to move the boat for a year or two to another country in the Mediterranean, or even that it is necessary to do so to avoid import taxes. Maintenance is something that can vary from year to year so that in one year the minimum maintenance necessary is carried out while in the next it gets a good refit.

The choice of boat for the syndicate will vary depending on the desires and wants of the partners. Most boats in boatsharing syndicates are middle of the road cruising boats between ten and twelve metres, but there is no reason why a syndicate should not get an out and out racing yacht or a thirty knot power boat. The boat should be of fibreglass construction for easy maintenance and all the gear must be reliable and sturdy stuff. The engine causes more problems than any other part of the boat and a major breakdown will not only cost the syndicate money, but can jeopardise the holidays of several of the members.

The boat should be under the flag of the country the partners live in with all the names on the registration and ownership papers. If any of the names of partners are omitted from the ownership papers, the syndicate will run into trouble in most of the countries in the Mediterranean where the authorities will assume the boat is being chartered. It is no use pleading ignorance and proferring bits of paper that show you are a syndicate member to the authorities – they want to see your name on the ownership and registration papers and if it is not there the boat will be held up, fined, or may even be impounded.

Setting up a boatsharing syndicate is not as easy as putting an advertisement in a magazine for partners, buying a boat, and sailing it down to the Mediterranean. The scheme needs planning and careful consideration over the choice of partners. Having pointed out the pitfalls I should add that boatsharing makes real sense, offering not only economy, but a group of people you are likely to become good friends with. One syndicate holds an annual ball for partners and friends. And if one syndicate doesn't work out for you, a new syndicate can be started learning from the mistakes of the previous one.

TIMESHARE

A number of years ago timeshare advertisements were splashed all over the national newspapers and glossy magazines: 'Sail your own boat in Spain, or France, or Greece, for two weeks of the year, every year, for a once only payment of 'X' number of pounds. Get a villa to go with it for two weeks of the year, for only another 'X' number of pounds.' There are fewer advertisements now, but timeshare companies are still around although often under different titles – timeshare has become syndicated yacht ownership, share yacht ownership, syndicated boatshare, or whatever mix of words can be dreamed up.

Basically timeshare is what it says it is: you buy a share in a boat for an amount of time, commonly two weeks, for a lump payment. You can then use the boat every year for that period until the boat is sold and the proceeds shared out to the timeshare customers. Prices for your option vary according to the time of year you want with high season the most expensive going down to the least expensive at the very beginning and end of the season. The timeshare company owns and maintains the boat and can sometimes arrange cheap flights.

It sounds a good idea, but in practice there are a lot of problems. Many companies went bankrupt a short time after selling most of the options, often in suspicious circumstances. After the receiver had paid off all the companies' primary debtors there was little left for the people who had put money into timeshare options – no boat, no money, and no holiday for the next ten or fifteen years.

A number of those companies still in business have not maintained the boats in good condition and you don't have to look far to find dissatisfied customers unhappy with the condition of the boat after a year or two. One of the problems was that the small print gave the company the freedom to charter the boat out for any slots that were not filled by timeshare customers and so the boat got bashed around on charter as well as being poorly maintained.

Recently an auction of unwanted timeshares took place that demonstrated how unsatisfactory some timeshare options have been. Of the timeshares up for auction only 20% sold and all of these sold at less than 50% of the original price. Many of the owners of the timeshares were selling them because they could not use the option in the allotted period, nor could they exchange the period for other dates as they had been led to believe, and with maintenance charges due every year as well as repayments on the timeshare itself, the financial burden had become too great for a very small return in the pleasure they thought they were buying. The Department of Trade and Industry has been looking into timeshares and the companies selling them, often with high pressure sale techniques, with the aim of establishing a code of practice and legal guidelines. At present their advice is not to sign anything until you are sure of what you are doing and what the whole financial commitment is, and always ensure that you have a 'cooling off' period after the initial commitment where you can change your mind and opt out of the agreement.

There are a few competently managed timeshare companies still in business and selling options on boats. If you are contemplating buying an option go out and look at the boats. Do not put up with being shown a boat 'like' the one you will get – demand to see the boat you will get. And if it all fails you can join the large number of other people who trade timeshares with one another, a trade so big that several companies have been set up to deal with reject timeshares. One timeshare owner of a boat summed up his feelings on timeshare companies like this, 'Avoid them like the plague, unless you happen to own the management company'.

A CONCLUSION – THE DESIRE TO GO

Human beings are endlessly ingenious at dreaming up reasons for choices that were never made. Far more important than acquiring the proper little ship for your voyage is the determination to go. We are all familiar with the stories of yachts equipped with every conceivable goody being lost on a reef and of the impossibly small and fragile boats that cross oceans. I have come across a kayak rigged for sailing with a vane steering gear, Webb Chile's Drascombe Lugger *Chidiock Titchborne* which he sailed from Port Said to Malta in 23 days, and a Hobie Cat and a Wayfarer that have cruised extensively in the eastern Mediterranean – not that I advocate such craft, but the power of concentrated thought and an iron determination can accomplish much more than a sluggish spirit in the 'right' boat. One of my favourite tales of fantastic endeavour concerns a certain Fred Rebell; foresaken in love, jobless in the great depression of the thirties, this extraordinary man decided to emigrate from Australia to America. Nobby Clarke tells the story in his *An Evolution of Singlehanders*:

> The American Consul gave him little encouragement: waiting lists . . . visas . . . immigration laws . . . But Rebell had overcome such difficulties when he had left his homeland, and he was not deterred.
>
> He bought a clinker-built, three-quarter decked, 18ft centre-board sloop for £20, which

In the end the desire to go is the significant factor.

was all the savings he had left. Finding a job building seaside cottages at the grossly underpaid rate of £1.50 per week, he managed to save some money — enough to buy some provisions for the projected voyage. He strengthened the boat by doubling the ribs and fixing an outside keel; he made a folding canvas hood to be fitted amidships for shelter; he packed dried food into old paraffin cans fitted with screw caps, and took on board 30 gallons of water.

He taught himself to navigate by studying in the Sydney Public Library, and then, because navigation instruments were too expensive, he actually made a sextant and a distance-run log and purchased two cheap watches which he carefully rated. His charts were all traced from an elderly atlas in the library, so ancient that later he 'discovered' islands which had been unknown when the atlas was printed.

He left Sydney on December 31, 1931 and after a great many desperate adventures, including riding out a hurricane, he arrived at Los Angeles on January 7, 1933. The voyage of nearly 9000 miles in an open boat had taken exactly one year and one week. The total cost including boat, food and everything, came to £45. He did not even have to pay for a passport, since he issued his own: 'The bearer of this passport, Fred Rebell, of no allegiance, is travelling from Sydney, Australia via Pacific Ocean, United States of America and Atlantic Ocean to his native town, Windau, in the country of Latvia. Description of bearer: Sex, male. Age: 46 years. Height 5ft 8 in. Eyes: blue. Complexion: fair. Dated this 3 March, 1932.

Equipping it

Murphy's Law: Everything that can go wrong will go wrong.
O'Reilly's Law: Murphy is an optimist.

A WORD OF CAUTION

Along with the small number of yachts that put to sea in a totally unseaworthy condition with owners who know little or nothing of seamanship or navigation, there is also the breed of owners who are too cautious by far and who believe that a yacht must be so elaborately prepared and equipped that they spend the best years of their lives doing just that only to find they would rather have been sailing in a less than perfect yacht. The most often heard comment in the Mediterranean from people cruising there is simply: 'Why didn't I do this before?' It is worth remembering that there is no final coat of varnish, no hull that does not show the wear and tear of visiting new harbours, no sail that never wears out or engine that does not need an overhaul, no electronic equipment that is the final state of the art, no navigation lesson that removes the uncertainty of a landfall, and nothing bar nothing that contains one's fears at the height of a gale, although a cup of hot soup helps. With this in mind regard the following comments with a sceptical eye and decide upon what you can reasonably afford in time and money *before* you leave, the rest you can catch up on along the way.

LISTS

I have often been accused of being a compulsive list-maker, but if you are going to get your yacht and yourself ready then you will need to draw up lists of essential jobs to do and stores and spares to buy. It gives me great satisfaction to strike items off a list either because I have done them or they have been relegated to another 'possible' list. Lists also enable you to organise your time to the best advantage and, as the day of departure draws nearer, act as a goad to your sometimes flagging spirits.

ENGINES

Most of the major manufacturers of marine engines can supply you with a recommended kit of spare parts. Obtain all the spares you think you may need before departure as they can be difficult to get hold of especially if you are venturing into the eastern Mediterranean. Not only may there be but one distributor in the major city, but often he will stock only a limited selection of spares, being primarily interested in selling new engines. Among the spares you should take include: a top-end gasket set (or at least a head gasket), several impellors for your raw water pump, spare v-belts, oil and fuel filters and a spare ignition key if you possess only one (don't leave them on the same ring). For a longer stay in the Mediterranean include another head gasket, a complete gasket set, a spare injector nozzle in a sealed packet, a water pump spares kit, a spare mechanical or electrical fuel lift pump and spare thermostat. If your engine doesn't have an efficient water trap in the fuel line then install one, as fuel in the Mediterranean is not always of the quality one might desire. An oil-changing pump (manual or electrical) is also useful if you plan to do your own minor maintenance.

All my comments thus far have been about diesels, if you have a petrol engine then my advice is to think about changing it for a small diesel. Not only is petrol prohibitively expensive in the Mediterranean countries but the chances of a lethal accident are multiplied in the high ambient temperatures the engine must work in. The risk of an explosion and fire is, I am convinced, greater from stored petrol than from gas bottles. Put some thought into stowage of the petrol for the outboard motor as well — vaporised petrol forms a lethal explosive mixture with between 1.4-7.6% of petrol vapour in a given volume of air. To your spares list remember to add sufficient items for your outboard (at least plugs, points, condenser, carburettor jet and shear pin) and generator if you have one. Also make sure your tool kit contains all the spanners you require although most tools can be bought in the Mediterranean.

If you are contemplating buying a new engine and intend to cruise extensively in the Mediterranean or elsewhere, obtain from the various manufacturers of marine engines their distribution network. When you have narrowed down your choice of engine on other criteria (cost, reliability, size, etc), then cast an eye over their spares outlets and certified workshops (noting if the latter can carry out warranty work) and listen for the hiccup from the salesman. Some of the major manufacturers have a pitiful scattering of distributors in a few countries while others will impress you with a booklet pin-pointing distributors and certified workshops in numerous countries. In Appendix IV I have listed the main distributor in each country for most of the manufacturers of marine diesels but not the network of agents and workshops (that would require an additional book).

TOOL KIT

The following list is the basic kit you should have for a longish cruise. While most tools can be bought in most of the countries around the Mediterranean, the odds are that you will need a tool you don't have when you are nowhere near a town to buy it. Make adequate provision for stowage of the tools. Most boats have two tool kits: a small one for everyday use with pliers, mole-grips, screwdrivers, adjustable spanner, insulation tape, shackle-key, old knife, *WD 40*, and any other bits and pieces commonly used; and the heavy duty tool kit which need not be instantly accessible. Stow the heavy duty tool kit in a dry place so the tools don't get rusty and if necessary wrap them in oily rags.

Engine
Complete socket set, metric or imperial depending on your engine.
Torque wrench
Set of open and/or ring spanners
Large adjustable spanner (big enough for the propeller nut and seacocks).
Medium and small adjustable spanners
Set of Allen keys
Set of screwdrivers

General
Some of the above will be used generally as well.
Medium and small mole-grips – probably the most-used tool on board.

Medium and small pliers
Pipe wrench
Claw hammer and small tack hammer
Steel tape rule
Medium wood saw and padsaw
Hacksaw and spare blades
Stanley knife
Medium wood chisel and oil stone
Small wood plane and *Surform*
Flat and ratstail files
Hand drill or rechargeable electric drill and set of drill bits.

Wotchamacallits
Insulation tape and self-amalgamating rubber tape
PTFE tape
Selection of stainless steel jubilee clips
Selection of stainless steel wood screws and self-tappers.
WD 40 and multipurpose lubricating oil
Sealing spray for electrics – *Waxoyl* is good
Waterproof grease
Silicone sealant
Assorted split pins and stainless steel seizing wire
Lengths of single and double core electrical wire
Seizing line and assorted cordage
Bungee cord
Bulldog grips
Assorted conical wooden plugs
Two part epoxy glue (*Araldite*) and general one-tube adhesive.
Gasket goo and contact adhesive
Rubber gasket material or old inner tube
Shackles of all shapes and sizes
Polyester resin and gelcoat, glass cloth and mat
Safety goggles, dust-masks, and thick plumber's gloves

Spares
Engine spares mentioned in the previous section.
Dinghy repair kit
Toilet overhaul kit or at least gaskets
Galley and bilge pump overhaul kits or at least spare gaskets.
Spare log impeller or spinner and depth sounder transducer.
Spare gas regulator and rubber gas tubing
Hatch rubber seals
Spare seacock of the most common size (commonly ¾″ or 1″).
Sail repair kit – spinnaker repair tape is essential for 'get-you-home' repairs.
Spare block(s)

Spare torch and batteries – you always drop one overboard or leave it behind at a barbecue in the summer.

ELECTRICS

If you haven't got decent batteries then get them and if you don't have two or more batteries with a changeover switch then get them too. One battery should be for engine starting and one or two, or three for domestic use. When living on board, your batteries are going to be very heavily used especially if you have all sorts of fancy electronic equipment to run and quite possibly a hi-fi and refrigerator as well. If you must have a generator to run your accumulated electrical goodies you should do your utmost to silence the engine noise and exhaust for others as well as yourself, there are too many otherwise tranquil anchorages spoilt by the spluttering of a generator that can be heard by everyone around but which to you on board the offending boat is only just audible.

Take a good supply of spare fuses and bulbs for all your lights (interior and navigation lights) as they can be surprisingly difficult to find. For some reason the manufacturers of interior lights, navigation lights, anchor lights, compass lights and so on use a variety of different sizes and types of bulbs. Likewise fuses are not standard either. Add in some spare switches and cable for basic electrical repairs even if it has to be of the 'get-you-home' type.

Many boats are now fitting 'black box' regulators to overrule the standard regulator on the alternators most marine engines are fitted with. Normally the standard regulator cuts down to a trickle charge after 10 or 15 minutes of charging. The 'black box' regulator monitors the charge in the battery and keeps the input from the alternator at a higher rate until the batteries are charged. The people I have talked to seem pleased with the results of fitting one of these 'black boxes' and the experts have given them their blessing. It is worthwhile purchasing a trickle-charger for when you are connected up to shore-power so that batteries stay topped up. Don't forget to arrange to have batteries trickle-charged through the winter if laying up ashore.

SAILS

Get any new sails you need before you leave as the cost of sails and sail repairs increases in direct proportion to the distance you sail in the Mediterranean and the quality is not always the best. In the U.K. you can shop around the numerous sail-makers and get exactly what you want. Whereas the cost of freighting out bulky sails (and for that matter any other bulky or heavy item) can add a substantial amount to the initial price tag. Then you must extract it from the tenacious grasp of the customs without paying import duties — a task that can be so convoluted and aggravating that like many others you may end up paying an agent to do it for you.

If you do not have a roller reefing headsail then think about getting one. I must confess I once thought that this bit of gear was for charterers and feeble minded folk, no real sailors used these toys on proper yachts! But after a season of sailing with one on flotilla I was converted: you can have exactly the right amount of sail out at any one time; one person can increase or decrease the sail area — a big bonus for night passages when you don't have to wake another person up; the sail is stowed out of the way increasing stowage space below and cutting down on the number of sails you would otherwise have to carry; and there is the psychological advantage of knowing you can instantly remove over 50% of your sail area making your cruising a more relaxed and enjoyable affair. The gear I use has been in use on one flotilla fleet for over six years now without any major failures. Considering the use and abuse charter boats get that is probably equivalent to some twenty years hard cruising by a careful owner.

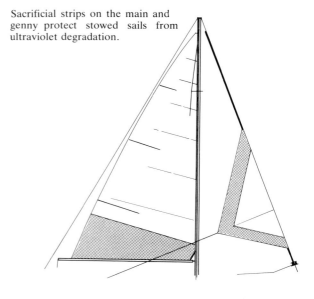

Sacrificial strips on the main and genny protect stowed sails from ultraviolet degradation.

Of roller reefing mainsails I have little experience and at present I am happy with slab (jiffy) reefing knowing I can bang a reef in early on and then reduce my foresail area from the cockpit, those owners who have luff roller reefing mains seem quite satisfied with them apart from the considerable initial cost. I have had my new mainsail cut without battens (thereby reducing the area slightly since it cannot now have a roach) as the batten pockets are a common place for sail damage to occur. With a leach line to stop the leach fluttering the sail does not set badly and probably affects my performance little given all the other factors which slow an overloaded cruising boat down. My sail is also made of new ultra-violet proof terylene which if not totally ultra-violet proof (the sailmaker sceptically reckoned on an additional 5% protection) is at least soft and pleasant to use from new. Because of the greater incidence of ultra-violet in the Mediterranean a mainsail cover should be used at all times and a roller reefing foresail should have a sacrificial strip protecting it when furled.

With a roller reefing headsail you need two other foresails: a storm jib and a cruising chute or spinnaker. The storm jib can have a wire bolt rope and be winched up tight from a strong point on the deck. If you have a cutter rig then you have the best of all possible worlds since in heavy weather you can simply roll up the foresail and plod along under reefed staysail. Add a cruising chute to your wardrobe and you're ready for anything the Mediterranean will throw at you.

AWNINGS

Your awning, an essential piece of equipment in the hot summer months, should be constructed to cover the cockpit and main hatch and must be quickly and simply erected when you need it. Anything that is complicated will sit in a locker most of the time while you sizzle outside wondering if it is worthwhile going through all the trouble of putting it up. For long stays in harbour a second awning to cover the cabin, front hatch and after cabin is a good idea. It should be constructed to be a comfortable height above the cockpit and side curtains (or one moveable side curtain) are useful for when the sun is low in the sky. Have the awning made from dark coloured canvas as light colours cause an uncomfortable glare and nylon or terylene materials flap and crack annoyingly in the slightest breeze.

A permanent awning under the boom is a good idea and I have constructed one on *Tetranora* (an afternoon of inspired labour and at little cost) which is simply aluminium pipe bent into shape with the awning laced to it and four aluminium struts bolted onto the top and screwed onto the cockpit coamings. A similar contraption flimsily constructed as an experimental idea on a friend's yacht has survived for five years and is now three-quarters of the way round the world. It provides welcome shade when sailing, keeps the dew off if you are sleeping in the cockpit, keeps some rain off and by the simple addition of a skin fitting in the middle it doubles as a rain catcher to augment your fresh water supply; but until you adapt to it it does restrict vision when sailing and makes getting in and out of the cockpit more difficult. With a little time, thought and money, a sophisticated affair could be constructed that rolled up on a roller like a blind from the boom gallows and attached to the spray hood. Alternatively the sort of Bimini hood American yachts use in Caribbean areas works equally well and looks good too.

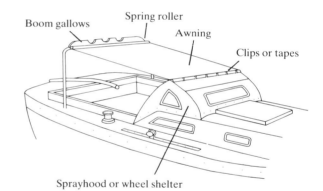

A roll-away awning.

Tetra now has a second generation permanent awning, dubbed the *African Queen*, which is simply a more sturdy version of the first. It needs to be sturdy as the supports are often used as a handhold for getting in and out of the cockpit. With side-screens it is just about another 'room', a back porch for *Tetra*.

NAVIGATION GEAR

You need far less than you might imagine (or be persuaded you need) from the array of glossy advertisements for interfaced *Satnav* or *Navstar*, on board DR computers, automatic RDF, Loran and Decca, talking echo-sounders and colour radar. You can manage quite well without any of

A permanent awning under the boom is a good idea. Note the kedge anchor stowed on the pushpit (chain is in a bucket on the aft deck) ready for berthing bows-to.

Awning design.
Note the pole at the aft end goes through the seam after awning is taken around the backstay. The pole rests on the backstay and supports the awning this way. (The pole can be your boathook.)

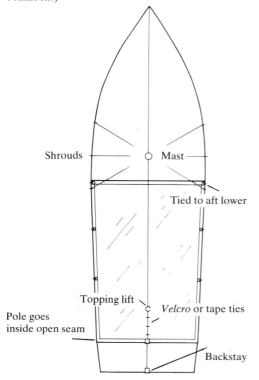

Shrouds — Mast

Tied to aft lower

Topping lift

Velcro or tape ties

Pole goes inside open seam

Backstay

An awning is an essential piece of equipment in the hot summer months.

these electronic aids relying on your compass, hand-bearing compass, (the mini-compass is by now justifiably popular or the small portable flux-gate type), log (one of the trailing types which although a nuisance to stream and retrieve are usually more accurate than through hull propellers and paddle wheels), an echo-sounder, a simple RDF set and a sextant. Even the last two pieces of equipment will fall into disuse for long periods when you are eyeball navigating along the coast or between islands.

Of course all the other bits of equipment are useful, but remember that complicated electronic aids need technicians who understand their intricacies to repair them when they go wrong and while the gap between affordability and sophisticated electronic hardware narrows, the gap between such hardware and competent repair shops widens the further you leave your home shores behind. It has become something of a stereotype to talk of the all-electric boat, harbour bound because the generator has broken down or the batteries have failed, yet there is some truth in the tale when I see large private and charter yachts spending more and more time in harbour having work done on this or that electronic installation or the power source for them. While the chip has given us affordable space-age technology still we do not have affordable space-age batteries but only clumsy and inefficient lead-acid cells that were originally patented in 1859 or the heavy and expensive nickel cadmium types. So even if your budget can include a selection of these electronic marvels do not rely totally on them or skimp on the basic tools for navigation which will probably cost less in total than a *Navstar* or whatever else you choose to pinpoint your position at the touch of a button.

When choosing electronic position finding equipment for cruising in the Mediterranean think about the following.

Satellite Systems

Satnav (Properly *Transit Satellite Navigation*). This early system relies on six operational satellites which send continuous signals to the receiver. By the Doppler effect, an apparent increase or decrease in the frequency of the waves, the receiver computes a position. With good satellite passes accuracy is given as around 200 metres, but in practice errors can be as much as a mile and sometimes more. *Satnav* is now cheap to buy and reliable, with later models automatically set up to receive the signals. The satellites will transmit until at least 1996, and probably for longer despite the introduction of the more sophisticated *Navstar* system.

Navstar (Properly the *Global Positioning System (GPS)*). This is the second generation satellite navigation system to be made fully operational for civilian users in 1991. Accuracy will be high, so high that even in the degraded civilian mode an accuracy of around 100 metres is possible with good reliability. Initially the cost of receivers will be higher than present prices for *Satnavs*, but the cost will no doubt come down with competition and increased production. *Navstar* will supplant *Satnav* and some of the hyperbolic position finding aids such as Decca and Omega.

Hyperbolic Systems

Decca With deregulation of Decca receiver production this system has recently become a cheaper and more sophisticated position finding aid. Decca coverage in the Mediterranean is restricted to the Strait of Gibraltar and part of the Spanish and Moroccan coasts and the sea area in between and it now seems unlikely that cover will be extended in the Mediterranean. Consequently a Decca set is pretty much useless for the Mediterranean.

Loran C A long range, low frequency radio aid that has been around for a while. In the Mediterranean the master station is at Catanzaro in Italy with slave stations in Spain, Lampedusa and Turkey. The accuracy of Loran C is usually within 300-500 metres although at the limits of the range, especially in the SE corner of the Mediterranean, errors can be greater.

The life of Loran C now seems likely to be extended well into the 21st century with the EC countries taking over the transmitters from the US Department of Defense in 1994. Even if Loran C lasts only until the end of the century, and the shortest life expected for the Mediterranean transmitters would be an extension by the US DOD to 1997 or 1998, it offers the lowest cost electronic position finding system at the moment. Loran C receivers have become more sophisticated and compact compared to earlier sets – the SAIT 6300 measures a minuscule 5.5H x 4.75W x 2.62″ (13.9 x 12 x 6.6cm). At present a Loran C receiver dedicated to the Mediterranean can be purchased for under £300. A Loran C receiver for world-wide reception with waypoints and interfaces can be purchased for under £500. This is cheap position finding and I have found it more than adequate in practice for the western and eastern Mediterranean on *Tetranora*. Most of the time an accuracy of better than quarter of a mile can be obtained with adequate signal reception.

Omega A very long range global system. The cost of receivers is high and I've yet to encounter a yacht using the system.

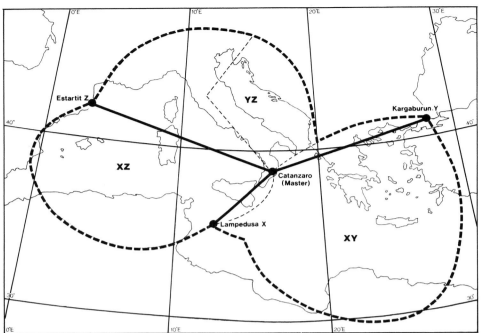

LORAN C cover in the Mediterranean

Right One of the new breed of small radars. This is the Apelco *LDR 9900* using a liquid crystal display. The unit measures 9″ x 7″ x 3¾″. The scanner is the size of a large frying pan. *Photo:* SAIT.
Far right The compact Apelco Loran receiver. *Photo:* SAIT.

RDF The cheapest form of electronic position finding equipment, but also the most difficult to use for consistent results and accuracy. RDF equipment has become more sophisticated in recent years, getting smaller and lighter, easier to use with a visual null light or meter, and digital dialling for frequencies. The Mediterranean is well supplied with radio beacons, particularly in the western Mediterranean, so given the low cost of the equipment it is worthwhile having it as a back-up to any other electronic position finding equipment, and for the impecunious it will be the primary position finding equipment. All the usual provisos on RDF bearings apply in the Mediterranean such as coastal refraction and the 'skip' effect from the ionosphere at night.

Radar Radar has long been thought of as big-ship gear. The new breed of radar equipment is considerably more sophisticated, easier to use, smaller, lighter and much cheaper. The new digital radar, as opposed to the old 'tubes', is an extremely compact bit of kit that can be usefully installed on yachts of ten metres or less. It is interesting that in an informal mini-survey I carried out amongst cruising yachts with both *Satnav* and radar, where I posed the question 'What if you could have either *Satnav* or radar, which would you choose for Mediterranean cruising?' the answers were around 80% in favour of having just radar. The reasons given basically boiled down to the fact that it offers an actual chart on which your position is pinpointed both day and night and in poor visibility, which can be compared to the chart and a course plotted to steer clear of all dangers – and all with great speed. However all stressed that in the beginning you need to get used to using radar and in this period care is needed in interpreting the picture.

Errors With the installation and use of electronic position finding equipment the following points should be kept in mind.

Mounting Electronic gear has got more robust and reliable, but even so it does not like excessive vibration and all equipment should be soft mounted on rubber bushes and mounted securely with an adequate number of fastenings. It must also be sited in a dry position because even equipment stated to be waterproof must be considered to be, at best, water resistant. Electronics and salt water just don't mix however reputable the manufacturer is.

Magnetic Interference All electronic equipment produces a magnetic field with some equipment, such as flux-gate compasses, producing

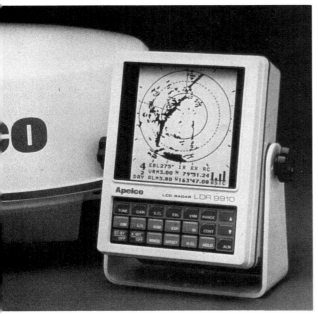

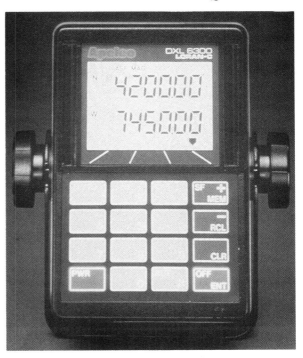

quite substantial fields. A common mistake is to mount equipment back-to-back on a bulkhead perhaps an inch or so thick. So a flux-gate compass, which should be at least three feet away from active magnetic interference or large ferrous objects, may be only inches away from say the speaker in a radio on the other side of the bulkhead. If equipment of any sort is installed or moved check all equipment in the vicinity to see it is not affected.

Radio Frequency Interference   Microprocessors, even simple ones, generate frequencies that if not contained may get into other equipment. All leads and connections to equipment should be shielded and in the installation check the effect of new equipment on the existing gear. A problem out of the control of the boat owner is radio interference from military installations, particularly the powerful listening posts in parts of the Mediterranean. On Cyprus the British run a listening post and several yachts have reported having everything wiped from electronic gear, including the time on a digital watch.

Surge   Fluctuations in the voltage and amperage supplied to equipment can cause problems, particularly to microprocessors. It is most likely to happen when starting the engine and the best policy is to simply turn all electronic gear off before you reach for the key.

Repairs   Sophisticated electronics require sophisticated repair facilities and in many parts of the Mediterranean such facilities just do not exist. While the local television repair shop will have a go at simple gear like a VHF radio or depthsounder, you cannot expect any good to come of it if you give him the *Satnav* or a radar set to tinker with. The best policy is to return it to the manufacturer who will have not only the expertise but also any specialist spare parts needed.

Accuracy   Not how accurate your position finding gear is, but how accurate the charts on which you plot a position are. Many of the charts for the Mediterranean were surveyed in the nineteenth century using astronomical methods to determine positions and it is now known that some islands, capes, headlands, rocks, and reefs are not at the positions given on the chart, mostly it is the longitude which is wrong. Most charts carry a notice stating any known discrepancies, but what is needed are new surveys and new charts comparable in accuracy with the new position finding equipment, which will obviously take many years to produce. In some cases these discrepancies can be a mile and a half and more, so that while you may know your position to within a quarter of a mile, the chart you are plotting the position on has an accuracy of just plus or minus one and a half miles. The necessity of simple coastal navigation techniques and eyeball navigation, and the usefulness of radar in this situation, should be obvious.

PILOTS AND CHARTS

If you are used to Admiralty charts then stick to them, they are still the best although German charts of the area run them to a close second. French and Italian charts are also good, though comparatively expensive. Turkish charts cover the Turkish coast well and are cheap. However, many Admiralty harbour plans are not worth bothering with, often being so out of date as to be useless and in any case failing to show many small harbours and anchorages suitable for yachts. There is a good selection of yachtsmen's pilot books for most parts of the Mediterranean which will save you money (you need a considerable folio of charts to cover what a pilot includes) and expand your cruising horizons by introducing you to harbours and anchorages not on Admiralty harbour plans. Admiralty pilots are fascinating once you have conquered the prose style but are not essential. The relevant charts and pilots for each Mediterranean area are listed in this book in the chapters covering the individual countries.

As you travel east you will encounter others travelling west and often you can swap charts and pilots with them, alternatively you may run across some yacht owners selling charts and pilots, the going rate is usually half the new price of a chart. If you need pilots then order them from England where for a small additional charge for postage and packaging you can get what you need from a chart agent or one of the big chandlers or direct from the publishers. I mention this because some of the booksellers in the Mediterranean will add an inordinate sum to the cost of the book (in Greece some booksellers were adding 300% to the cost of my pilot for the area!).

SELF STEERING GEAR AND ELECTRIC AUTOPILOTS

Your choice is between a wind-vane and an electric autopilot. I have used both and if you can afford to then I recommend you to do likewise.

Self-steering gear

The following points favour wind-vane self-steering:

They can be cheaply fabricated for some types of yachts. Mine cost £25 (Malta) and was welded up by a Maltese blacksmith and put together by me. It is agricultural (all galvanised or mild steel, wooden bearings, rubber hose and jubilee clips) but it works.

Being a mechanical system it is comparatively easy to repair wherever you are. If necessary you can probably do an emergency repair yourself.

No power is required, apart from the wind.

The gear is efficient in strong winds and seas, the power generated being proportional to the wind.

Being set to the wind the gear will not accidentally gybe a yacht if the wind changes direction.

The disadvantages are these:

A wind-vane steering gear is not cheap to buy if you cannot fabricate one yourself.

The gear will not steer a compass course and requires constant adjustment if the wind is flukey. This criticism is overrated in the discussion of the merits of which gear to buy: it takes as little time to adjust a wind-vane gear as it does to adjust an electric autopilot.

The gear is bulky and clumsy in harbour when, if moored stern-to, it may be damaged if the yacht is pushed onto the quay.

The gear will not steer the yacht if motoring and sometimes not even in light following winds. On a multihull where the apparent wind changes quickly as it accelerates and stops, wind-vane gears do not cope well.

Electric autopilots

Points in favour of an electric autopilot:

For small yachts (up to 10 metres) the initial cost is not great, but for bigger yachts the cost of a good autopilot is getting close to the cost of vane gear.

It steers a compass course and takes the tedium out of motoring and sailing in light airs when a wind-vane cannot cope.

It is compact, being hidden away in the bowels of a yacht or easily removed from the cockpit on smaller craft.

For a motor-boat it is of course the only thing and for a multi-hull it may be the only thing depending on the design.

The disadvantages are these:

It is difficult to repair an electric autopilot especially in the eastern Mediterranean. The best solution is to return it to the manufacturer as repairs by repair shops, even by the manufacturer's representative, are not always what they should be. On a small yacht one solution is to carry two of the more portable autopilots so that when one dies it can be dispatched for surgery while the other takes over.

Most auto-pilots do not cope well in strong winds and big seas although this depends to some extent on the yacht in question.

Either/Or?   As I mentioned at the beginning, if you can afford it, get both. I use my small portable autopilot for motoring and in light following winds and the wind-vane gear when sailing, in that way both gears are working at their best. The autopilot is not being asked to do a task beyond the powers of its little electrical motor and the wind-vane gear is happily working with the boat and its sails. If you must choose then it is best to get an autopilot for Mediterranean sailing, but go for a second generation microprocessor controlled job. I lost my vane steering gear when a dredger in Greece raised its cable too quickly and neatly snipped the gear off the back of *Tetra*. Since then I have relied

The speed at which an autopilot works is critical. It should be able to put the rudder across from one side to the other in 15 seconds at the most when under load. Any longer and it will not be able to match sudden movements such as the boat luffing up when you are sailing hard on the wind. And faster is better.

Yaw control and rudder gain controls allow flexibility in different wind and sea conditions. Yaw control introduces a deadband sector where the autopilot will not respond unless the course deviates, say plus or minus five degrees. Rudder gain varies the amount of rudder movement an autopilot will introduce in a given situation.

Second generation autopilots have a microprocessor sensing course deviation, rudder gain, and yaw, and from this work out the optimum response. As conditions change the microprocessor adjusts the response of the autopilot so that effectively you have a 'thinking' autopilot. Wind-vane sensors for autopilots where deviations from the wind direction activate the autopilot were ineffective and downright dangerous on early models. With second gener-

Wind-vane self-steering. *Tetranora's* cost £25: an agricultural affair welded up by a Maltese blacksmith, but it worked well.

on an Autohelm 2000 and on most points of sail it copes, though not downwind in heavy seas.

There are a number of important things to look for in an autopilot, especially if it is going to be your sole system of automatically steering the boat.

ation autopilots the information from a wind-vane is coupled to information from the helm by the microprocessor and a response made on this basis.

DODGERS AND SPRAY HOODS

A spray hood adds so much to your comfort when sailing hard that I cannot think of sailing without one — it confers some of the advantages of an enclosed wheel shelter with none of the disadvantages. Make it a sturdy affair as it is most disconcerting to grab hold of a hood to find it folding itself away while you are off balance.

Similarly dodgers give protection from the wind and spray and as with a spray hood add to your privacy whilst in harbour. If you sew pockets on the inside of the dodgers then odd pieces of rope, shoes, torch, shackle key, knife and other odds and ends can be conveniently stowed there.

VENTILATION

If you can afford air-conditioning and want to run your generator all day and night all well and good, otherwise additional cowls, perhaps a hatch over the saloon, and most importantly a wind-scoop will add to your comfort down below. A wind-scoop to funnel air down the fore-hatch or a saloon hatch can be bought or quite simply made (the designs I favour are shown below) and it works as well in harbour as when you are anchored off, without needing constant adjustment. It does not have to be very large to funnel enough air below to keep

you cool and remove cooking smells, in fact if it is too large it may cause a minor gale making it uncomfortable below and impossible to use when it is very windy. Sometimes a small 12 volt fan is recommended but they are not efficient and give nothing like the movement of air that a wind-scoop does.

A wind scoop makes life below bearable in the summer.

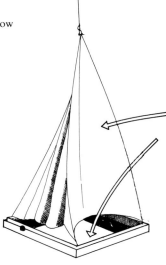

A spray hood so adds to the comfort when sailing hard that I cannot think of cruising without one now.

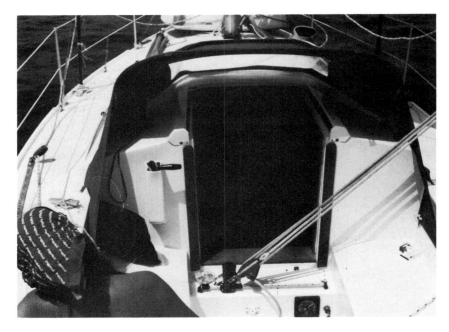

Wooden crossbar folds for stowing

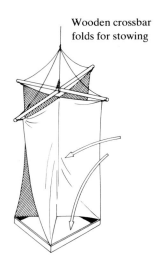

Some novel ideas have evolved for wind-scoop design. This is a giant nylon cowl.

PARAFFIN OR GAS

There was a time when paraffin was considered the only thing to use on a cruising boat, now the choice is more difficult. Gas is clean, efficient and easy to use: no pouring the methylated spirits into the cup to pre-heat the burner; no scorched deckhead and singed eyebrows; no blocked burners and gummed up jets. But paraffin burners still have some advantages. Even a small cruising yacht can carry nearly a season's supply of fuel and with adequate spares the burner will last forever. You can also use the same fuel for lighting and heating and above all it is safe. This last factor is the most persuasive as a paraffin cooker, although it will singe your eyebrows, will not explode and if the fuel should leak out it is not a real hazard.

But have the dangers of storing liquid gas on board been exaggerated? With a carefully installed system and an outboard gas locker that drains overboard, with the cook and crew trained to turn the gas off at the bottle after they have finished with it and with a regular inspection of the line and junctions (use soapy water on the junctions to see

if gas is escaping) and a gas alarm (although they do not all seem to be reliable), then liquid gas is a viable alternative. In the Mediterranean it is becoming harder all the time to find paraffin and furthermore it contains a high percentage of water and other impurities which block up the jets. In some countries (France is the worst) the cost of alcohol required to initially heat the burner is prohibitive. The types of cookers that use paraffin in a blow-torch affair to pre-heat tend to destroy the top of the burner in a short time so that spare burners must be carried. A newly designed burner that electrically pre-heats and burns under a solid element may overcome all previous problems with paraffin and provide a safe cooker that is easy to use and clean in operation, but I have yet to see one in action.

It is sensible to install a paraffin tank with a tap so that you can easily fill the cooker (and the Tilley lamp and heater). A good idea is to have the tank in a cockpit locker with the tap over the galley sink so that any paraffin that spills is easily dealt with. At any rate carry two jerry cans for paraffin so that when one is empty you can refill it whenever you come across a supply.

Camping gaz can be found throughout Europe although the difference in price for the same size cylinder is remarkable — it costs approximately twice as much in France as it does in Spain. In some parts of North Africa, *Camping gaz* is virtually unobtainable. Calor Gas bottles can be refilled everywhere in Europe but it may take longer elsewhere, alternatively you can buy adaptors to fit local bottles though this does leave you with a collection of adaptors at the end of your travels! If you plan to stay for some time in a particular country then it is worthwhile getting an adaptor and switching to the local bottles. It would be foolish to travel without two of the large (32lb) Calor type bottles and at the very least two 3kg *Camping gaz* bottles.

Would I choose paraffin or gas? I have used both throughout the length and breadth of the Mediterranean and to some extent my answer would depend on what other things I run on the same fuel. On *Tetranora* the cooker, the heater, the Tilley lamp (it provides additional heating in the winter but is too hot for the summer), a hurricane lamp for an anchor light, and the lamps in the saloon all run on paraffin. If the cooker was one of the new electric types with a solid element and it sported an oven I would be ninety per cent happy as it gives one a great feeling of independence to know you can take on fuel to run everything for a season. But I am tempted by the ease of gas and the fact that you can have a grill and an efficient oven in a compact and relatively cheap package so that if I were choosing again it would be gas. That time came with this edition of the book. My old paraffin cooker and the heater expired after seven years of faithful service, and probably another decade or more of service to previous owners. Paraffin is getting more and more difficult to find in some of the Mediterranean countries, so I bought a gas cooker for *Tetranora*. It will be interesting to see how long it lasts. I predict five years or so service looking at its construction. And how will I get on looking for *Camping gaz* on some Greek island where the local shop forgot to order replacement bottles or the supplier forgot to put them on the ferry. Perhaps I'll go back to paraffin?!

I have encountered a number of boats with all-electric systems: cooking, heating, refrigeration and hot water. Most of them have a small gas bottle and burner to make a cup of tea or coffee because it is so much bother to start the generator just to boil the kettle. Electricity may be clean and easy to use but it is not efficient where a yacht cannot regularly plug into a mains supply (which is everywhere except for Gibraltar, parts of Spain, southern France, northern Italy and Malta).

If you have a gas system check to see if it is propane or butane. While a cooker can usually run on either, the bottles you have may not be suitable for storing propane. Propane is stored at approximately three times the pressure of butane and consequently a butane bottle MUST NEVER BE FILLED WITH PROPANE. If this happens the butane bottle will vent gas if it has a pressure relief valve or may split the steel cylinder: either could be catastrophic. In hot climates like the Mediterranean a cylinder should never be more than 70% full or else when the gas expands in the heat it may vent or split the cylinder. For practical advice on the do's and don'ts of gas I recommend you get hold of a copy of Calor Gas's *Notes For Blue Water Yachtsmen* which can be obtained from: Calor Gas Ltd., Appleton Park, Slough SL3 9JG, United Kingdom.

SHOWERS

As well as for your own hygiene you need one to wash off after swimming in the salty Mediterranean which is considerably more saline than the large oceans and the adjoining Black Sea. For this reason it is a good idea to have one rigged on deck as well as one below. A deck shower can be powered by an electric pump or by a foot pump and it is best situated on the foredeck or aft right away from the cockpit. A portable shower, either the pressurised type akin to a garden spray outfit, or one of the 'sun-showers' (a black plastic bag with hose and shower rose — something you can easily construct yourself) are practical and cheap, with the latter you use only the amount of fresh water in the apparatus and you can use the former type inside or outside, adding hot water from the kettle when the weather gets cooler. If you install an electric or foot-powered shower it would be wise to install a separate fresh water tank — it is surprising how easy it can be to empty a tank, especially when you have guests taking showers as well.

HEATERS

Oh yes, you will! The summer may be hot and settled but the winter nights are cold. It occasionally snows in Marseille, Genoa, Venice, Athens and Istanbul and in Malta and the Bay of Tunis you will get freezing fog and rain that chills your bones. To keep the boat dry and yourself warm install a heater before you go. One of the drip-feed diesel types or pressurised paraffin heaters with a chimney to take away moisture and nasty smells (any of the Taylor models are good value), work well. Alternatively the diesel heaters where an electric fan blows heat through a number of ducts around the boat (the *Wallas* and *Eberspacher* have been recommended) work well, but are more expensive than 'stove' types.

A solid fuel heater is pretty much a nonsense in the Mediterranean where driftwood is difficult to find (keep it for barbecues ashore) and coal is expensive and difficult to store. Free-standing heaters such as bottled-gas fires or paraffin-wick heaters are smelly and produce so much water vapour that the interior will drip with condensation no matter how well insulated you believe your deckhead to be. A Tilley lamp will provide a good light as well as some heat although this too produces water vapour but it is useful in the early spring and late autumn when you may need some form of heating and the hatches can be left open to waft moisture away. If you are in a marina with shore power a small 220V fan heater is a useful and instant form of heating.

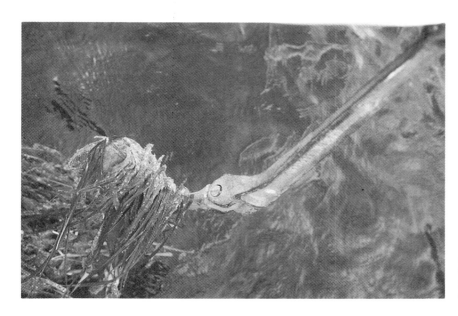

If your anchor collects a clump of weed like this it won't hold – period. Pull it up, clear the weed off and start again.

ANCHORS

The choice and defence of types of anchors belongs to that category of conversations-to-be-avoided which includes politics, religion and relations. Yet I'll venture my opinions.

Bruce My number one anchor, although one should buy a size heavier than that recommended. The Bruce is strong (drop-forged), it has no moving parts, it digs through weed easily, it holds well on a short scope, it will dig itself in when you swing on your rode, it can hook on rocks, and it breaks out easily. Its disadvantages are that it is difficult to stow on deck and it can be rendered totally useless if it picks up a rock inside its claws.

C.Q.R. A good bower anchor that is the only alternative to the Bruce. It gets through weed well and will dig itself in when you swing around it. I have heard that the sharpness of the point on a C.Q.R. critically affects its ability to dig in quickly. Its disadvantages are that the point easily picks up clumps of weed making it useless until raised and cleared and it doesn't hold well on rocks.

Delta A new anchor that looks similar to the C.Q.R. but has no moving parts. Its one-piece construction makes it strong and it is designed to turn itself to a holding position however it lands. It looks good and it will be interesting to hear how it works in the 'rough'.

Fisherman A good storm anchor but not one I would use for a main anchor — it is too easy for the rode to wrap around the flukes or stock and render it useless. The Fisherman gets through weed easily, is good on rock, and gets through soft mud to firmer stuff when all the plough types skid along the top. An excellent kedge especially when anchoring and taking a long line ashore.

Danforth My choice for a kedge. A light Danforth is a good anchor for mooring bows-to. It digs in well and has good holding power in a straight line. It is not a good bower anchor as the rode can easily foul the flukes as you swing about it.

Grapnel types Useful for mountain climbing and as a dinghy anchor. I have never thought much of either the folding grapnel anchors or the large grapnels common in the eastern Mediterranean, they are useful only on rocky bottoms and in the canals.

Ideally an 8 ton yacht should carry a 15kg Bruce or a C.Q.R., a 12kg Fisherman and an 8kg Danforth. The Bruce or C.Q.R. would be on all 5/16″ (minimum) chain, at least 50 metres, the Danforth would be on 5 metres of 5/16″ chain and 25 metres of nylon warp (it doesn't want to be too heavy or cumbersome), and there should be 10-20 metres of chain and a 50 metre nylon warp for the Fisherman. The last warp is also useful if you want to take a line ashore and tie it around a tree or rock as is common practice in anchorages where the depths drop off quickly (in Spain, Greece and Turkey there are many anchorages where it is prudent to take a line ashore). An anchor winch is also useful, enabling any member of the crew to get the anchor and chain up, the choice is a difficult matter for most modern winches are constructed of aluminium alloy and quickly corrode, the white aluminium oxide electrolytically welds stainless bolts and cast aluminium into a corroded lump that is nearly impossible to dismantle and repair. Electric anchor winches suffer from the same corrosion problems and also consume a lot of amps. If you can find a winch made of bronze or galvanised iron then you should snap it up as they are difficult to find.

In many parts of the Mediterranean the sea bottom is hard sand or mud covered with thick weed and the problem is to get the anchor through the weed and holding on the bottom. My standard practice is to let go a scope of at least 4:1 and go astern with the engine until the rode is taut and stays so. This may sound extreme but all too often an anchor will hook a lump of weed or simply sit on the bottom until a good puff of wind blows you astern and the anchor drags. When going astern under power, if the anchor does not bite early on then it will often pick up a clump of weed which can be cleared by raising the anchor. All too often I have seen a yacht pull up its anchor complete with a clump of weed and attempt to set it again and again without removing the weed, no doubt wondering all the time why it will not bite. One advantage you do have in the Mediterranean is that the clear water enables you to see a patch of sand free of weed to plonk your anchor in, getting it right the first time.

MARINAS

In Mediterranean marinas you must berth stern or bows-to using a variety of methods to keep you off the quay or pontoon. The common methods of berthing in a marina are outlined here, though there are of course minor variations from place to place.

Laid moorings A chain sinker from a laid mooring of some sort is connected to a rope which is either tailed to the quay or to a small buoy. When you come in you must either pick up

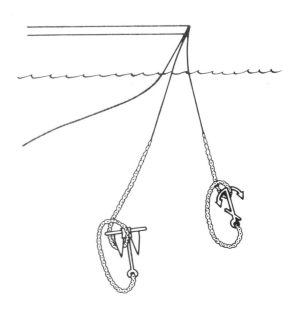

Why the Fisherman and Danforth do not make a good bower anchor. The chain or rope can easily wrap round the flukes, rendering the anchor useless.

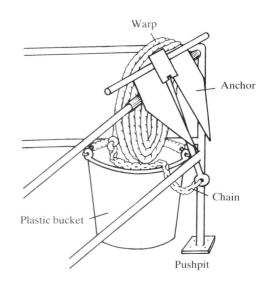

Stern anchor arrangement for berthing bows-to.

the small buoy or the rope and pull the mooring line tight, tying it off when the lines to the quay are made off. The lines are often dirty and may have sharp barnacles or coral worm on them, so wear gloves to prevent damage to your hands. If you get to the chain it is usually

Going bows-to has a lot of advantages: more privacy, an easier manoeuvre to carry out, and you can get into places where you cannot go stern-to.

To make going bows-to easier have the kedge anchor ready stowed on the stern – it doesn't take much as this photo shows!

best to tie a line onto it (use a rolling hitch), or pass a line through a link if it is large enough, rather than cleating off the chain itself which can cause damage to the topsides and deck.

Posts and large buoys A line must be passed around a post or through the top of a large buoy and the ends tied off when the lines to the quay are made off. It is best to have a long line looped around the post or through the buoy rather than a single line tied off as the latter makes leaving difficult, especially in strong winds or crowded conditions.

Finger pontoons Nose in and tie up alongside the pontoon with springs to keep the boat off the quay. Be careful when jumping down onto a pontoon as it will probably bounce down until there is enough buoyancy to support you.

BERTHING MEDITERRANEAN STYLE

In the Mediterranean you will be going stern or bows-to in most harbours. Whether you like it or not you will have to get used to doing it in a confined space with perhaps gusts of wind making manoeuvring difficult. To cut down on the panic that so often accompanies berthing stern or bows-to for the first time it is essential to have everything ready before you start to manoeuvre.

Going stern-to is a straightforward matter, although difficult the first few times, and only entails getting the stern lines ready and putting fenders out to prepare for it. Have someone letting the chain go who knows what he/she is doing.

Going bows-to you can arrange the anchor, chain, and rope in an easily handled arrangement that makes letting go and recovering it much easier.

I have a plastic bucket tied to the pushpit and sitting in the corner of the aft deck. The bucket holds the chain and warp and the anchor itself stows on the pushpit with its flukes over the top rail secured with bungee cord. A piece of reinforced hose-pipe, the sort used for toilet pipe, over the top rail to stop it being scratched by the anchor or the chain as it is paid out completes the outfit. This arrangement takes the bother out of going bows-to since the anchoring gear is ready for instant use without scrabbling around in the cockpit locker for it all. Refined versions of my somewhat agricultural arrangement include elaborate anchor lockers on the aft deck, rollers such as those used for reeling in garden hose for the anchor warp, a bow-roller on the stern, and even an anchor winch mounted on the aft deck.

LIFE-RAFTS

More and more cruising yachtsmen are thinking twice about buying a conventional life-raft and I am one who would not spend a lot of money on one again. Instead I would buy an inflatable dinghy (such as the Tinker Tramp) and equip it with a canopy and survival kit of flares, water, concentrated rations, fishing lines, solar still, etc, or even better a rigid dinghy (preferably aluminium) with buoyancy tanks and sailing gear, that can also be equipped with canopy and survival kit. Apropos a rigid dinghy, it can also be equipped with a detachable length of inflatable tubing which attaches round the topsides to give it all the advantages of an inflatable craft, extra buoyancy, stability, instant fendering, with none of the disadvantages. Inflatable tubing for rigid dinghies is now commercially manufactured and can be custom-made for most types of dinghy.

Tinker Tramp sailing for fun. *Photo:* J. M. Henshaw (Marine) Ltd.

One of the reasons I would now opt for an inflatable or rigid dinghy instead of a conventional life-raft (apart from the fact you can propel yourself to safety), is that you can check over your survival gear yourself. I don't want to scare you with horror stories (and they are legion) but some of the life-raft servicing agencies, apparently licensed by respectable companies, have checked and certified life-rafts that on later inspection had to be scrapped. If you want to have your life-raft reliably checked and serviced then have it done in Gibraltar, France, Italy, Rhodes or Cyprus and insist on seeing it unpacked (as much for your own edification as for your own security) so that you know just what is included in the survival kit — you may want to include additional items as the manufacturer's standard kit is often on the mean side.

Tinker Tramp with survival canopy rigged. *Photo:* J. M. Henshaw (Marine) Ltd.

RADIOS

I go cruising to get away from telephones, telexes and the like so I have no ambition to hook myself up via V.H.F., C.B., or single side band. On *Tetranora* there is a V.H.F. radio that was installed when I bought her, but I rarely use it. V.H.F. is useful if you are in distress, for weather forecasts, advising harbour authorities that you require a berth, cruising in company and for making telephone calls, but except for distress, the area for its other uses is pretty much confined to the countries west of Italy and Malta, excluding North Africa. In the eastern Mediterranean V.H.F. transmissions from a yacht will often be ignored or at best handled brusquely, as the shore stations are considered the domain of commercial shipping.

Amateur or ham radio has been of vital importance in emergencies when a maritime mobile rig

A range of refrigeration systems. For the Mediterranean a system without a holding plate is not worth considering. The best system is one with the compressor driven off the motor like the *Thermocool* system on the right of the picture. *Photo:* SW Mfg.

in contact with other amateurs has saved the yacht. An amateur radio operator must have a 'ticket' to operate the set, if you don't have one you may find that a lot of other operators won't talk to you. In an emergency a legitimate operator will, of course, talk to a 'pirate', but amateur radio has a lot more to offer than being just a radio link in an emergency. You can get up-to-date navigation and pilotage information from someone who is there or has been there recently, latest marina charges, the name of a good restaurant or bar, news of friends who have safely arrived, all sorts of useful information. In Appendix I there are the addresses of the relevant licensing authorities. In Britain the U.K. Maritime Mobile Network, established some ten years ago, is in daily contact with maritime amateurs on the 20m (14MHz) HF band. Contact them at 0800 and 1800 ZULU on 14303 kHz. Information is then passed on world-wide.

Citizens' Band radio is not yet well established on yachts in the Mediterranean. If you are buying a set in the U.K. it will be (legally) an FM type. Many of the sets outside the U.K. are AM types so it may pay to wait a while before getting one to see which system will be most used in the area.

REFRIGERATORS

If you are going to do it then do it right with one exception. There are many so-called marine refrigerators on the market and although they will work well in Britain, many are not efficient in the high ambient temperatures of a Mediterranean summer.

Heat absorption types On the whole do not work well, producing a small reduction in temperature for a big reduction in battery condition — except when they run on bottled gas. Although the manufacturers do not recommend gas powered refrigerators for yachts, (they are made for caravans and campers), I have seen a number installed and working well, one yacht even had its gas powered refrigerator on gimbals so that the pilot light remained on and the refrigerator worked when sailing. A gas powered refrigerator carries the same risks as gas cookers and the installation should be carefully thought out and constantly checked.

Compressors The old fashioned and well-tried compressor still comes out tops in the refrigerator league but how you power it is the problem. If you run it off your batteries they will be flat in no time. The solution is to run the compressor off the motor via an electromagnetic (or other) clutch and use a holding plate; with such an arrangement (sold commercially under the trade names *Frig-o-boat*, *Thermocool*, and others) proud owners have told me they can power a 4 cubic foot deep freeze and an adjacent 3 cubic foot refrigerator by running the motor for an hour in the morning and an hour at night. Having sampled ice cold beer from such an arrangement I can vouch for its efficiency but unfortunately the initial cost of this system is more than that of any other. So if you are going to do it — do it right.

Installation When contemplating a refrigerator don't consider front opening types where every time you open the door the cold air 'falls out' so that the compressor must work twice as hard to keep things cold. You can go some way towards alleviating the problem by fencing in the bottom half of a front opening fridge with clear plastic (attached by *velcro* or something similar) and put items you use least often in the bottom. Most commercially made refrigerators are inadequately insulated and could anyway usefully have another inch or two of polystyrene around them, with top opening types don't forget to insulate the top as well.

The humble ice-box should not be forgotten when considering refrigerators. In most Mediterranean ports, especially fishing harbours, ice can be found and this is the cheapest form of refrigeration. A block of ice will last two days in most ice-boxes, throw a few chemical cold-packs in, (the manufacturers have thought of a delightful miscellany of names: *Eskimo, Penguin, Snowflake, Chemi-cold, Nuova Ice*) and the icebox will remain cool for another night. Ideally an icebox whould be constructed in the galley extending into the cockpit locker so that ice can be dumped in from the cockpit. A metal plate could then separate the box in the cockpit from that in the galley so that the galley compartment is used for provisions and the cockpit box for provisions of the liquid variety. One cruising man who uses ice in preference to a refrigeration system summed it up like this: 'ice is nice and freons for peons'.

TENDERS

Most yacht tenders are inflatables because they are easy to stow and a good one will give many years' service. But try rowing an inflatable against a moderate sea and wind and its disadvantages are readily apparent, they are not good boats to row and in an emergency, say when you have to lay a second anchor, this becomes an important factor — it is just the sort of time that the outboard which powers your inflatable decides not to start or is swamped by a wave. The only alternative to a rigid dinghy by way of a tender is a folding dinghy; several models are made including one which folds lengthways, takes up no more room than a windsurfer when collapsed, and is easily stowed on the deck along the guard rails.

But no folding dinghy comes close to a rigid dinghy for strength and that solid feeling under you as you row through the swell with a second anchor. Most yachts over thirty feet can find a convenient place on deck to stow a rigid dinghy — either

Sailing tenders. When the wind is free you can zip ashore without you or your outboard huffing and puffing.

immediately forward or aft of the mast. Davits are a nonsense on small yachts. Not only do they look silly but they get in the way when going stern-to, provide extra windage, make it difficult to install a wind-vane, and hang a lot of weight in the wrong place adversely affecting a yacht's trim.

I favour aluminium dinghies for strength, durability and easy maintenance. A friend just completing a circumnavigation still uses one over 30 years old, much battered and patched but still in everyday use. Whatever material a rigid dinghy is constructed from, it should have buoyancy tanks built into it and adequate fendering. One of the advantages of an inflatable is that it does not damage the topsides. A useful addition, especially if you have children, is a sailing rig so that when the wind is free you can zip ashore without you or your outboard motor huffing and puffing. For the children it will provide hours of fun and teach them the rudiments of sailing.

BICYCLES

Many larger yachts carry small foldaway models that greatly increase your range ashore. No messing about with bus timetables, haggling with taxi drivers or in the end walking for miles. On small yachts room for a couple of folding bicycles can generally be found, I carry one stowed in the forepeak but I must confess that when first confronted with the idea I was dead against it. But in Greece a few weeks of cycling from the Olympic Boat Yard to Lavrion some two miles away soon convinced me of its usefulness and now I don't regret a penny of the purchase nor the space the bike takes up. Apart from everyday shopping in the winter it has taken me to some nearby but too-far-to-walk places I might never have visited. It constantly surprises me how many yachtsmen spend four or more months in one place in the winter yet never explore the surrounding area. Perhaps with bikes they might, and moreover, it is good for the lungs and better for the spirit.

ELECTROLYSIS

Because you have never had problems with electrolysis in colder more northerly waters is no reason to believe you will not have problems in the warm salty Mediterranean. On my second boat I had to replace the stainless steel propeller shaft after a year because I took insufficient care to ensure it was protected, I failed to bridge the rub-

ber pads on the flexible couplings which effectively insulated the anode from the shaft. Numerous other yachts have lost propellers, skin fittings and rudders and some have sunk as a direct result of electrolysis. One yacht from a reputable boatbuilder had a bronze skin fitting attached with stainless steel bolts, the bolts corroded, the fitting dropped off, and the water inlet for the engine became a water inlet for the yacht.

The Mediterranean is warmer and saltier than most other seas so that electrolysis proceeds at a faster rate — putting your yacht in a saltier sea is something like going from a six volt system to a twelve volt one. A sacrificial anode, bonded to the engine, gearbox, shaft (with a bridging connection over the flexible coupling!), rudder stock and nearby skin fittings will go a long way to solving these worries. M. G. Duff manufacture good quality anodes and fitting kits with detailed instructions for fitting them.

Owners of steel and aluminium boats need to pay special attention to electrolytic problems, some sling anodes over the side, attached above water to the steel hull, whenever they are in harbour — presumably to cut down on loss from anodes attached underwater. Another system, used on some commercial ships, is to trickle a small positive charge from the ship's supply through the hull. I shudder to think what must happen to any yacht moored close to a vessel using such a system.

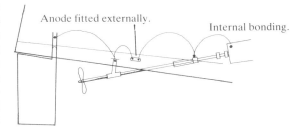

Anode fitted externally.

Internal bonding.

Correct anode bonding.

Every yacht has a mixture of metals underwater, thus leading to electrolytic problems, so one should not presume that because your yacht is constructed of wood or G.R.P. it is free from electrolysis. Even worse is the electrolytic corrosion that goes on in engines cooled by raw sea water. Some engines have a sacrificial anode in the block that should be changed more frequently than the manufacturer recommends, others can be fitted with such a sacrificial anode but yours may not, so check with the manufacturer and get in a supply of spare anodes. One engine with an alloy head and without a sacrificial anode, lasted just one year in the Mediterranean before the head was so eaten away as to be useless.

WORDS AND MUSIC

With the technological advances made in the last decade you can now carry your sound system with you. A short wave receiver can be cheaply bought and will repay your investment many times over listening to the B.B.C. World Service. It is without doubt the best radio service in the world, better, dare I say it, than the B.B.C. Home Service, and certainly better than private stations with their ubiquitous morning chat shows and middle of the road muzak. For a modest sum you can get a digital short wave receiver that will lock onto the exact frequency you require and stay there. You will need a radio of some sort for weather forecasts on medium wave frequencies anyway.

Cassette players have come a long way in recent years; today in a small unit you can get quality reproduction from a twelve volt player. Cassette tapes enable you to carry your music in a compact and reliable form. A 'Walkman' is well worth getting for those long night watches so you can listen to your favourite music, be it the latest offerings from the bubble-gum music brigade or Mozart, or perhaps you could learn the language of the country you are going to next, all without disturbing those off-watch. For that matter you can use it in daylight hours as well so as not to disturb the others on board with your Spanish language course or the Pet Shop Boys.

GANGPLANK

For mooring stern-to you will need a gang-plank or *passerelle* which vary from exquisite creations with guard-rails, carpet and recessed lights to a humble plank with a hole in one end so it can be attached to the boat. If you are making a gang-plank put some wheels on the end so it doesn't annoy you and your neighbours as it rasps on the quay, also thin anti-skid strips across the plank are more useful and practical than a guard-rail on one side. Even if you moor bows-to, a short gang-plank is useful with the outer end on the jib halyard to keep it clear of the quay. If you get the chance have your pulpit modified to make boarding easier, you could have a lift up gate or the pulpit could be a U-shape at the bows so that you can easily step aboard.

A U-shaped pulpit makes getting on and off easy when bows-to.

You will be swimming more often, so make it easy to get back on board.

SWIMMING LADDER

You will be swimming more often and when you do you need to be able to get back on board easily. Most of the rope or plastic affairs that hang over the side are difficult to use — although if you hang a fender behind these ladders it is easier to get a toe-hold on the rungs. A solid wood or stainless ladder is best and with a little thought it can be permanently installed on the transom. Some boats have a clever arrangement whereby part of the pushpit folds down to form a swimming ladder. Although primarily for pleasure use a swimming ladder can be invaluable for getting someone who has fallen overboard back on the boat.

Equipping yourself

Diogenes c. 380 B.C.

Alexander the Great . . . asked him if he lacked anything. 'Yes,' he said, 'that I do; that you stand out of my sun a little.'

In Plutarch's *Life of Alexander*

(Alexander, to his credit, is supposed to have retorted that if he was not Alexander he would have liked to have been Diogenes.)

In Gibraltar, the Balearics, Malta and a few other harbours elsewhere throughout the Mediterranean you can find disillusioned yachtsmen contemplating selling their yachts and everything in them to return to the life they fondly thought they had left behind. A large part of the problem is money or rather the lack of it. It is a nightmare being broke in a foreign country, far from the benevolent arms of the community you once lived in, where the state (you hope) provides and friends and family comfort you. What was a minor problem at home can take on the dimensions of a catastrophe in foreign parts: a doctor's bill, a repair job on the engine, a trip home to see an ailing parent, someone who owes you money and is mysteriously away when you call. Some can survive on very little, I know of one yachtsman who survived through a winter on potatoes and an egg or two, but for most of us things crop up which weaken and break the spirit unless we are in some way prepared for them.

But lack of money, and worse, the things you didn't budget for that erode both your bank balance and your spirit, may only be part of the reason why not everybody fulfills the long planned-for dream. After all many yachtsmen, not all of them young, fit men ready to turn their hand to anything, enjoy cruising around the Mediterranean on miniscule budgets. A little forward planning to equip yourself for the voyage is just as important as equipping the boat. Here are some hints:

MONEY

So you need it, but not as much as might be thought if you are prepared to budget. If you have an expensive lifestyle at home and wish to take all the trappings with you then you must budget for that, jot down what it costs to live for a month and add half again: *Remy Martin,* Danish smoked bacon, Stilton and the *Sunday Times* will all cost a lot more in the Mediterranean when you can get them. But if you live like the natives, drink the local wines, make do with local sausages and goat's cheese and read a fifth hand *Time* passed along from another yacht, then your living costs plummet dramatically. It is all common sense, or uncommon sense, because there are many who fall by the wayside.

Apart from your basic living costs you will need a fund for any contingency which may crop up: a shredded genoa, an engine on its last legs, a yard bill rather higher than you expected. Even if you have a brand spanking new yacht you will need this security fund, a figure which varies even more dramatically from person to person. I am quite happy to get my spending down to a figure that horrifies even my close friends, when money is in short supply I lower my expectations and living standards keeping only enough in reserve to buy the basic necessities and the air fare to somewhere where I know I can get a job. Others have a sizeable nest egg and property that enables them to weather just about any disaster that might occur.

On the subject of money I should mention ways and means of changing money. For Europe the simplest and easiest way of changing money is by

Eurocheques with a *Eurocheque* card. These are issued by the major banks for which they make a charge. If you use one of the major credit cards such as *Access* or *Visa* these are useful to get cash advances in larger towns or to get you out of a jam should you suddenly need to hop on a plane or pay a hospital bill. Charge cards such as *American Express* are less useful since you can only get money from an *American Express* office. With all these cards there are lots of restaurants, boutiques and shops at the upper end of the market who will take them. In out of the way places you may have difficulty changing *Eurocheques* but in Gibraltar, Spain, France, Italy, Malta, Greece, Turkey, Cyprus and Israel you are unlikely to encounter problems. (See the relevant section for each country.) In Yugoslavia, Tunisia and Morocco you can change *Eurocheques* in the larger towns and in tourist resorts. In Europe you should still carry a supply of travellers' cheques and out of Europe a larger wad of the same for most of your money changing. Along with travellers' cheques it is a good idea to carry a supply of cash in hard currency. American dollars are still the best, but sterling, German marks or Swiss francs are also easily negotiable. This cash is useful in out of the way places and can save your skin even in Europe. In 1982 all of the banks in Italy were on strike for nearly two months and only my supply of sterling and American dollars kept me going.

Having money cabled to a bank is bothersome; you may have to wait around in a busy city until it comes through, and it invariably arrives late. Cabling for money is more often than not a disaster, the telexes and cables often get delayed and I once waited for two weeks to get money after an expensive telex because the bank in Malta had 'lost' the telex for ten days. It would have been quicker and less expensive to write to the bank in the first place.

INSURANCE

Medical Insurance   Falling ill abroad can cost you a lot of money and may become one of those catastrophes that exhausts your finances and breaks your spirit if you do not have insurance. In the Mediterranean a modest cover of around £10,000 for medical expenses can be obtained quite reasonably, the policy should cover medical expenses for hospital treatment, doctor's fees, drugs and ambulance fees, it may also be worthwhile getting cover for repatriation should treatment not be available in a particular country.

Travellers from E.C. countries can get urgent treatment free or at a reduced cost, but only for temporary visits to another E.C. country. Whether a yacht cruising for a year in

. . . but if you live like the natives living costs plummet.

Italian waters is a temporary visitor or not is a thorny question. To get such treatment you should obtain leaflet S.A. 28/30 *Medical Treatment during Visits Abroad* from your local Department of Health and Social Security office, at the back is *Form CM1* which you send in not more than six months before you leave. You will then be sent *Form E 111* which you carry with you and present when you receive treatment abroad. Malta and Yugoslavia have reciprocal medical agreements with the United Kingdom so that you get free or cheaper medical treatment in these two countries.

Remember that medical insurance and reciprocal medical agreements (E.C. or others) do not normally cover previously existing illnesses nor do they cover pregnancy, abortion, nervous disorders, dentistry or cosmetic surgery. Also in some countries, particularly in North Africa, you will find that doctors want to give you the works: vitamin courses, wide spectrum anti-biotics, suppositories, anything they think they can prescribe in order to claim as much as possible from the insurers. Some judicious bargaining is in order here.

On the subject of doctors I will say that contrary to popular opinion, medical treatment is good throughout Europe including Italy, Greece and Cyprus. In Yugoslavia and Turkey medical treatment is good in the large cities and in large tourist resorts. In Northern Africa medical resources vary dramatically between city and village.

Boat Insurance Insurance for a yacht in the Mediterranean is only a little more expensive than insurance in home waters; normally the rate is between one and one and a half per cent of the total value of the boat for a fully comprehensive cover, not an excessive amount for your home and means of transport. There are insurance firms in the Mediterranean countries which will insure your yacht but some caution is needed here – if you have a good marine insurance broker at home then stick with him.

Nearly all insurance policies for the Mediterranean cover everything west of 30°E and exclude anything east of that. The excluded area includes the trouble spots of the Middle East: Cyprus, Syria, Lebanon and Israel, it also includes part of the non-troubled Anatolian coast of Turkey so that cover for this area if you are going there involves an extra premium, though you may be able to negotiate to include just Anatolian Turkey and Cyprus under the normal cover.

Warranties Much of the equipment you buy is covered by a warranty in the country you bought it in but once you leave you may as well be on the Moon as far as many manufacturers are concerned. Check to see if a warranty will be honoured after you have left. Whether it will be or not see if you can get the manufacturer's handbook for the equipment you have on board. Often you can repair equipment yourself or at least give someone else a fighting chance if you have the manufacturer's handbook but remember this will in most cases invalidate warranty agreements.

CONSULAR ASSISTANCE

Just what a consulate offers to those of us abroad is a mystery to me and many others. Much of their 'work' appears to be attending cocktail parties to meet other diplomats, attending official functions which are difficult to distinguish from the cocktail parties, and attending functions to drum up trade which end up as cocktail parties. Their other activity is endlessly telling you they cannot help. I'm being a bit unfair, but not a lot. The following list of what a consulate can and cannot do is from the HMSO pamphlet on *Consular Assistance Abroad*. I quote.

What a Consul can do
Can issue emergency passports.
Can contact relatives and friends and ask them to help with money or tickets.
Can advise on how to transfer funds.
Can at most posts (in an emergency) advance money against a sterling cheque for £50 supported by a banker's card.
Can, as a last resort, and provided that certain strict criteria are met, make a repayable loan for repatriation to the U.K. But there's no law that says the Consul must do this and he will need to be satisfied that there is absolutely no one else you know who can help.
Can provide a list of lawyers, interpreters and doctors.
Can arrange for the next of kin to be informed of an accident or a death and advise on procedures.
Can contact British nationals who are arrested or in prison and, in certain circumstances, arrange for messages to be sent to relatives or friends.

Can give some guidance on organisations experienced in tracing missing persons.

What a Consul cannot do
Cannot pay your hotel, medical, or any other bills.
Cannot pay for travel tickets for you except in very special circumstances.
Cannot undertake work more properly done by travel representatives, airlines, banks or motoring organisations.
Cannot get better treatment for you in hospital (or prison) than is provided for local nationals.
Cannot give legal advice, instigate court proceedings on your behalf, or interfere in local judicial procedures to get you out of prison.
Cannot investigate a crime.
Cannot formally assist dual nationals in the country of their second nationality.
Cannot obtain a work permit for you.

A STEADY TRADE

To borrow a phrase from Tristan Jones. It is possible to find work in the Mediterranean with just a willing pair of hands but it is easier if you have a trade or a profession. Of the professions, only doctors, dentists and engineers find employment easily; lawyers, teachers, middle management executives, town planners and anybody else who falls under that much misused term — professional — will find it extremely difficult to find work away from home. A steady trade is the thing especially if it has anything to do with yachts. If you are a proficient marine engineer (I mean engines), know about marine electrics or electronics, a rigger, boat carpenter, G.R.P. specialist, welder or sailmaker, then you will invariably find work from other yachtsmen or charter fleet operators. You may have to work illegally but on private yachts that is no problem, you simply sign on as crew. As in so many other fields a ticket stating a certain degree of competency can mean nothing, while a job well done, a word of mouth recommendation from another yachtsman, can mean as much work as you can handle. The cruising community soon sorts out the charlatans from proper craftsmen whether the latter have a ticket or not.

Whether you have a trade or simply a willing pair of hands that can scrape and wield a paintbrush, do not expect to arrive somewhere and find work the next day. There will be a period in which you will find little or none at all until word gets around that you are looking for gainful employment and you are a reliable worker.

CHARTERING

Many people spend a lot of money building or buying a yacht in the belief that they will be able to charter it for three months of the year and have the rest to themselves. There are many reasons why you cannot do this and some why you should not.

In most of the European Mediterranean countries it is illegal to charter a foreign flag yacht. This is so in Spain, Italy and Greece where you must pay import duty, sign away half your yacht to a national of that country and remit a certain amount of the charter fees in its currency; the paperwork and complications are overwhelming. In France you must pay T.V.A. (French V.A.T.) at around 18% before you can charter. In Yugoslavia, Turkey, Cyprus and Tunisia you can charter a foreign flag yacht subject to certain regulations which usually involves employing an agent. In the countries where you must import your yacht before you charter it, not to do so risks crippling fines and in some cases imprisonment with seizure of the vessel.

But if despite these difficulties you still seriously contemplate chartering your yacht then I recommend you to get in touch with the tourist office of the country concerned as the regulations do change. An even better source of information will be a British based charter company operating in the country you are thinking about, they will know the latest regulations and, more importantly, will have practical advice to offer. Some of these companies take private yachts under their wing for a fee and/or a percentage of the profits, but you should satisfy yourself about their organisation before the commitment of your pride and joy to their care as there are a lot of cowboy firms around.

One legal loophole that some charter yacht owners use is to pick up passengers in one country and clear for another country. For instance you might pick up charterers in Italy and clear for Yugoslavia, but if you are doing this from the same place every two weeks or so, officials will inevitably realise what is going on and although they cannot stop you they will find reasons to make life uncomfortable. Thus you should keep a low profile and not flaunt your rights.

Assuming you have organized to charter somewhere, then you must find charterers and there is an increasing number of charter boats chasing a limited market. A single yacht owner is at a disadvantage against the big charter companies who can afford to run an office and advertise extensively,

LIVING ABOARD

Samuel Johnson did not much care for it: 'No man will be a sailor who has contrivance enough to get himself into jail; for being in a ship is being in jail, with the chance of being drowned . . . A man in jail has more room, better food, and commonly better company.' I'm sure the good doctor would have looked askance at people choosing to live on a yacht and in bad weather I occasionally wonder why I'm not ashore — until I live ashore when I can't wait to get back on board.

The rewards are many. Where else can you change the view from your back door when you want to? Change your neighbours when you don't like them? Live in the middle of a bustling city one winter and in a peaceful anchorage the next? Share a community that is bonded by simply owning a yacht however humble, but which is loose enough not to suffocate you? There are many rewards but a few pitfalls as well. Before you commit yourself to life aboard a yacht, try it for more than a weekend. Many couples find that problems normally submerged by a routine life erupt when they are together for twenty four hours a day in a confined space. Minor aches in an everyday relationship can become a major pain on board.

Much can be done by the skipper (inevitably male) to involve the other half (almost inevitably female) in the project. Some of the happiest couples cruising around the Mediterranean have divided the skills needed for the voyage quite equitably, the man will usually look after the engine, heavy chores such as raising the anchor and sails and repair jobs within his scope such as welding or boat carpentry. The woman will do the navigation, probably most of the cooking and repair jobs such as sail repairs. Both should share the route planning and the night watches. I am not so 'liberated' that I enjoy rippling muscles on a woman hauling up the anchor nor so blind that I cannot appreciate a woman who excels at boat carpentry or welding.

One thing I am adamant about is that your crew must know how to sail the boat and how to start the engine and manoeuvre under power – there are numerous stories of tragedy at sea because the crew did not know how to turn a yacht around and rescue a skipper who had fallen in the water. Friends of mine tell of a yachtsman who picked up two female crew in Australia and set off across the Indian Ocean. In light winds with the yacht ghosting along at just over a knot he fell overboard and the two girls, not knowing how to turn the yacht around or start the engine, watched him swimming

Couples should divide the skills needed for a voyage and boat maintenance equitably.

and for this reason I would advise you to think hard about chartering your own boat for an income. It is a full time occupation, not something you can dabble your toes in and come out refreshed.

One alternative worth thinking about is working as a skipper or mate on a charter yacht for a limited period. Many of the larger charter companies require free-lance skippers for inexperienced charterers. Often you will be working illegally with the connivance of the owners, but over a short period this is no real problem. Again a low profile will keep you out of trouble. Another line of work is delivering yachts in and out of the Mediterranean, a job that gives you a lot of freedom but often imposes punishing deadlines. After a friend of mine was drowned en-route from Britain to the Mediterranean because, I believe, the delivery deadline forced him to leave in weather he normally would have avoided, I no longer take on deliveries that leave little or no margin for bad weather. After all it is your life out there and if you would not leave in your own yacht, why should you in someone else's?

after the yacht until they could see him no more. They were rescued four days later drifting helplessly around the middle of the Indian Ocean. A few days instruction to your crew on the rudiments of sailing and handling a yacht under power will give you peace of mind and may save your life.

A loosely related matter is the attitude of those who live aboard to 'them' on the shore. Some live-aboards seem to think that people on the shore, shopkeepers, marina staff, tradesmen and the like, are out to rob them of every penny they have just because they live on a yacht. Their perverse logic turns this on its head and states, and I have heard this stated quite blatantly, that it is therefore legitimate to abuse shore living folk, especially if they are foreign. The worst sympton of this misbegotten 'philosophy' is the yachtsman who leaves a marina early in the morning without paying his mooring charges or other bills, others anchor off marinas and row ashore to have showers, do their washing and deposit their garbage.

It is a fact that in some marinas the charges, especially in the summer, are expensive for what is offered. Electricity and water charges may be out of all proportion to what one would pay living in a house ashore, but the yachtsman who knowing this chooses to stay in the marina and run up bills he has no intention of paying is nothing less than a thief. He demeans himself and worse he tarnishes the image of live-aboards. The next cruising yacht arriving in that marina may find themselves being treated inhospitably because the last cruising yacht skipped harbour early in the morning leaving unpaid bills.

In many of the countries around the Mediterranean, but particularly in the poorer ones, people living on yachts are regarded as affluent if not downright wealthy. It is difficult to explain to say a Greek or a Turk that you are not extremely well-off, that you perhaps have little else but your yacht and a precarious income working where you can, when any Greek or Turk worth his salt knows that only the very rich have yachts, even small ones. Even worse, you are a tourist as well and therefore idle as well as rich. Consequently prices are rounded off to the nearest hundred Italian lira, the nearest ten Greek drachmas, the nearest fifty Turkish lira and so on. You are never overcharged an excessive amount, probably no more than ten per cent at most and if you keep an eye on prices then any exorbitant additions to your bill are soon spotted and a bit of judicious haggling will win you respect and save a few pennies. In the eastern Mediterranean this haggling over prices is custom-

ary, anyone who doesn't agree on a price for a service beforehand is considered a fool who has too much money for his own good; this means agreeing on a price for a taxi before you hire one or the price of a repair job before it is started. To quibble afterwards is unbecoming and petty.

DOCUMENTS

All on board need valid passports. If you have one of those difficult passports, like a South African or Bermudan passport, then you will need visas for many countries around the Mediterranean and some you may not be able to visit. Even with a normally innocuous New Zealand passport one needs a visa to visit Yugoslavia. Get the visas you need before you leave home to avoid disappointment later.

If you have a U.K. passport then you can visit all countries bordering the Mediterranean without a visa except for Albania, Syria, Libya and surprisingly, Egypt. If you have a U.S. passport then you can visit all countries without a visa excepting Albania, Syria, Egypt, Libya and Algeria. In Egypt a yacht arriving without visas for those on board will not be turned away, but will be issued with them at the port of entry.

For your yacht you will require some sort of document detailing the name, home port, length, tonnage and registration number. The new registration papers provided by the Small Ship's Register administered by the R.Y.A. (application forms from R.Y.A. Technical Department, R.Y.A. House, Romsey Road, Eastleigh, Hants. SO5 4YA) should in practice prove adequate for all countries around the Mediterranean. The older Part I Registration (still needed to prove ownership), the *Blue Book*, is of course still accepted and may be preferred in some countries not familiar with the new small ship's papers.

In addition to registration documents it is well worth your while to have a ship's stamp made, this can be cheaply made to your own design and will repay its small cost a hundredfold. Nothing impresses an official more than to get a ship's stamp on crew lists and other sundry bits of paper. I must point out that you will be dealing with a great deal of paperwork in the Mediterranean where it is a fact of life. In Britain the least bit of paperwork interrupting our messing about in boats is regarded as an intolerable interference so that when the Mediterranean official encounters this attitude there are occasional hiccups and the paperwork inexplicably takes longer than it should. An attitude that smacks of paternalism — 'just smile at the natives, nod and pretend not to understand' — will only serve to lengthen already lengthy procedures, better to try and understand that these officials are underpaid beings caught in a bureaucratic web. Otherwise patient endurance must suffice. One thing which is particularly annoying but about which you can do little is to have officials come aboard in heavy shoes and boots. Asking them to remove the offensive footwear is difficult and in any case I hesitate to demand that of a customs official who might then decide to be difficult.

To be on the safe side it is worth getting some sort of certificate attesting your ability as the captain of your ship. If you do not have an R.Y.A. Yachtsmaster's certificate then the R.Y.A. Helmsman's certificate is worth getting, the latter can be obtained upon proof of cruising experience, usually from a recognised yacht club member. It is worth bearing in mind that even your much valued Yachtsmaster's certificate that you laboured long and hard to get may be sniffed at in some countries. It doesn't have your photograph on it!

In some countries (Yugoslavia, Spain, France and Italy for example), proof of insurance may be required though it is not always asked for. Check with the yachtsmen who have recently cruised in a particular country and have the requisite papers with you, to be on the safe side.

MAIL

In most of the Mediterranean countries mail can be sent care of *poste restante* but be sure to tell those writing to you to allow time for the mail to arrive. The drawbacks of sending mail to *poste restante* are several: you are tied to a certain place at a certain time especially if important mail is being sent there; in some countries mail is sent back after a short time and owing to the vagaries of the weather you may arrive one day after your mail has been sent back; and if your mail is there you can have problems getting it away from post office employees. Always check under your first name, your yacht's name, and 'Esquire', as well as under your surname.

The system I use is to have all my mail sent to one address in Britain from where it can be sent to a *poste restante* or a private address as convenient. I have found marinas, banks, tourist offices, friends of friends resident in the country and yacht clubs alternative addresses to using *poste restante*.

Take some care arranging for your mail to be forwarded, you will attach more importance to it when it comes less frequently — probably because it is likely to contain fewer bills than before, and even bank statements don't seem to convey the doom and destruction they once did when you are relaxing with a drink a few thousand miles away.

PETS

If you can't possibly do without an animal friend on board you must accept that your cruising will be curtailed in a number of ways. Animals arriving in Malta on board a yacht must be put in quarantine for twelve months or destroyed, usually the latter. Gibraltar, France, Italy and Greece have regulations concerning inoculations and certificates for animals arriving on a yacht and although they are rarely enforced it would be wise to get your pet inoculated against rabies and distemper and get a certificate to that effect. Remember you cannot take your pet back to Britain without putting it into quarantine, any re-introduced illegally can be destroyed and the owner fined a considerable sum.

Most cruising folk agree that a cat makes the best pet on board being just as aloof and independent afloat as it is on shore — except at feeding times when it suddenly becomes affectionate and vocal. I think the cat's abilities as a rat catcher are overestimated and it should be regarded as a good friend rather than a useful animal. Most cats adapt to life onboard remarkably well except for getting on and off the yacht when bow or stern-to – if there is a little slop and the boat is moving they seem to experience difficulty judging when to jump, but fortunately they swim well when they have to. Dogs do not adapt so well to life on board and mostly seem to be marking time between trips ashore for fun and other things, however they are useful as a watchdog and are better rat catchers than cats.

Cats and dogs do not exhaust the choice of pets: I have come across a parrot (a vicious dirty bird), canaries (noisy), a duck (always incontinent), a monkey (a naughty six year old child), terrapins (the tank was emptied and they were wrapped in a damp dish cloth when it was rough), and a lizard (a useful mosquito catcher).

One of the problems of having a pet aboard is the time you spend running around after them. In harbour cats and dogs like to go ashore and explore. Owners seem to be continually looking for them and in addition you must feed them and collect litter for the dirt box. If your cat or dog likes fish, a small fish trap is a good investment, and occasionally you will catch something you can eat. If the animal is addicted to a proprietary brand of pet food then you will need to stock up on it. Try to wean them off it if you are going to spend some time in the Mediterranean as it is impossible to find in many places.

MEDICAL

Your first requirement is a good first aid handbook. *The Ship Captain's Medical Guide* H.M.S.O., *The Yachtsman's Doctor* by Dr. R. T. Counter and *A Traveller's Guide to Health* by Lt. Col. James Adam are all good. The manual should be put somewhere readily accessible. The first aid kit proper should contain at least the following:

Sterilised lint and bandage packs.
Sterile burn dressings.
Adhesive dressing (a roll of non-waterproof tape and individual waterproof dressings).
Cotton wool.
Disinfectant *(Dettol)*.
Antiseptic *(Savlon, T.C.P.)*.
Mild painkiller *(Aspirin, Veganin)*
Anti-histamine cream (for insect bites and stings).
Calamine lotion (burns and rashes).
Diarrhoea treatment (Kaolin and morphine, *Lomotil, Enterosan*).
Wide spectrum antibiotic *(Ampicillin, Tetracycline)*.
Anti-seasickness tablets.
Forceps and scissors.

This is the most basic kit you should take. In addition I would seriously suggest you add the following:

Suture strips (instead of stiches for wounds).
Antibiotic ear drops (for local ear infections from swimming).
Antibiotic powder (for infected wounds).
Eye drops.
An aerosol burn treatment *(Burneze)*.
An aerosol sting treatment *(Waspeze)*.

Most of these items can be obtained over the counter or on prescription from a doctor once you explain what you are doing. In the Mediterranean many of these items (antibiotics, antihistamines) can be obtained over the counter without a doctor's prescription. You should check out any allergies you or your crew might have to classified dangerous drugs before you leave.

Stock up on any special medication you are on (for high blood pressure, angina, diabetes, etc.) before you leave, the medication will be available in most countries but it may well be under a different brand name. Get a list of equivalent drugs under different manufacturer's brands or make some arrangement for medication to be sent you. The 'pill' can be bought over the counter in many countries but again the brand name may differ for the same pill from a different pharmaceutical company. Most doctors will prescribe a six month supply once you explain what you are doing and can suggest similar brands available abroad.

Insects, especially mosquitos, are a nuisance on board so stock up on insect repellants, I find Oil of Citronella works as well as the more expensive proprietary brands if you don't mind its peculiar smell. If you are especially allergic to mosquito bites then it is worthwhile having screens made for the hatches and any opening ports, these can be simple affairs of plastic mesh framed in wood for the hatches and framed in wire for the ports. On the subject of mosquitos, remember that parts of southern Turkey, Syria and parts of Egypt and Tunisia are classified by the World Health Organisation as malarial risk areas. Although I have heard of only one person on a yacht who has contracted malaria in this area, if you are at all worried then carry a supply of tablets (such as *Comoquin* or *Pyrimethamine*) for protection.

Cockroaches can be a problem on board and apart from the chance they may carry diseases, the very presence of these furtive scuttling little animals revolts most people. Cockroaches can get on board in all sorts of ways. If you are alongside they will simply stroll onto the boat. If you forget to keep your gangplank raised above the quay, they will make a dash for it and get aboard that way. One of the most common ways that they get aboard is as eggs laid in the cracks of cardboard boxes and these eventually hatch to give you your own private colony. And if you are alongside local fishing boats cockroaches can climb over the fenders and get on board. There are few boats cruising in the Mediterranean that don't, at some time or other, have to deal with these unwelcome visitors. The only real solution is to have the boat fumigated. In a number of countries such as Malta, Italy, and Spain there are professional companies who will do this. I haven't had any experience of the fumigation 'bombs' you can buy in some chemists, but you would certainly have to close the boat up and leave it as long as possible for these to work. There are a number of other solutions. In

Greece you can buy cockroach powder that poisons the little monsters. In Cyprus and Malta you can buy cockroach 'hotels'. This is a box you fold so that there is an entry at each end and into which the cockroaches are enticed by a bait they can't resist – a friend suggested it was a pheromone of a sexual variety. The floor of the 'hotel' is sticky so that the cockroaches get stuck on it once they go for the bait. It really does work. You can also get a bait which contains boric acid. After the cockroach has had a meal, the acid crystallises in the gut of the unfortunate creature and spears it from the inside. Insect sprays only tend to slow the cockroach down, which is useful for crushing them, but won't get at a quickly multiplying brood somewhere in the bowels of the boat. In the end the best remedy is prevention so take every precaution to stop them getting on board by going stern or bows-to and leaving carboard boxes on the quay.

Incidents of typhoid and hepatitis have been reported, any suspect water should be treated (water treatment tablets such as *Helazone* can be bought) or boiled. I have never experienced problems from tap-water anywhere in the Mediterranean but avoid using well water or water stored in cisterns for drinking purposes. Fruit and vegetables should be washed in water with a few grains of potassium permanganate (Permanganate of Potash or Condy's crystals) dissolved in it to kill any nasties but the chances are that you will contract typhoid or hepatitis after eating ashore rather than from local fruit and vegetables or the local water supply.

Recently a report indicated that there maybe a danger of Legionnaire's Disease from a yacht's water system. A fresh water tank with stagnant water in it could grow *Legionella* bacteria where temperatures are 20° to 40° Celcius, although the bacteria can survive in temperatures up to 60°C once it has developed. Apparently the most likely way of contracting the disease is inhalation of water particles when showering. I should stress that only one yachtsman contracted the disease out of four on board the yacht where the sample was taken from, and this is the only known case. Cleaning the tank and removal of sludge and the addition of a weak sodium hypochloride (common bleach) solution will kill off the *Legionella* as well as any other nasties in the fresh water system.

Although you may be going to the Mediterranean in search of the sun, you should also guard against it especially if you have a fair skin, so stock up on sun tan and sunburn lotions. Lips should be also protected from chapping by sun and wind with a chapstick and sensitive appendages like the nose protected with a barrier cream such as *Sun Block* or *Uvistat* (protection factor 15). Invest in several pairs of good sunglasses especially if you have pale coloured eyes, I find the dark polarised sunglasses made for the ski slopes the best. A good sun hat or visor completes the ensemble.

If you wear spectacles or contact lenses then carry a spare pair. Just as important is the optical formula for these so that they can be made up locally if need be.

It should go without saying that everything discussed and suggested here should be talked over with your doctor who can provide expert advice and locate the latest information on drugs and their availability.

I have left the subject of vaccinations to the end. No vaccinations are required before you will be permitted to enter any Mediterranean countries. However the D.H.S.S. in Britain recommends certain vaccinations for the following countries.

Cholera Recommended in Turkey, Syria, Lebanon, Egypt, Libya, Tunisia, Algeria and Morocco.

Typhoid Recommended in Spain, Italy, Malta, Yugoslavia, Greece, Turkey, Cyprus, Syria, Lebanon, Israel, Egypt, Libya, Tunisia, Algeria and Morocco.

MAL-DE-MER

Most people suffer at some time or other from seasickness, some more chronically and more often than others. I was recently seasick for the first time in ten years and though not incapacitated, it humbled me to think about the various remedies available, especially for those who are chronically afflicted. The following is a brief round-up of remedies.

Tablets A number of antihistamines are on the market: *Avomine*, *Dramamine*, *Marzine RF*, and *Stugeron*. Of these *Stugeron* is widely accepted as the most effective. They all cause drowsiness to some extent, though *Stugeron* to a lesser extent than the others. These pills must be taken before setting sail, sometimes up to 4 hours prior to going to sea, their effect is minimal once someone begins to feel seasick. Other tablets such as *Phenergan*, *Kwells*, and *Sereen* contain hyoscine hydrobromide which has a sedative effect and leaves the sufferer drowsy.

Scopoderm disc A small elastoplast disc which is stuck behind the ear four hours before sailing. It contains hyoscine hydrobromide which is released slowly into the bloodstream and is said to reduce the sensitivity of the inner ear without causing undue drowsiness as it does in tablet form. The disc will work over two to three days and tests seem to indicate a good success rate. It is available only on prescription, cannot be used by young children, and for a minority does have some side effects such as minor drowsiness and one or two reports of mild hallucinations!

Homeopathic cures A number of homeopathic treatments are available: *Nux Vomica 6*, *Cocculus Indicus 6* and *Ipecac 6* tablets. I have not tracked down any results from these. A number of old salts swear by natural remedies such as ginger, glucose and Vitamin B12. Ginger seems to be the favourite.

Sea bands Elasticated bands with a small plastic knob sewn into them can be purchased and when slipped over the wrist the knob is supposed to press on the *nei-kuan* pressure point, an acupuncture point that reduces nausea. The problem is hitting exactly the right point – something an acupuncturist spends years learning to do.

Generally Someone who is seasick should be kept warm, but should stay in the cockpit if possible. Watching the horizon seems to have a curative effect while down below, apart from the absence of a horizon, any odours, diesel, gas, cooking food, will be enough to induce vomiting. When seasick try to eat something like dry bread or crackers, and drink plenty of water as vomiting causes dehydration. Someone who is mildly nauseous can be given something to do, operating a winch or even helming can reduce nausea. If you are regularly seasick at the onset of a voyage take the advice of a friend of mine who would eat only tinned pineapple because, he said, 'It tasted as good on the way up as on the way down'.

GUNS AND THE NON-COMBATANT

On my yacht there is no place for a gun. And I believe if you are cruising only in the Mediterranean then you too have no need of firearms.

Rumours of piracy in the Mediterranean are laughable, at least they would be laughable if the possible consequences were not tragic. I have seen the armoury on one yacht whose owner believed there were well armed pirates around: a pump action shotgun, a .22 pistol, a .22 rifle, and a high velocity rifle. I shudder to think of the consequences if the owner of this arsenal came across anybody acting in what he believed to be a suspicious manner; he told me he had heard that small fishing boats put out from the south coast of Italy with violent intentions. Now, I know that small fishing boats will come out along this coast and ask for American cigarettes, but I would hardly describe the kids in them as violent thugs even though their boathandling is erratic to say the least. Off Israel a patrol boat will stop you before you enter Israeli waters, at night it is possible you could mistake the patrol boat for a marauding pirate. In the first instance this yachtsman might kill or maim innocent Italian children. In the second he might find himself blown out of the water by the vastly superior fire power of the patrol boat.

If however you feel you must arm yourself there is I believe an alternative. One is to carry a Very pistol or one of the rapid fire mini-flare launchers that are readily available on the market. In Britain a Very pistol is classified as a firearm and the owner must have a licence, but in Italy, for example, it can be bought over the counter, without a formal licence being required. (However it is usual to notify the police and customs). A Very pistol or flare launcher can be vaguely aimed at an intruder to discourage him from whatever he might have been going to do and would be sufficient to stop most instruders, the noise and flash of an exploding flare should deter all but the hardened professional.

Being raised on a farm another deterrent comes to mind: the high voltage electric fence used to keep cows grazing in a certain part of the paddock. These systems usually run off a twelve volt battery and consume very little current. I see no reason why the lifelines around a yacht should not be hooked up to such a system providing it is insulated from the rest of the craft. The device will register when a charge is given (i.e. the system is earthed), usually by a loud click. Thus it can be monitored and when installed will 'tell' you when an intruder has touched the live wire. Certainly anyone who has encountered an electric fence can tell you that you don't try to touch one again. The whack of the high voltage electric shock is a deterrent that works well and yet will not harm anyone. The sea or a wet dinghy is an excellent earth. My only hesitation in recommending such a system concerns possible rapid electrolysis should the system accidently earth through the yacht itself. But as I have said the gadget tells you, by clicks or a meter, that it is being discharged and so it should be an easy matter to detect any accidental earthing and eliminate it.

You will have difficulties with the authorities if you carry a firearm on board in Malta, Greece, Turkey and Cyprus and probably in Israel and Algeria as well. Anyone who takes a firearm to Syria, Lebanon or Libya is simply asking for trouble. Customs officers in all countries always ask if you have a firearm aboard and while you could conceivably hide it as customs searches are haphazard affairs when made at all, I would not advise this. Should you be thoroughly searched for any reason and a firearm that was not declared unearthed, then in some countries you face a prison sentence. In my mind the penalties for carrying a firearm on board in the Mediterranean far outweigh the remote possibility of it being useful or used.

BOOKS

The only reason for my buying a larger yacht would be so I could put more books aboard as books are old friends and companions on voyages of fact or fiction. They fall into two categories, reference books and books for relaxation and enjoyment.

Your reference books will include the necessary Admiralty publications and pilots for safe passage making and any specific small boat cruising guides for the countries you will visit. I find the Admiralty pilots, although written with big ships in mind, make for fascinating reading although some find the prose style difficult to conquer. Almanacs such as *Reeds* or the newer *Macmillan* contain much useful information which is usable long after their ephemeral tables are out of date. The Admiralty *List of Lights* and *Reeds' Mediterranean Navigator* are also useful, each covering the Mediterranean and Black Seas in one volume, and should be carried. For general navigation I like Kenneth Wilkes' *Practical Yacht Navigator* and *Ocean Yacht Navigator* and I wouldn't be without Eric Hiscock's *Cruising Under Sail* and *Voyaging Under Sail* (now in one volume) although Bob and Nancy Griffiths' *Blue Water* comes a close second. On heavy weather sailing I choose the slim *Handling Small Boats in Heavy Weather* by Frank Robb and another slim volume I constantly refer to is *Instant Weather Forecasting* by Alan Watts.

Other general reference works to do with cruising in one way or another should include a good book on knots and splices, but not so large that is an effort to get it out of the shelf; a good galley cook book is also necessary, there are many to choose from. A book on diesel engine maintenance and one on boat electrics as well as the specific handbooks for your yacht's engine and electrical equipment should be carried, circuit diagrams for the latter should also be available to any electrician not familiar with your system. The *Yachtsman's Eight Language Dictionary* is useful when it comes to explaining technical trouble to the natives.

Reference books to the flora and fauna greatly add to your enjoyment. On flora, one volume, Oleg Polunin and Anthony Huxley's *Flowers of the Mediterranean* is outstanding. For the sea the Hamlyn guide to *The Flora and Fauna of the Mediterranean Sea* is excellent. There are also Hamlyn guides to *Birds of Britain and Europe, Shells of the World* and *Trees of Britain and Europe. The Yachtsman's Naturalist* by Maldwin Drummond and Paul Rodhouse is another useful reference work.

On the individual Mediterranean countries I find the *Blue Guides* published by Black way ahead of the competition although the *Collins Companion Guides* also maintain a high standard. There are other good guides which do not belong to any particular series.

In the Mediterranean you should carry *The Odyssey* and *The Iliad*. Ernle Bradford's *Ulysses Found* is a fascinating yachtsman's commentary on Odysseus' voyage. The voyages collected and recorded by Richard Hakluyt are interesting as is Fernand Braudel's *The Mediterranean in the Age of Phillip II* (two volumes) containing a wealth of information on Mediterranean nautical history which repays struggling with its academic style; add to these titles Lord Byron's *Childe Harold's Pilgrimage*, some of the Hornblower series, some Hammond Innes, and some Monserrat and your bookshelves will begin to bulge.

In addition to the books you will not want to part with, you must have aboard a selection of paperbacks for swaps. Often the first words you will be greeted with after you have tied up next to another cruising boat will be: 'Have you any books to swap?' Cruising folk divorced from television and the atrophied imagination it encourages, turn to books. Usually they are swapped on a one-to-one basis but of late many have resorted to an inch-for-inch (or cm-for-cm) basis — as if an inch of Harold

Where else but on a boat can you change the view from your
back door when you want to? Change your neighbours. Live in
a bustling city one winter and in a quiet village the next.

Robbins was worth an inch of Nicholas Monserrat!

One book you will constantly refer to is your visitors' book. Often I have leafed through the pages of mine remembering pleasant evenings and sharing again the laughter and cheer of meeting the company of another cruising boat. My visitors' book is not the conventional one which allots a few mean lines for particulars and a postage stamp space for comments, but rather a large plastic-covered blank-paged book where a visitor can use up for comment as many pages as he or she likes and there is plenty of space for photographs and cards, it is more akin to a scrap book. Whether or not you have children on board, you will need other amusements like *Scrabble*, chess, backgammon, *Go* and a pack of cards. A musical instrument, if you play one, is solid gold at a barbecue or party. If you don't play then perhaps this is the time to learn.

PHOTOGRAPHY

If you know nothing at all about cameras then I suggest you get a small automatic camera using 35mm film. The well tried Pentax 'zoom', Olympus XA1, Konica C35 series and Canon *Sure Shot* belong to this category. Half frame, 110 or 110 disc cameras, are not worth bothering with and 120 film is not compact enough for the traveller.

One step up and well worth looking at are the 35mm automatic single lens reflex cameras such as the Olympus OM101, Nikon F30 or Pentax P30; and the new breed of autofocus cameras such as the Olympus AZ-300, Nikon F401 or Canon EOS series. These are virtually foolproof. There are a large number of manual and automatic single lens reflex 35mm cameras to choose from but beware of those containing sophisticated electronics on a boat.

The first camera I used was a manual Pentax with through-the-lens metering, with a mechanical shutter and mechanical winder, the only electrics being the meter and the flash connection. It was simple, easy to use, robust and it produced good pictures. Seduced by the new electronic cameras I bought one, and experienced nothing but trouble with the electronic shutter and the automatic exposure electronics. Had I thought about it I would have realised that in conditions where there is often salt spray or a salty atmosphere which quickly corrodes and destroys delicate electronics that it would soon malfunction and this is exactly what happened to my aperture priority camera. I abandoned it and went back to the sort of manual exposure camera with mechanical shutter that I had before — and it keeps going! To be fair later automatic and programmed cameras are significant improvements on the earlier models and have proved more robust and reliable.

If you are adding lenses to your equipment then first get a wide angle lens (28mm-35mm) for shots on board and secondly a 135mm or 200mm lens, or something like a 70-200mm zoom lens. There is no need to have a vast array of lenses when for most purposes the wide angle lens or the normal 50mm or 55mm lens will do. Get an ultraviolet filter, or better a polarising filter, both to cut down glare, penetrate haze and to protect your lens.

If you want to take underwater pictures then the Nikonos III or IV are in a class of their own, the new Nikonos IV has an automatic exposure meter and this is a great help. These cameras are completely waterproof and produce good quality pictures. If you don't want to take underwater pictures but believe that such a camera will be useful for action pictures when the spray is flying — then I must say it is not because they are too clumsy and difficult to use under normal conditions. Better to tape a plastic bag over your normal camera than to struggle with a fully fledged underwater camera above the water.

Most people will want to use colour negative film if they are are not aiming to sell their pictures. (Reproduction is normally from transparencies or black and white). Away from home film is expensive and can be from old stock so if you can get visitors to bring you a supply of fresh film then do so. Film processing varies radically in the Mediterranean. In Gibraltar, Spain, France, Italy, Malta and Greece it is quite good but elsewhere the processing can be very bad indeed and it may be better to post your films back to Britain to avoid disappointment. Some dedicated amateurs do their own processing on board, but this is a very difficult task within the confined space of a small yacht. (However see what Eric Hiscock has to say on this subject in *Voyaging Under Sail*.).

When taking photographs in the Mediterranean be cautious about working in military areas or near large industrial sites. I was once arrested in Greece for taking a picture of a harbour that had an electricity generating plant on the other side, the film was confiscated but otherwise I escaped unscathed. However, wildlife photographers in Turkey have been imprisoned for taking pictures near military installations. I suspect that the powerful telephoto lenses wildlife photographers often use (500mm-1000mm) made them appear even more suspicious than might have been the case had they carried cameras with 50mm lenses. In certain areas, especially near borders, you will often see signs saying photographs are forbidden, the sign may say this in English, or have a picture of a camera with a diagonal red stripe through it. Obey it.

Getting to the Mediterranean

The Worst Voyage:

Mr William Smith of Norfolk sailed from Scotland to Great Yarmouth in August 1978. Showing great independence of mind, en route, he missed Bridlington Harbour by 400 yards and rammed a jetty; at Yarmouth he overshot by 90 miles and ran aground off Kent.

A full-scale search for the boat was hampered by the change in its appearance. When it left Scotland, it was black with one mast. When rescued, it had two masts and was painted green. 'I passed the time while I was aground redecorating,' Mr Smith explained.

Entering Yarmouth Harbour, he scraped a floating museum, collided with a small coaster and hit an entrant for the Tall Ships race. He also knocked several guard rails off a trimaran and got the ropes of the cargo vessel 'Grippen' wrapped around his mast.

Describing the voyage as 'Pleasant with no hassle or worries,' Mr Smith said he planned sailing to Australia next.

Stephen Pile *The Book of Heroic Failures*

There are three possible ways of getting to the Mediterranean from England. The direct route sailing down the English Channel is to turn left into Biscay off Ushant and left again into the Strait of Gibraltar, an open sea passage of about a thousand miles. The alternative route is to cross France by the inland waterways, using rivers and canals you can potter through the heart of France to emerge on the Mediterranean coast some 200 locks later. A hardened few go up the Rhine and Main rivers and are trucked overland to Kelheim or Regensburg on the Danube. In 1993 the Main-Danube Canal will open so it will be possible to go by water through the heart of Europe to the Black Sea. The route you choose will be dependent on a host of factors not the least being your sailing experience and your own personal prefence.

Professional yacht delivery skippers usually choose the sea passage, it being the quickest and least fussy. With a full diesel tank and fair winds you can reckon on turning the corner into the Mediterranean within ten days of departure from the U.K. Most of us are not in such a hurry so that the trip can be broken up into more digestible chunks. From Ushant, many cross the Bay of Biscay to somewhere on the northwest coast of Spain like La Coruña, then down the Spanish and Portuguese coasts as weather and time allow until you arrive at Gibraltar.

On the sea passage you will need to have more experience than you need for the waterways route as Biscay has an evil reputation and there is often bad visibility along the Spanish and Portuguese coasts. The Strait of Gibraltar alone can give you a headache with adverse winds and the shipping of all nations pouring in and out. However, without in any way wanting to play down these very real dangers, I will say that in a seaworthy yacht and with careful planning, the passage is not the nautical obstacle course it is sometimes made out to be. Many yachts regularly cruise the Atlantic coasts of Spain and Portugal and a number of new marinas have been built along the coast for yachts permanently berthed there. Approach the voyage in the right way and you will enjoy some good cruising en-route to the Mediterranean.

Going through the French inland waterways, a yacht usually enters the system at Calais or Le Havre for the river Seine above Paris from whence there are three alternative routes to the rivers Saône and Rhône and eventual entry to the Mediterranean. An alternative inland route is through the Brittany canals between St Malo and St Nazaire, though they are very shallow. From St Nazaire you can sail a short distance down the coast to Bordeaux on the river Garonne and re-enter the inland waterways on the canal latèral á la Garonne and canal du Midi which connects with the Mediterranean ports of La Nouvelle, Agde and Sète. This canal du Midi route is often used by yachts returning from the Mediterranean to avoid the long passage round through the Strait of Gibraltar.

Whilst getting to the Mediterranean through the inland waterways does not of course require the same seamanship and skill that a sea passage does, nonetheless the journey should be carefully planned. More than one yacht has come to grief in the fast flowing rivers that link the canals to the sea and while currents, weirs, sloping locks and passing barges may not convey the menace of a Biscay gale or of tidal currents through the Raz de Sein, one still cannot afford to underrate them.

The Outer Sea Passage

Before deciding how to take your yacht to the Mediterranean, the following points for and against the sea passage should be considered.

The sea route may be the only one you can take because of restrictions on draught, breadth (for multi-hulls especially) and air height. Many modern motor yachts with built up cabins and flying bridges are too high to pass under some of the canal bridges.

If you are not port-hopping down the coast, this passage is the quickest. Professional delivery skippers choose it, not only because they can get on and keep sailing as long as the weather holds, but also because they do not have to prepare the boat for the canals by unstepping the mast, fitting fendering and so on.

If you like coastal cruising then the outside passage offers interesting passages with day-hops possible except for a few stretches of coast. In my opinion the west coast of France is a superb cruising ground and further south the Atlantic coasts of Spain and Portugal are rated highly by those who have cruised there.

You will need more experience to do this passage and more sea-time than for the hop across the channel into the canals. If you do not have adequate sea-time and the requisite navigation skills then you must cast around for an experienced crew, which can lead to further problems if adverse weather holds you up and your crew, with limited time off, have to return to jobs and loved ones.

The Bay of Biscay can be fearsome in a gale; for the most part, passages across are trouble-free in the summer but in the spring and autumn the gale frequency increases with the approach of the Equinox. Old sailing masters dreaded Biscay where the ungainly square riggers could be embayed with winds from the south through west to north and whilst modern yachts may be more weatherly to windward, it still pays to treat westerly gales in the Bay of Biscay with respect lest you find yourself embayed. Fog or a morning sea mist often occurs along the Atlantic coast of NW Spain and Portugal which can greatly reduce visibility.

Fishing boats are a hazard all along the coasts of Spain and Portugal. At night many do not carry regulation lights and some no lights at all.

As you approach the Strait of Gibraltar you will encounter increasing numbers of ships entering and leaving the Mediterranean. Traffic separation zones are in operation off Cabo Torinaña, Cabo Carvoeiro, Lisbon, Cape St Vincent and in the Strait of Gibraltar but except for the latter, these are sufficient distance off the coast not to bother the coast-hopping yacht unless for any reason you must cross them. At night particular care must be taken of rogue ships outside the traffic lanes.

PILOTS
Admiralty *Bay of Biscay Pilot (NP22)*.
Admiralty *West Coast of Spain and Portugal Pilot (NP66)*.
North Biscay Pilot. RCC Pilotage Foundation. Adlard Coles.
South Biscay Pilot. Robin Brandon. Adlard Coles.
The Atlantic Coasts of Spain and Portugal. RCC Pilotage Foundation. Imray.
North Brittany Pilot. RCC Pilotage Foundation. Adlard Coles.
Brittany and Channel Islands Cruising Guide. D. Jefferson. Stanford Maritime.
French Pilot (Four volumes). M. Robson. Nautical.

See
Inland Waterways
of France.
for dimensions
and routes

North Sea

ENGLAND

LONDON

English Channel

DUNKERQUE
CALAIS
ST VALERY *Nord* *Somme*
LE HAVRE *Seine* *Oise*
ROUEN *Marne*
PARIS
Lek
Waal
Maas

Meuse
C de l'Est *Moselle* *Rhine*
NANCY
VITRY LE F TOUL *Marne au Rhin*
Loing *C de l'Est*
MONTEREAU *Marne à Saône*
Lat à la Loire *Saône*
Nivernais *Bourgogne* *Rhône au Rhin*
DECIZE *Centre* CHALON

REGENSBURG
Danube
DONAUESCHINGEN
BASLE

Ushant
BREST
Brittany
Vilaine
ST MALO *Rance*

ST NAZAIRE *Nantes à Brest*
NANTES

LA ROCHELLE

Atlantic Ocean

ROYAN
Gironde
FRANCE

Bay of Biscay
BORDEAUX *C. lat à la Garonne*

LYON
Rhône

AVIGNON
TOULOUSE ARLES NICE
C. du Midi SETE P.ST LOUIS
P.LA NOUVELLE MARSEILLE

ITALY

Corsica

C.Finisterre
LA CORUNA
BAYONA

SPAIN

Sardinia

PORTUGAL

Balearic Islands

Mediterranean Sea

From
the Azores

LISBON

VILAMOURA

GIBRALTAR
Strait of Gibraltar

NORTH AFRICA

0   100   200
Kilometres

Routes from the United Kingdom to the Mediterranean

The French Inland Waterways

The following are the advantages and disadvantages of the inland waterways route.

After crossing the channel your navigation problems are over until you reach the south coast of France. If you are short on sea-time and your navigation is not up to a long sea passage then the journey through the inland waterways is the logical choice, but remember you have to cross the Channel and be able to navigate once you get to the Mediterranean.

Bad weather won't hold you up as it might do on the open sea passage. In early spring or late autumn the trip through the waterways would probably take a little longer than the sea passage but in winter it could conceivably take less time.

In most inland waterways, (the stress being on 'most'), there are lots of safe and attractive places to tie up for the night with no worries about the wind turning round in the night or of having to catch an early tide. Locks are closed at night and so your rest will not be disturbed by the wash from barges passing in the wee hours.

The inland waterways are not just a convenient short cut to the Mediterranean. They run through picturesque countryside, towns and cities rich in history, by riverbank and through forest full of wildlife and wildflowers, through some of the finest wine growing regions in the world. Like a good wine the waterways should be tasted and appreciated and not rushed over.

There are however some disadvantages to the passage through France. There are restrictions on length (immaterial for most boats because of the other restrictions), breadth, draught and air height

French Government Tourist Office.

Opening the sluices in a lock *(écluse)*.

(the maximum height above water) which vary for the different rivers and canal systems. For the through routes to the Mediterranean the maximum dimensions are these:

Length   In most of the locks the maximum length that will fit is 30 metres (98ft 5in). In the Brittany canals the maximum length that will fit the locks is 25 metres (82ft 6in) so unless you own a barge designed for the canals your breadth, draught and height are likely to be the critical dimensions.

Breadth   In most of the canals the maximum breadth (without fenders!) that can fit into the locks is 5 metres (16ft 5in). In the Brittany canals it is 4.5 metres (14ft 9in).

Draught and air height   The maximum dimensions for draught and air height vary as follows:

St Malo to St Nazaire 1.30 metres max. draught, 2.40 metres max. air height

Le Havre to Paris 2.50 metres max. draught, 5.97 metres max. air height

St Valéry to Paris 1.80 metres max. draught, 3.40 metres max. air height

Calais to Paris 2.18 metres max. draught, 3.68 metres max. air height

Paris to the Mediterranean (via the central canals — canal du Centre, canal de Bourgogne) 1.80 metres max. draught, 3.38 metres max. air height

Paris to the Mediterranean via the Marne canals 1.80 metres max. draught, 3.40 metres max. air height

Bordeaux to the Mediterranean, (canal latéral à la Garonne and canal du Midi) 1.60 metres max. draught, 3.00 metres max. air height.

The canals are closed for certain periods *(chômages)*, usually in the autumn and the winter, for maintenance. You can obtain a list of the *chômages* for the coming year from the French Government Tourist Office. In most cases a section of the canal is closed for a month or so, but rarely more than three months, and if this section lies on your route you must either choose an alternative (if there is one) or be prepared to wait until the maintenance work is completed. Like roadworks the repairs to the canals always seem to take longer than first anticipated. In recent years the drought conditions in France have further reduced water levels in the canals. If you can, go through in the spring when water levels are generally higher.

To go through the canals you must unstep your mast and lash it on the side-decks or the cabin top. At the beginning and end of the waterway system it is not difficult to find a crane to do this but you need to reserve a couple of days for this operation at either end.

It is surprisingly arduous work getting through the locks, and it is the locks after all that dictate your progress. One soon adapts to the rhythm of working the locks but at the end of the day you can be quite worn out as most people tend to overestimate the number of locks they can get through in a day. It is best to allow an extra twenty per cent of your passage time for a relaxed trip through the inland waterways.

CANAL EQUIPMENT

Fenders   You will need lots of fenders and also a number of old motor car tyres, four as a minimum and the more the better within reason. Some hardened brown water cruisers recommend wrapping fenders and tyres in plastic bags but I have found that any grit that gets between the polythene and the hull rapidly scratches your topsides; canvas bags over fenders and tyres are the best solution or alternatively, paint the tyres white so the topsides are not too badly marked. Whatever you do there is bound to be some marking.

Warps   You will need at least two 30 metre lines substantial enough to take the strain in the locks and the strain from passing barges when you are moored up. For a six ton boat get at least 14mm diameter, for a ten ton boat at least 20mm diameter.

Boathooks   Have at least one stout boathook about 2.5 metres long and preferably two. Most of the commercially produced hooks will break in no time with the punishment they get in the locks. You will need a boathook for alternately hanging on and pushing off the locks sides and for pushing off when you go aground.

Torches   You will need one with a strong beam to double as a searchlight (if you don't have a deck mounted light) when negotiating any tunnels as well as for messing around mooring up for the night and finding your way back from the local *brasseries*. A couple of smaller torches are also useful.

Canal anchors   While the traditional rond anchor is useful, a couple of hefty iron stakes and a large hammer are cheaper, easy to stow, and quite as effective. You will need these for tying up on the side of the canal where there are no trees or other suitable points for taking lines to. A Danforth also works reasonably well in firm ground if you hammer the flukes in.

Horn   A fog horn, lung-powered or operated by a compressed air cannister, is perfectly adequate for letting the lock-keeper know you have arrived and want to lock through, you normally give one long blast. Once the bush telegraph knows you are coming the lock-keeper ahead will be expecting you and you do not then need to disturb the peace of the country.

A plank   Not necessarily a *passerelle* as you will sometimes want to use it outside your fenders as a fender board when tying up against piles. It is also useful for getting ashore when you are moored some distance out from the canal bank.

Mast support   You may need to construct trestles on which to rest your mast if it will not lie along the pulpit and pushpit or on the side-deck. Old carpet or foam strip is useful for cushioning and lots of tape to bind up the rigging. It is best to remove the masthead light(s), wind speed and direction recorders, and to reverse or remove the bracket for the aerial(s) so they can be taped to the mast for protection. The odds are that if you leave anything projecting from the top of the mast it will be damaged. If the mast rests on top of the cabin ensure you have calculated this addition into your maximum air height.

CANAL CRUISING

Barges   Barges come in different sizes depending on the section of the inland waterways you are in. In the Seine and the Rhône huge pusher tugs shunt a train of lighters and these vessels are more akin to small ships than the barges which operate in the canals proper. In the maritime Seine, sea-going ships of large tonnage go up as far as Rouen, similarly sea-going ships ascend the Gironde to Bordeaux. Fortunately there is plenty of room for this traffic in these rivers, so that avoiding these monsters is no problem. In the canals the barges *(péniches)* are smaller but then so are the canals. An oncoming barge pushes a hill of water in front and leaves a disturbed wash behind it but after encountering oncoming barges a few times you will learn to take the hill at an angle and to cut across the wash behind to minimise rocking and rolling about.

Locks   Passage through these is not as traumatic as some make it out to be. They come in different shapes and sizes and varying degrees of sophistication, a number still being manned, others automated and gargantuan such as those on the Rhône.

Some locks, such as are found in British waterways, are manned but mechanical and thus require little action from yacht crews other than a need to tie up to the bollards and hang on, once entry has been made. If they are unmanned and automated one either twists a handle hanging down from an overhead wire before reaching the lock or a 'magic eye' detects your presence and opens the lock gate. On such locks there are traffic lights to direct you, red — wait, red and green — stand-by, and green — enter the lock. Once you are tied up inside, you push a green button to continue the locking cycle or a red button to stop the whole process should anything go wrong. Normally you have two or three minutes to get clear of the lock after the cycle is complete and the gates have opened.

In the old fashioned locks you normally lend the keeper a hand to open the sluices and one of the lock gates as well as taking lines ashore.

Lock procedure   In most of the locks, except for the manned automated ones on the rivers, you get quite adept at nosing into the bank to land a crew member then reversing off to wait for the gates to open. Once inside, a single breast line from the bow up and around a bollard and back to a winch or cleat in the cockpit is sufficient to hold the yacht. After a bit of practice you will have no problems controlling the boat with this single line which is easily whipped off the bollard for a speedy exit from the lock.

Barges have priority at locks; when they leave keep a good grip on your lines as the wash from the propeller is considerable and can throw a yacht about quite as much as the inrushing water from the sluice gates. Normally the engine should be kept going in the lock and it can be useful at times to put it into gear slowly going forward to counter the surge from the sluices. In locks with sloping sides (there are not many) you must have a number of tyres ready to drop down under the water to keep you off the sides, alternatively I would strongly recommend that you chat up a barge owner and go through tied alongside his vessel. You can then nip out first, let him pass, and do the same in the next lock until you are through the series of sloping locks.

Mooring up There are not as many places to moor as you might imagine, especially on the Seine and the Rhône. In many of the canals it is too shallow near the sides for keel yachts to moor up to the canal bank, nor can you stay in or immediately outside a lock for the night. Your plank will come in useful for mooring off the bank in sufficient depths so that passing barges do not dump you on the bottom. Having said this there are still numerous attractive places, especially in some of the villages and towns, where you can berth for the night. On the whole there are few marinas but a small charge may be made at some quays if facilities are provided.

Regulations Most of the inland waterways (exceptions being the rivers Seine, Rhône, Gironde and the large commercial canals) are closed at night, or, more accurately, the locks do not operate then. During the summer, locks are open from 0630-1930 and in the winter from 0700-1800 (local time). On the Seine and the Rhône you may not navigate at night unless accompanied by a pilot. In all of the inland waterways commercial craft have the right of way and priority in locks and you keep to the right hand side of the channel or canal.

Speed limits In the canals the speed limit is 3¼ knots, a limit which is not closely observed by commercial craft. In many of the canals there are 'clatter-boards' at the sides of the canal which float up and bang back down again when you are creating too much wash. On the Seine and Rhône the speed limit is 8 knots up to 20 tons and 13½ knots over 20 tons.

French Government Tourist Office.

One of the Rhône locks.

53

Road signs   You will come across a number of 'road' signs in the canals and rivers which should be followed religiously, especially those showing the channel and dangers. Only the common signs are shown below.

Dangers   In the canals there are no real dangers provided you follow the 'road' signs and exercise some basic canalmanship. On the rivers, particularly in the Seine, Saône, Rhône and Garonne, you must be a little more cautious.

Seine   Some of the guides say you can make it from Le Havre to Rouen on one tide. Perhaps if you have a powerful engine you could, but for more modestly powered craft this is simply not possible, especially in the winter and the spring when the current in the river, fed by numerous tributaries, significantly holds up the tide. You can moor at Caudebec-en-Caux and Duclair on laid moorings if you fail to make Rouen. Remember navigation is prohibited at night without a pilot. Although you can usually find a crane at Rouen to take down your mast, it is best done at Le Havre where there is a crane at the yacht club.

Approaching bridges in the Seine there can be considerable eddies and swirls around the bridge supports. I know of at least one yacht that was badly damaged under a bridge, being swept onto it by the eddies in a moment's inattention. In Paris there used to be berths only at the Touring Club of France and these were uncomfortable with the constant wash from passing craft. Now the new Port de Plaisance de Paris-Arsenal at the entrance to the old Canal Saint-Martin just upstream of Notre Dame provides berths out of the stream and with all facilities right in the heart of Paris. There is something wickedly hedonistic about berthing your own boat in the middle of Paris – linger over it.

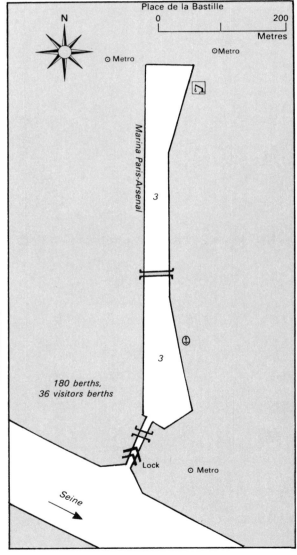

Paris (bridges not shown)

Port de Plaisance de Paris-Arsenal

Saône Navigation is not difficult as long as you follow the marked channel, the worst hazard the *cléonages*, the training walls which direct the current so it will scour the main channel. They are just above water except in the winter and spring when they may be just below, so stay in the main channel and you will have no problems with them; stray and like a number of folk you can badly damage your boat on them. Like the Seine there are few places to moor up: Châlon and Lyon are best.

Rhône Now it is canalised, this river does not provoke the fear it once did. Although you need no longer take a pilot, it is wise, indeed necessary, to get a copy of Vagnon's *Carte Guide de Navigation Fluviale No. 5 Rhône*. Armed with this and following a barge you should experience no problems although you may at times be alarmed by the overfalls and sluicing currents in this mighty river. After struggling up the Seine you will be sluiced down the Rhône in three or four days and like the Saône its biggest danger is the *cléonages*. Again there are few places to stop for the night: Condrieu, L'Epervière, Relais de Roches, Avignon, La Courtine marina (shallow) Arles and Port St Louis du Rhône (where there is a crane for stepping your mast).

Gironde and Garonne You must work the tides to get from Royan to Bordeaux and then to the lock admitting you to the canal latéral à la Garonne. You can easily carry one tide from Royan to Bordeaux but low powered craft may have difficulty getting from Bordeaux to the first lock in the spring and winter when the river is considerably swollen by rain. The estuary and the Garonne river are well buoyed but if in doubt follow a barge from Bordeaux to the first lock. There is a crane at Bordeaux for unstepping your mast.

FRENCH INLAND WATERWAYS GUIDES

Notes on the French Inland Waterways. Cruising Association. Constantly updated. Excellent value.

Les Cartes Guide Vagnon de Navigation Fluviale. Vagnon. Les Editions du Plaisancier. Editions are in French, English and German. You don't need them all but No. 5 covering the Saône and the Rhône and No. 7 covering the Garonne and canal du Midi are highly recommended.

A Cruising Guide to the Lower Seine. E. Howells. Imray.

Les Carte Guides de la Navigation Fluviale. Editions Cartographiques Maritimes. Useful, but Vagnon's guides are better.

Inland Waterways of France. D. Edwards-May. Imray. The standard reference giving all the essential data and general information.

France — The Quiet Way. Liley. Stanford Maritime. More evocative than straight descriptive but charming for that.

Through France to the Med. Mike Harper. Gentry. Covers Le Havre to the Mediterranean and the canal du Midi to Bordeaux well.

Through the French Canals. Philip Bristow. Nautical. Least useful.

Cruising French Waterways. Hugh McKnight. Stanford Maritime.

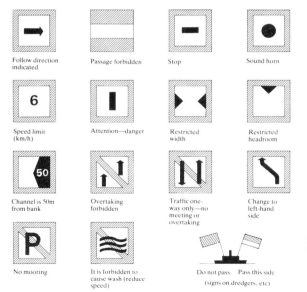

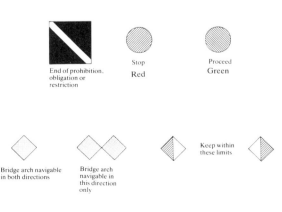

signs on French Waterways

The Danube

Little is heard about this route, and most of what is heard turns out to be myth, but a significant number of craft travel down this mighty river en route to the Mediterranean every year. It is gradually being canalised making navigation easier than it once was, and once the Main-Danube Canal is finished in 1993, it is likely an increasing number of boats will take this intriguing and interesting route to the Black Sea and thence to the eastern Mediterranean.

From northern European waters a boat can go up the Rhine and the Main to somewhere like Erlangen or Nuremburg where you can arrange to be trucked overland to Kelheim or Regensburg. The Rhine is quite a swift flowing river in places and you will need a decent sized engine to get up it, although you may be able to arrange a tow up the more powerful sections of it. Once into the Main, which is pretty much canalised, the current is much less than on the Rhine.

On the Austrian section of the Danube.

An intrepid few go down the Danube to the Black Sea and then to the Mediterranean. This is Budapest on the Hungarian section of the Danube.

The Danube is a different beast altogether to the French inland waterways. It flows through seven countries; four of these are in the eastern bloc and one is an independent socialist/communist state. From the top you go through: Germany, Austria, Czechoslovakia, Hungary, Yugoslavia, Bulgaria and Romania. It is advisable to get visas to all countries below Austria in advance to speed up what can be a very slow bureaucratic process, and certainly you should get visas in advance for Czechoslovakia, Bulgaria and Romania. In Czechoslovakia, Bulgaria and Romania, you will have difficulty getting provisions, sometimes even bread and fresh vegetables can be hard to come by, and accordingly you should stock up well before leaving Germany or Austria.

Despite the difficulties involved, the trip is one I can thoroughly recommend for adventurous souls. Unless you have blinkered eyes many of your preconceptions of eastern bloc countries will be shattered, a few will be confirmed, and you will see some spectacular and memorable sights and scenery and meet a lot of wonderful and extremely kind people. It is not a trip to be undertaken lightly and you will have more than a fair share of bureaucratic hassles, but even so you will see a part of Europe that few take the trouble to look at, on land or water, and you won't regret it.

READING
Sailing across Europe. Negley Farson. Century Hutchinson. Absorbing account of taking a small yacht down the Danube between the wars.
Black Sea and Blue River. John Marriner. Rupert Hart Davis. O.P. Marriner takes *September Tide* up the Danube to Vienna in the early sixties.
The Improbable Voyage. Tristan Jones. Bodley Head. Ripe tales and racey prose, as always a good read.
The Danube – A River Guide. Rod Heikell. Imray. Contains information for pleasure craft to get to the Mediterranean using this route.

From across the Atlantic

The usual route from the U.S.A. and the Caribbean is to Bermuda, to the Azores, and then to Portugal or Gibraltar.

Bermuda
The Bermuda islands are surrounded by coral reefs so good up-to-date charts and a lot of care are needed if you are not going to add to the numerous wrecks already on the coral. Bermuda Harbour Radio monitors VHF channel 16 on a 24 hours basis and will talk you through the reefs using their powerful radar to keep tabs on your movements. Most yachts make directly for St Georges where you clear customs at Ordnance Island. A yacht should leave in early spring for Bermuda, February or March being the most popular, to avoid the hurricane season of May to November.

The Azores
Reckoned to be a 2½ week trip on average from Bermuda. Yachts usually clear into Horta where Peter's *Café Sport* is justifiably popular with cruising folk. There are numerous delightful anchorages and harbours around the group of islands and it is well worth planning to spend a little time pottering rather than pushing on straightaway for Portugal or Gibraltar.

To the Mediterranean
From the Azores you can head for Portugal, to somewhere like Vilamoura, or head straight for Gibraltar. The passage to Portugal usually takes a week to ten days and to Gibraltar ten to twelve days.

READING
The Atlantic Crossing Guide. RCC Pilotage Foundation. Adlard Coles.
The Yachtsman's Guide to the Bermuda Islands. Michael Voegeli. PO Box 1699, Hamilton 5, Bermuda.
Cruising Guide to the Azores. R. and J. Silverman. Horta, Azores.
The Atlantic Islands. RCC Pilotage Foundation. Imray.
Street's Transatlantic Crossing Guide. W. W. Norton and Co.

Leaving the Mediterranean

From Gibraltar many yachts will be heading off across 'the pond' if they are not going down the Red Sea or back to northern European waters. After Gibraltar a yacht will head for Madeira or more likely the Canaries before crossing to Barbados or dropping further south to the Cape Verde Islands before the crossing.

Madeira
Although the prospect of visiting Madeira looks promising few yachts used to because of the poor anchorage there. Recently a marina has been built at Porto Santo with room for 20 yachts on two pontoons and it is likely more yachts will call in here now.

Canaries
Most yachts head for the Canaries, a group of seven islands lying just over fifty miles off the African coast. They make for the Canaries in September to November to be ready to cross in December or January. Yachts traditionally aimed for Las Palmas on Gran Canaria, but it is a dirty

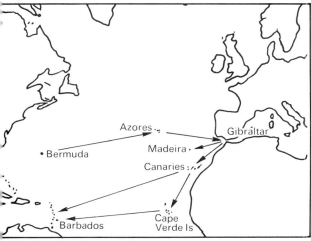
Routes across the Atlantic.

cluttered harbour with very few visitors' berths and given the relaxed attitude of the authorities you are better off going elsewhere. Try Arrecife or Naos on Lanzarote; Castillo on Fuerteventura; Puerto Rico marina on Gran Canaria; Radazul marina on Tenerife; or Santa Cruz on La Palma. A yacht should plan to spend a little time pottering around the islands as there are numerous small harbours and anchorages dotted around the islands away from the concrete blots on the landscape that house the multitudes flown in every day on package tours.

Cape Verde Islands

These lie to the southeast of the Canaries and are useful as a further staging post before crossing 'the pond'. Going further south to the Cape Verde Islands has the advantage that it puts you squarely in the Trades and most yachts take less than twenty days from here to Barbados. Because the islands are in the Trades, 20-30 knot winds blow day and night covering everything in dust and making many anchorages rolly. The islands are poor, so few provisions are available, and the authorities, though courteous, will hold your passports.

READING

The Atlantic Crossing Guide. RCC Pilotage Foundation. Adlard Coles.

Street's Cruising Guide to the Eastern Caribbean. Volume I. W. W. Norton and Co.

Wintering over

There's a great deal to see and do in the Mediterranean so it is not surprising that increasing numbers of boats are wintering over before pushing on to other parts of the Mediterranean. Some get accommodation ashore, but most spend the winter on board.

Before you choose a spot to spend the winter in think about what there is to do and see ashore. While cinemas, pubs, bars, restaurants, bookshops, and access to public transport may all seem peripheral to the real concerns of a safe harbour, facilities such as water and electricity, and how much it is all going to cost – most people need diversions ashore in the winter. Bicycles are useful for getting around locally and with cheap public transport the winter is an ideal time to make excursions to places of interest – there are fewer tourists around and prices are lower. In many of the countries you can go skiing, even in such unlikely places as Greece and Turkey.

The following list of areas details the popular spots where yachtsmen congregate for the winter. It is not exhaustive, after all you can winter almost anywhere that's safe from winter gales, and some do in the most out of the way places.

Gibraltar Liked for good facilities, hauling, cheap flights and its 'Englishness'.

Spain Algericas, Estepona, Marbella, Alicante, Almerimar, Palma (Mallorca). Liked for good winter climate, facilities, hauling, and cheap flights.

France Port Camargue, Martigues, Marseille, Hyères, Port Cogolin, Port Grimaud, Antibes. Liked for facilities, hauling, good bars and restaurants, easy access.

Monaco Liked for bustling and sophisticated life ashore.

Italy San Remo, Rapallo, Portoferraio, Cala Galera, Fiumicino, Ischia, Sibaris Marina. Liked for facilities, hauling, good bars and restaurants, easy access.

If you are leaving the boat ashore a good winter cover protects it from dust and stops the sun getting at the brightwork.

Malta Liked for good winter climate, facilities, hauling, good bars and restaurants, cheap flights.

Yugoslavia Dubrovnik. Liked for hauling, cheap cost of living.

Greece Gouvia, Levkas, Athens, Portokheli, Crete, Rhodes. Liked for good winter climate (Crete and Rhodes), cheap cost of living, bars and restaurants.

Turkey Kuşadasi, Bodrum, Kemer. Liked for cheap cost of living, bars and restaurants ashore.

Cyprus Larnaca. Liked for good winter climate, facilities, hauling and its 'Englishness'.

Tunisia El Kantaoui. Liked for its good winter climate, cheap cost of living.

LEAVING A BOAT THERE

Once down in the Mediterranean many people want to leave the boat there and return home for the winter. Some have to work to replenish funds for the next season's cruising, others prefer the comforts of a house to life afloat in the winter months. With increasing numbers of charter flights in the winter or late autumn and early spring to some Mediterranean countries, it works out cheaper to base a boat in the Mediterranean including flights back home than it does to keep it in some of the more expensive marinas in northern Europe, and you get guaranteed sailing in the summer. For whatever reasons you are leaving a boat, there are a number of important decisions to make and some work to do if the boat is to be safe for the winter.

To haul or not?

It is quite feasible to leave a yacht in the water over the winter provided it is in a safe marina with good security and ideally a few friendly cruising folk who are wintering over to keep an eye on it for you. Personally I would always haul a boat out of the water for the winter as, if I am not going to be there, it all seems so much safer to have the boat standing on solid ground and for most boats it does not do them any harm and may do some good. A wooden boat left in the water can be at risk from teredo and gribble. A glass fibre boat is less likely to get osmosis if it is allowed to dry out for the winter. Steel and aluminium boats may suffer from electrolysis problems in the water. Whatever material a boat is made of it needs just one faulty seacock or skin-fitting to fail and the boat sinks.

Preparations for laying-up afloat

Take off all sails, including the roller-reefing foresail, and wash and stow.

Remove all loose gear above deck such as anchors, spinnaker pole, inflatable and oars, liferaft, sheets, boathook and *passerelle*.

Turn all sea-cocks off and turn off battery switch.

Have a cockpit cover made and cover all brightwork and exposed mechanical gear such as the anchor winch and sheet winches with buckets or plastic containers. Do not cover winches with plastic bags taped over as this encourages condensation.

Ensure you have adequate warps ashore that are protected from chafe both on the quay and on the boat.

Pull the boat well off the quay and if possible use two permanent moorings to hold you off. If in doubt about marina moorings, put an anchor down as well.

Make sure someone reliable is keeping an eye on your pride and joy.

Laying-up ashore

Another short checklist:

Winterising the engine

Run the engine to operating temperature. Drain or pump out the engine oil.

Refill with fresh engine oil.

Drain the saltwater cooling system.

Flush the engine through with fresh water. The easiest way is to disconnect the inlet pipe and put it into a bucket of fresh water and run the engine – refill the bucket several times. Drain the fresh water from the engine.

Mix fresh water and antifreeze at a ratio of 4:1 and run the water/antifreeze mixture into the engine.

Remove and store waterpump impeller.

Check the anticorrosive zincs if you have them and replace if necessary.

Remove air filter cover and spray *WD-40* or similar into the air intake while turning the engine by hand.

Turn engine to compression stroke.

Fill fuel tank to avoid condensation.

Wipe engine with an oily rag or a mixture of *Vaseline* dissolved in petrol, or spray with *WD-40*, to avoid external rust.

In most places you get hauled out by travel hoist.

Remove all sails and wash and stow.

Remove all loose gear from the deck and stow below.

Flush the toilet out with fresh water and a little detergent.

Remove seacocks, grease and replace.

De-tension the standing rigging.

Remove all carbon-zinc batteries from equipment.

Remove the main batteries and arrange for them to be trickle charged.

Wipe all surfaces with a weak bleach solution to stop mould growing.

Open all lockers, lift up bunk cushions, lift floorboards, to allow air to circulate around the boat.

Have a heavy duty boat cover made that can be securely fastened, preferably under the boat. The cover is as much to stop dust getting in and protect brightwork, as to stop rain.

Boatminders

Are a breed apart. You only seem to get good ones or bad ones, there is no in-between. Ask around residents for recommendations since too many are unreliable and will not carry out everything you have contracted for. On numerous occasions I have checked boats during bad weather where owners had paid substantial amounts for it to be looked after, but which hadn't been checked for weeks. In Appendix I I list a few addresses of reliable boatminders.

Popular spots for leaving a boat

As in the other list, this one makes no claims to be exhaustive, but is simply a list of places that have proved popular to leave a boat for the winter, either afloat or ashore.

Gibraltar

Spain   Algeciras, Estepona, Marbella, Alicante, Palma (Mallorca).

France   Port Camargue, Martigues/Port à Sec, Hyères, Port des Embiez, Port Cogolin, Port Grimaud, Antibes.

Italy   San Remo, Rapallo, Portoferrario, Punta Alla, Santo Stefano, Cala Galera, Porto Cervo, Sibaris Marina.

Malta

Yugoslavia   Dubrovnik, Split, Trogir, Kremik, Biograd, Zadar, Rovinj, Novigrad, Punat.

Greece   Corfu, Levkas, Nidri, Zea, Kalamaki, Lavrion, Porto Kheli, Rhodes.

Turkey   Kuşadasi, Bodrum, Kemer.

Cyprus   Larnaca.

Tunisia   El Kantaoui.

The Mediterranean

These seamen, like their forefathers, rely upon no winds unless they are right a-stern, or on the quarter; they rarely go on a wind if it blows at all fresh, and if the adverse breeze approaches to a gale, they at once fumigate St Nicholas, and put up the helm. The consequence of course is that under the ever varying winds of the Aegean they are blown about in the most whimsical manner. I used to think that Ulysses with his ten years voyage had taken his time in making Ithaca, but my experience in Greek navigation soon made me understand that he had in point of fact, a pretty good 'average passage'.

Eothen. A. W. Kinglake

VITAL STATISTICS

Geology The Mediterranean we see today is in geological terms a comparatively young sea. About 70 million years ago there was no recognisable Mediterranean but open sea, the Great Tethys Sea which stretched from the Indo-West Pacific region (between Europe and the continental land mass to the south) to the Atlantic. Over millions of years Arabia swung up to Turkey to block off the Indian Ocean so that the Mediterranean was a gulf of the Atlantic. Around 40 million years ago Africa began pushing up towards Europe and with this compression and the detachment of chunks of land the features we recognise today had formed by about 9 million years ago. Some 6 million years ago the Mediterranean was actually closed off from the Atlantic and dried up into what could be described as a briny puddle, the floor of the present day Mediterranean is covered in thick layers of various salts dating from this time. About 5½ million years ago the Atlantic burst through the barrier, (whether this was caused by an earthquake or a rise in the sea-level is unknown), and the Mediterranean once again became a sea joined as it now is to the Atlantic by the narrow Strait of Gibraltar.

The enormous forces that moved continents and moulded the Mediterranean and buckled the land to form the mountains are still in evidence. Today the African land mass or 'plate' pushes north, the Iberian plate east, the Apulian south, and the Eurasian plate west. At the collision points of the plates lie the Mediterranean volcanoes, along them run the fault lines which give rise to earthquakes like that on November 23 1980 which killed 5000 people in Southern Italy and demolished countless buildings leaving some 400,000 homeless. The earthquake is said to have caused more damage to ancient Pompeii than the eruption of Vesuvius that preserved it in ash in A.D. 79.

Climate The Mediterranean is typically defined by the geographer as the region between the olive tree in the north and the large palm groves in the south. It is a long skinny sea lying between the latitudes of 32°N and 44°N, a difference in latitude which although not great, nonetheless contains a distinct climatic zone. To some extent this zone is contained by the mountains around the perimeter which are: to the north, the high mountain ranges of Europe — the

Pyrenees, the Apennines, the Alps and the Dalmatians; to the east, the lofty Taurus mountains, the Amanus range in Turkey and Syria and the Lebanese mountains; and in the south the Atlas ranges.

The two gaps in the mountains around the Mediterranean, the great Sahara desert and the Atlantic Ocean, combine to give the classic definition of the Mediterranean climate of hot dry summers and mild wet winters. In the summer the desert contributes the heat, the clear blue skies and a great thermal air mass that significantly influences the winds in the summer. The winter is the domain of the Atlantic when depressions drop into the Mediterranean and generate high winds and rough seas, along the way bringing heavy often torrential rain.

The Atlantic influence is historically recorded in the prohibitions against sailing in the winter that we know of. The Greeks proscribed shipping in the Aegean in the winter and Roman ships were ordered to be laid up between October and April. In the 13th century the maritime law of Pisa, Venice and Ancona forbade ships to put to sea between St Andrews Day and March and even up until the end of the 18th century the shipping of the Levant did not sail between the 26th October and the 5th May.

One of the monsters of the Atlantic influence is the Genoa lee cyclone caused when a depression moving down across Europe encounters the Alps which then funnel it into the Ligurian Sea where it deepens. The cyclone then moves east across the Mediterranean lashing the coasts with high winds and torrential rain. Often a *mistral* follows and the cyclone can cause a *bora* to howl down the Adriatic. The effects of the Genoa lee can be dramatic. In December 1980 I was in a small harbour on the south of Evia in Greece where for two days Force 10-11 winds caused shipping to seek shelter in the bay until by the third day there were over thirty ships ranging from supertankers to coasters anchored in the roadstead. On land over ten inches of snow fell overnight at sea level and all electricity and communications were cut. A contrast with the Saharan summers that the yachtsman should be well aware of!

The Sea Perhaps the most striking feature of the Mediterranean is the virtual absence of tides. The small area of the sea is little influenced by the gravitational pull of the Sun and Moon and the narrow Strait of Gibraltar shuts out the Atlantic tides so that at Gibraltar the range at springs is only one metre and at Naples and Alexandria it is just half a metre.

A winter sea. It is just possible to see the size of the swell beyond the breakers.

Although gravitational forces have little effect on the waters of the Mediterranean, other hydrological factors are at work moving it. In the summer the Sun causes massive evaporation in the sea's eastern basin. The rivers flowing into the Mediterranean can replace only a small part of this water and most of the water to replace that lost by evaporation pours in from the Atlantic through the Strait of Gibraltar where about one million cubic metres flow in every second. Water circulates around the Mediterranean in approximately an anticlockwise direction subject to the lumps of land in its path but this is only on the surface, the more salty waters of the eastern Mediterranean (about 39 parts of salt per 1000 compared to 35 parts per 1000 for the Atlantic) sink and flow slowly westwards to spill over the sill at Gibraltar into the Atlantic. It takes about 180 years for the total volume of water in the Mediterranean to be renewed.

The volume of water being turned over is not all that large in comparison to the Atlantic, Pacific and Indian Oceans. Its area, 1,146,000 sq. miles, is about 1/140th of the total sea area of the world but its volume is a miniscule 1/355th. Its mean depth is 1500 metres but at its deepest in the central eastern Mediterranean it gets down to 4602 metres which is only slightly more than the mean depth of the Atlantic.

Paradoxically one of the attractions of the Mediterranean for the yachtsman is the considerable depths close to the coast. The absence of large areas of continental shelf (see map 72) mean that it is possible to sail very much closer to the land than in many other places, the exceptions being the northern Adriatic and the eastern and southern coasts of Tunisia.

For pottering yachtsmen the size of the Mediterranean is irrelevant. After all it is only 2300 miles long and nowhere wider than 500 miles, so the world girdler — in search of open sea and long passages — must look elsewhere. But what is relevant is the abundance of cruising areas to be explored — the bits of land in the sea.

The Land   Samuel Johnson thought the Mediterranean the proper place to travel to: 'The grand object of travelling is to see the shores of the Mediterranean. On these shores were the four great empires of the world — the Assyrian, the Persian, the Greek and Roman. All our religion, almost all our arts, almost all that sets us above savages, has come to us from the shores of the Mediterranean.'

Today there are nineteen countries around the Mediterranean (including Monaco) bridging Christian Europe, Islamic Africa and Asia Minor. In this small sea one moves not only between very different countries, often separated by only a few miles of coast, but between regions in any one country like Sicily in Italy where regional differences are reflected in the architecture, cuisine, dress, dialect and customs.

This profusion of lands and peoples going far beyond the strict geographical boundaries of the countries provides one of the joys of sailing in the Mediterranean. For those like myself who are fascinated by old ruins, there is the best collection in the world in the Mediterranean and along with Dr Johnson we can ponder on the origins of the civilized world. The grand object of sailing in the Mediterranean is to see the shores and not just go sailing.

. . . along with Dr Johnson we can ponder on the origins of the civilised world.

Pollution A closed sea that takes 180 years to renew its waters is especially vulnerable to pollution. Anything dumped into the waters of the Mediterranean stays there for some considerable time whereas in the Atlantic the tides sweep pollutants away from the shores. The most visible pollutant in the Mediterranean as in other oceans of the world are hydrocarbons: tar, crude oil, diesel and petrol. Tankers flushing out their tanks at sea, spillage at loading and refining installations, and dumping and the pumping of oily bilges cause the blight which affects the sea and coasts, despite the introduction of laws prohibiting the dumping of oil in the sea and the provision to impose heavy fines.

Although tar is a visible pollutant, and I suspect there are few beaches in the world not blighted by tar to some degree, there are many more dangerous invisible pollutants. The rivers of the heavily industrialised countries of Europe bring heavy metals, pesticides, detergents and other dangerous chemicals into the sea. This invisible pollution is more damaging than any other and so severe that there is now an area off Marseille where industrial sediment has oozed over about a square kilometre of the sea floor; it is even marked on the chart as a polluted zone.

Add to all this the raw sewage that ends up in the sea, not only from residents but also from the temporary summer population of tourists, and the picture looks a sorry one. Many of the cities dump raw sewage straight into the sea through antiquated sewers which are simply overburdened with the additional tourist population, the inevitable outcome being an outbreak of an infectious disease such as the cholera epidemic of Naples in 1973.

Until recently little was being done to put the brakes on pollution in the Mediterranean. However in 1975 the United Nations Environment Program managed to get the 17 nations around the Mediterranean (xenophobic Albania declined to participate) to contribute to a massive clean-up and to implement tight controls on pollution. The Council of Europe is also implementing a clean-up of sewerage systems in the Mediterranean running into millions of pounds. In many of the countries an awareness is growing that the Mediterranean cannot be taken for granted and must be cared for, resulting in controls which will inevitably affect yachts. In some countries at the moment only charter yachts are required to have holding tanks although the majority can fine yachts for

Marine life for the 'pot'.

pumping bilges and toilets in harbour and for throwing garbage overboard. TBT antifouling containing tin has been banned in France.

I mention all of this not to discourage one from going to the Mediterranean, after all pollution is an unpleasing fact of life wherever we go on this globe, but to discourage further contributions to the disgraceful abuse of the sea. In France and Italy there is a growing green lobby. Numerous sea areas off the French coast have been made into conservation zones. In Italy a referendum has banned the construction of nuclear power stations and those in operation will be closed down. Despite all my comments the Mediterranean remains an idyllic sea, Homer's wine-dark sea that no travel brochure photograph can do justice to – a sea that those of us who travel upon should take care not to stain.

Aide-memoire for the yachtsman to avoid polluting his environment.

Do not throw non-biodegradable refuse over the side. If you are within 2-3 miles of the coast do not throw biodegradable but visually polluting refuse such as whole fruits or vegetables, cabbage and lettuce leaves, orange skins, etc. over the side as they float for a long time and wash up on the beaches and scavengers like gulls do not appear to relish them.

Bring refuse ashore for proper disposal.

Avoid spilling fuel or pumping out oily bilges within 3-4 miles of the coast. Break down the diesel/oil mixture in the bilges with a mild detergent before pumping it out.

Avoid using a sea toilet if there are toilets ashore. Pump out holding tanks to shore tanks or when you are well out to sea. Avoid using strong disinfectants in toilets – the marine life doesn't like it either.

Avoid using strong detergents for washing up.

Avoid using damaging cleaning chemicals for the hull and deck.

Avoid scrubbing down the bottom in confined places as the residues of an antifouling harms marine life.

Use mild antifoulings and avoid those with tributyl tin – banned in Britain since 1987.

Do not empty solvents and paint residues where they can leach into waterways or the sea.

Do not empty waste oil or diesel into or near the sea. Dispose of it in sealed cans with the rubbish or in the special receptacles provided in some harbours.

Ashore do not light fires where the surrounding vegetation could catch alight or in strong winds. Always keep a bucket of water handy.

When snorkling do not disturb the marine life unduly by removing plants or animals – unless you are going to eat it.

Marine Life Contrary to popular belief the Mediterranean is not teeming with marine life. There is not the variety nor the prolific life that exists in other warm seas such as the Pacific or the Red Sea. There are several reason for this. The small tidal range means that there is little littoral life, that life that lives in the zone between the tides, to feed and shelter other species. The comparatively small area of continental shelf exacerbates this absence for many organisms need warm shallow water for part if not necessarily all of their life cycle. As previously noted only in the northern Adriatic and the shelf off Tunisia is there a large expanse of shallow water and as we might expect these two areas are rich in marine life.

The famous clarity and blueness of the Mediterranean points to another reason for the relative paucity of marine life, it is poor in plankton which most larval stages of fish and some adults need to feed on. The plankton poverty is worst in the eastern Mediterranean, although the Black Sea, fed by many fresh water rivers, is consequentially rich in plankton. It is interesting to note that the sardine catch off the mouth of the Nile was five times greater before the Aswan High Dam trapped the river's nutrients — now distributing them over the land instead of into the sea.

However the yachtsman will not be disappointed by the marine life in the Mediterranean, simply because he is on the water all the time and thus in the best position to see anything in it. Dolphins, tunny, turtles, flying fish, swordfish, sunfish and occasionally whales will be seen. On passage from Malta to the Ionian I was accompanied for three days and nights by a large school of tunny that adopted *Tetranora* as mum, only leaving as I approached Cephalonia. By the seashore you will see wrasse, mullet, giltheads, combers, crabs, starfish and at dusk, octopus hunting for dinner; with a mask and snorkel the warm waters are a delight to explore but be careful you don't get sunburnt on your back and neck as you drift over the sea bottom.

Most denizens of the deep, such as the octopus, have more to fear from us than we do from them.

A short history of yachting in the Mediterranean

Such is our insular historical perspective that we like to think that yachting began with the restoration of the monarchy in 1660 and the pleasure craft of Charles II and his cronies, not in the warm waters of the Mediterranean some fifteen hundred years earlier. Certainly the word yacht from the Dutch 'jaghte' meaning a small, fast ship, was introduced in this period to describe the royal pleasure boats, but yachting in this sense and in the meaning it picked up later has been around for longer than this.

Royal yachts have been around since the Egyptians with the earliest known royal pleasure craft belonging to the Pharaoh Cheops. At around forty-four metres (143 ft) he used it on the Nile and liked it so much he had it buried with him in the Great Pyramid at Giza. When the Ptolemies came along in the fourth century B.C. a whole fleet of royal yachts were built. Ptolemy IV had big ideas about the sort of royal pleasure craft he wanted and had a catamaran constructed that was ninety-two metres (300 ft) long with a deck nearly fourteen metres (45 ft) wide and what can only be described as a miniature palace eighteen and a half metres (60 ft) high erected upon it. This construction was towed up and down the Nile so that Ptolemy IV could survey and rule his kingdom in some comfort and style when on the move.

For flair and dramatic effect none of the rulers of Egypt could top the performance of Cleopatra. When she was summoned to Tarsus by Antony, Cleopatra intended to create an entrance he wouldn't forget. Plutarch describes Cleopatra's approach to Tarsus in 41 B.C.:

'She came sailing up the Cyndus on a galley whose stern was golden; the sails were purple, and the oars were silver. These, in their motion, kept tune to the music of flutes and pipes and harps. The Queen, in the dress and character of Aphrodite, lay on a couch of gold brocade, as though in a picture, while about her were pretty boys, bedight like cupids, who fanned her, and maidens habited as nereids and graces, and some made as though they were rowing, while others busied them about the sails. All manner of sweet perfumes were wafted ashore from the ship, and on the shore thousands were gathered to behold her.'

Cleopatra invited Antony on board for dinner and from there on in he was captivated by the Egyptian Queen and they were rarely separated.

They died together, committing suicide, after Antony failed to wrest the Roman Empire from Octavius.

The Roman Emperors showed the same predilection for royal pleasure craft as had the Egyptians. The demented Caligula had several, the largest of which was over sixty metres (200 ft) long. It was a well made craft sheathed in lead to stop teredo and gribble getting at the planking, and boasted such amenities as dining halls, a garden, baths, a brothel, and private chambers. After Caligula was dispatched Nero continued the tradition of opulent royal craft with a resplendent gilt and ivory creation on which he held lavish banquets.

What of lesser mortals in this era of grandiose royal pleasure craft? It is likely that there were rich aristocrats around who had sailing yachts constructed or converted one of the small tubby trading boats for pleasure use. The problem is that nobody wrote about it, or if they did it was lost as happened to so many of the ancient works. That is except for one important exception. The first concrete reference we have of sailing for pleasure comes from the Roman poet Catullus.

Catullus is not widely read today, but in his time he instigated something of a revolution in poetic circles writing lyrical and passionate poems with a gut feeling to them, pungent epigrams that can still shock, and poems of descriptive verse that is both evocative and accurate. He was born around 84 B.C. and died at an early age in 54 B.C. Catullus began writing when he was fifteen or sixteen, but the period describing his yachting endeavours occurred a few years before his death. His brother died in the Troad and Catullus went to visit his grave. While he was in Bithynia on the Asiatic shores of the Black Sea he decided, for whatever reasons, to have a yacht built.

near Cytorus
before you were a yacht
you stood
part of some wooded slope
where the leaves speak continuously in sibilants together.
Pontic Amastris
Cytorus
–stifled with box-wood–
these things
my boat affirms
are common knowledge to you both.

He calls his yacht a 'bean-pod boat' and in common with most boat owners asserts 'that she's been the fastest piece of timber under oar or sail afloat'. The sailing boats of this period looked much the same over a thousand year period – short and broad double-enders, a twenty metre boat would have had a beam of around six metres and carried a squaresail on a stubby mast. Essentially they were not too far removed from the double-ended caique, the *tre-handiri*, seen in Greece today. The sail was set on a yard nearly twice as long as the mast, the yard itself being constructed from two saplings lashed together and with a sheet from either end led back to the steering oars. The sail could be reefed by brailing it upwards to the yard in strong winds. Some of these boats also carried a small sail, the *artemion*, on a steep bowsprit, and in very strong winds this would have been the only sail up. It also aided stability downwind and would have helped with the boat on a broad reach. These boats could be rowed in a calm or into harbour, but they were not anywhere near as fast under oars as the sleek galleys of the time.

In his yacht Catullus sailed out of the Black Sea, through the Bosphorus and Dardanelles into the Aegean. Here he sailed to Rhodes and through the Cyclades and probably around the Peloponnesus where he turned north to sail up the Adriatic to the river Po.

> Call as witness
> the rough Dalmatian coast
> the little islands of the Cyclades
> Colossan Rhodes
> the savage Bosphorus
> the unpredictable surface of the Pontic Sea.

He then sailed up the Po and the Mincio to a short distance from Lake Garda. He must have had the yacht hauled overland because he describes her as lying under his villa at Sirmio on the lake:

> Finally,
> no claim on the protection of any sea god
> on the long voyage up to this clear lake.
>
> These things have all gone by.
> Drawn up here
> gathering quiet age.

Poem 4 transl. Peter Whigham

Catullus was not just a passenger on these trips. In various poems he accurately describes the winds, navigation, storms, and his boat in a manner only someone intimately acquainted with the sea could do. In this fragment he describes the afternoon breeze getting up in the Aegean:

> Zephyr
> flicks the flat water into ridges
> with a morning puff,
> the sloped waves
> loiter musically,
> later the wind rises
> & they rise,
> they multiply
> they shed the sun's sea purple as they flee.

Poem 64. transl. Peter Whigham

And in this fragment reveals an awareness of the basics of navigation by the times of sun rise and sunset and the appearance of certain stars:

> Who scans the bright machinery of the skies
> & plots the hours of star-set & star-rise,
> this or that planet as it earthward dips,
> the coursing brightness of the sun's eclipse.

Poem 66. transl. Peter Whigham

Catullus died at Sirmio with his yacht drawn up on the shore of Lake Garda when he was only thirty years old. For over a thousand years his poetry was lost until the codex was discovered, so the story goes, wedging a wine barrel in Verona at the end of the thirteenth century. How many more works have been lost describing innocent pleasures on the water in those long ago times is something we will never know. Catullus himself would no doubt have made further voyages had he lived longer – he had that hunger to break loose and go travelling that a yachtsman needs.

> Now spring bursts
> with warm airs
> now the furor of March skies
> retreats under Zephyrus . . .
> and Catullus will forsake
> these Phrygian fields
> the sun-drenched farm-lands of Nicaea
> & make for the resorts of Asia Minor,
> the famous cities.
> Now, the trepidation of departure
> now lust of travel,
> feet impatiently urging him to be gone.
> Good friends, good-bye.

Poem 46 transl. Peter Whigham

Not until the nineteenth century do we again have a record of yachting in the Mediterranean. It is likely that in Byzantium, Venice, Genoa, and other centres of wealth in the intervening period, the aristocracy and rich eccentrics had sailing boats constructed and sailed them for pleasure, but there are no records of adventures such as those of

Catullus. We know, of course, that poor Shelley was drowned while sailing with friends in Italy. Percy Bysshe Shelley was at La Spezia and set out to sail to Leghorn with Edward Williams, a sailor Charles Vivian, and Captain Daniel Roberts who had built the boat. They arrived safely and five days later set out to sail back. A storm blew up in the evening and the boat was seen to sink off Viareggio, the bodies were washed ashore ten days later on July 17th 1822. Byron and Leigh Hunt who were in Leghorn hurried down and made the funeral arrangements, the bodies had to be burnt because of quarantine laws, and that is about as much as we know of Shelley's yachting endeavours or of Roberts who had the boat built. Byron himself liked boats but knew little about them, being as interested in the flamboyant captains and crew of the ships he chartered when in Greece as in the boats themselves.

In the middle and late nineteenth century the Victorians took to yachting in a big way. One of the first accounts of a yachting cruise is to be found in E. M. Grosvenor's *Narrative of a Yacht Voyage in the Mediterranean during the years 1840-41.* Grosvenor and his family cruised in the 217 ton R.Y.S. *The Dolphin* for a year exploring many of the harbours and islands from Gibraltar to Turkey. The Americans, always keen to visit decadent and ailing Europe, sailed a number of large yachts across to the Mediterranean, sometimes with odd notions about the object of the cruise. In 1816-17 George Crowninshield Jr. sailed the opulent *Cleopatra's Barge* to the Mediterranean. George Jr. was obsessed with Napoleon and intended in a mercy mission to convey Napoleon's wife, the Empress Marie Louise who was ensconced in Rome, to the erstwhile Emperor exiled on St. Helena in the middle of the Atlantic. As it turned out Marie Louise was quite happy in Rome with a large part of the fortune amassed by Napoleon and a lover to help her spend it – she declined the offer and poor George Jr. sailed back home where he died not long after. In 1853 Vanderbilt visited the Mediterranean in his paddle-wheel schooner, but was little impressed and returned home after a short stay and rarely ventured onto a yacht again. Not long afterwards the eccentric and extravagant newspaper owner, Gordon Bennet Jr., the man whose name became an exclamation for anything outrageous, cruised around Europe and the Mediterranean for an extended period. Bennet Jr.'s eccentricities became a by-word in his own time. He abhorred playing cards and would have his crew and passengers' baggage searched for any offending pack. If he found a pack of cards he extracted a sly revenge by taking out the four aces and throwing them away before returning the pack to the bag. He didn't like beards and no-one on board was allowed to have one. One of his newspaper editors who stubbornly refused to shave his beard off followed the boat from port to port until he finally resigned from the paper in disgust. In one port when a troupe of actors came aboard he was so delighted with their performance that he sailed off with them and would not return until they had performed their entire repertoire.

Most visitors to the Mediterranean were rather more restrained than this. In 1895 *With the Yacht, Camera, and Cycle in the Mediterranean* by the Earl of Cavan was published. In it he details his voyage from Gibraltar to Turkey in the 200 ton schooner *Roseneath* and has reproduced a considerable number of remarkably crisp photographs. His book is typical of several of the period and reflects the ideas of the well-heeled aristocracy and what they considered to be the proper way to go cruising. These are the Earl's ideas on the proper yacht for such a cruise:

> Two or three strong, good masts, in proportion to the size of the vessel – masts, I mean, upon which leg of mutton sails of tanned or waterproof canvas could be set – will be necessary of course . . .These sails should give her a stability at sea, which the majority of our Mediterranean yachts sadly require. With so many interesting ports at easy distances the one from the other, the whole way between Gibraltar and Constantinople, there can be no reason for going at a speed exceeding ten knots, which speed could easily be obtained under steam and sail. The dislike to going afloat would thus be much lessened in the minds of those who may not be good sailors, their comfort also would be enormously increased, and providing that time is not of overwhelming importance, I am certain that owners at the end of their cruise, will feel more satisfied with yachts such as I have described, than they could be with any greyhound-built vessel, of which such numbers are now to be seen in the Mediterranean.
>
> . . . As to the size of the vessel, she should certainly not be less than 150 tons. As to how large she should be, must, of course, depend upon the means at the disposal of the owner, and the purposes for which he requires her.

In the Edwardian era more yachts began to make the voyage to the Mediterranean and although many of these were still in the category of little ships, there were numbers of smaller yachts under twenty tons as well. Many of the larger yachts of this era are still around, cared for by loving owners with lots of money or earning their keep as luxury charter yachts. In between the wars it was popular to combine a shooting and yachting expedition, woodcock and deer in Albania, wildfowl in Greece, boar in Turkey, but the Earl of Cavan was able to advise that 'Lions cannot now be found within a day's rail of any yacht anchorage in North Africa' and 'they will be unusually lucky if they return with one specimen'.

After the Second World War an increasing number of small yachts began to cruise the Mediterranean. Small yachts had been shown to be capable of extended voyages with the exploits of Humphrey Barton in *Vertue XXVI* and Adlard Coles in *Cohoe*. The Mediterranean had its own unsung heroes with the voyages of A. G. H. Macpherson in *Driac II* before the war and the more relaxed cruises of Ernle Bradford in his Dutch botter *Mother Goose* after the war. Right up until the Sixties a voyage to the Mediterranean was an adventure equal to a voyage to the South Seas or the Caribbean, not in distance and days at sea, but in the sense of an adventure that offered excitement and the unknown. The western Mediteranean was barely known and the eastern Mediterranean little visited at all.

In the late Sixties and into the Seventies the numbers of charter boats began to gradually increase. At first most of these were yachts, large and small, with a skipper and crew, but smaller boats for adventurous bareboat charter also began to make an appearance. In the 1970s the Yacht Cruising Association put the first flotilla yachts in Greece. The concept of flotilla sailing was an immediate success and flotilla holidays spread to other parts of Greece, Yugoslavia, Turkey, Italy, France, Spain and eventually back to England from whence the idea had originated. More and more private yachts began to cruise around the Mediterranean and in a sense it has become the playground of northern Europe.

It is easy to get the impression that the Mediterranean is full to the brim with yachts, both charter and private. It is not. In some areas you will sail for weeks without seeing another yacht and far from feeling claustrophobic, you will begin to look around for another yacht for company and to swap experiences with over a drink or two. Sail out of high season and you have the Mediterranean virtually to yourself. Around the highly populated areas and popular charter spots you will see large numbers of yachts, but get away from them and the indented coast and large numbers of islands provide a sanctuary for those who will want to explore and discover a deserted cove or two.

Looking back across the Strait of Gibraltar to the Rock from the Algeciras-Tangier ferry.

In most of the Mediterranean the land drops straight into the
sea and keeps going straight down so that you can potter along
the coast a short distance off and 'sight see'.

Information charts

On the following pages charts summarise aspects of Mediterranean climate, currents, sailing routes. A resumé of Mediterranean history is also presented in a series of small scale, generalised maps. This information can be applied to the descriptions given for each country.

The radiobeacon charts on pages 82-84 are to be used in conjunction with the lists of radiobeacons given for each country.

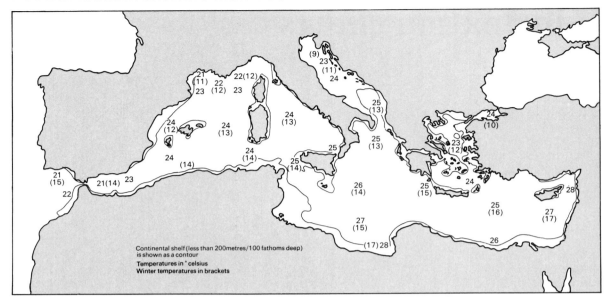

Average sea temperatures in summer and winter.

In the spring and early summer the sea heats up slowly from the winter low with maximum sea temperatures being reached in August and September. The sea then cools down slowly until the winter lowest average temperature is reached in January and February.

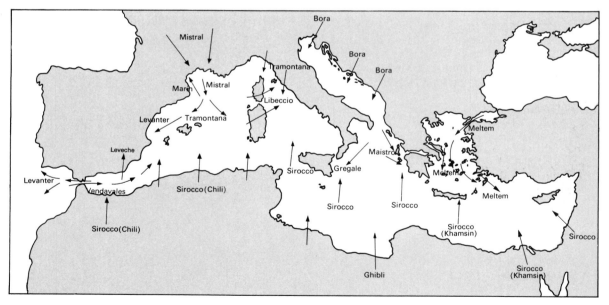

Local winds

These winds are not necessarily the prevailing winds, in fact they are often strong winds which interrupt the usual prevailing winds. Only the common names of winds are given here and not the many local variations.

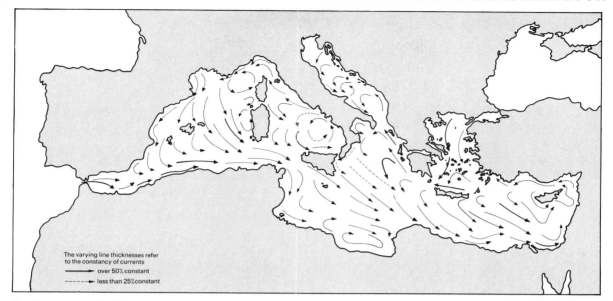

Surface currents. January

The basic anti-clockwise rotation of water around the Mediterranean from the Strait of Gibraltar can clearly be seen in the winter, although the flow is complicated by the bits of land jutting into the sea and the large islands in the way.

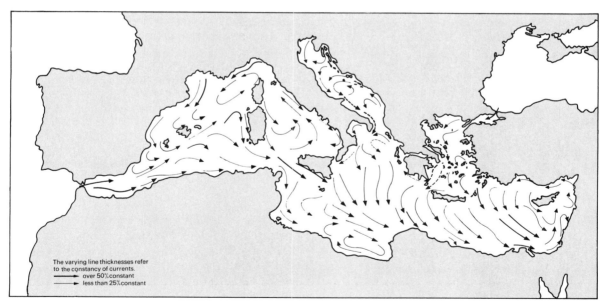

Surface currents. July

The anticlockwise flow of water is still evident in the summer although the massive evaporation of water in the eastern basin distorts the flow compared to the winter pattern. In the channels between islands and around headlands the flow may increase and where the flow is contrary to the wind direction there may be overfalls and broken water.

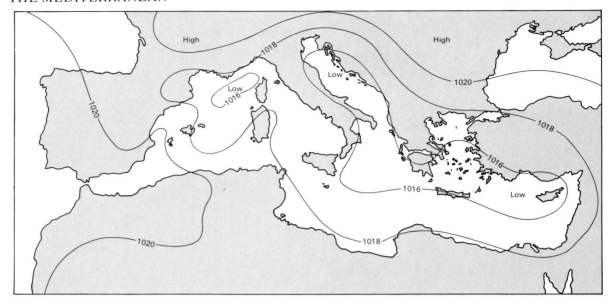

Air pressure. January
The Mediterranean air pressure gradient in the winter is unusual inasmuch as it is less than the air pressure gradient in the summer.

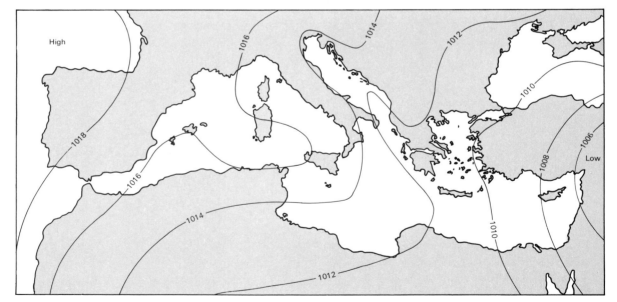

Air pressure. July
The air pressure gradient in the summer is considerable with a difference in values from the N and W sloping down to the S and E. The stable gradient over the Aegean is responsible for dragging the *meltemi* from the Black Sea around the Aegean to Rhodes (see map of Local Winds p.72).

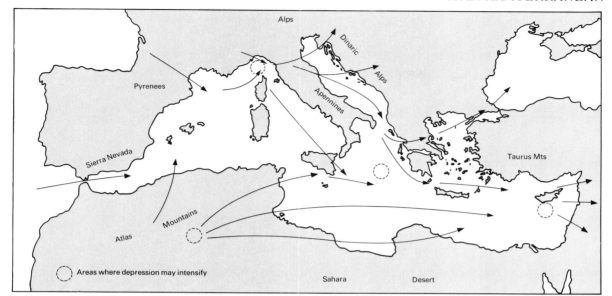

Tracks of depressions into the Mediterranean

Depressions enter the western Mediterranean from the Atlantic and travel across to the eastern Mediterranean on fairly predictable tracks. The speed at which the depressions travel is not so predictable, they can stop for no apparent reason and then move off again at high speed. The depressions may intensify in certain areas with the area in the Gulf of Genoa producing the worst effects – the Genoa lee cyclone.

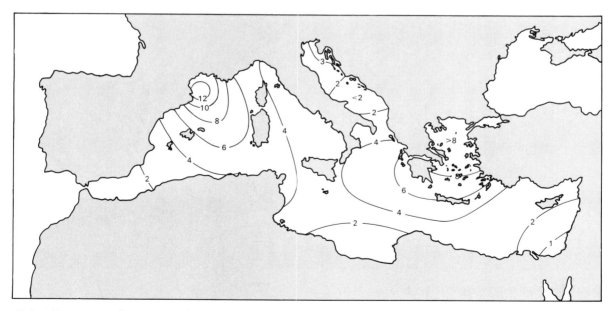

Gales. Percentage frequency of gales in the winter

This map shows the average recorded gale frequencies, but there are also strong local winds which do not figure on this map. The frequency of gale force winds in an area is likely to be higher than shown here.

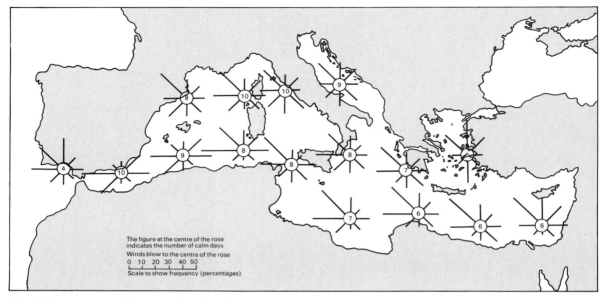

Wind directions and frequencies. April

It can be seen that although winds from the NW sector prevail in the spring, there is also a significant proportion of winds from other sectors.

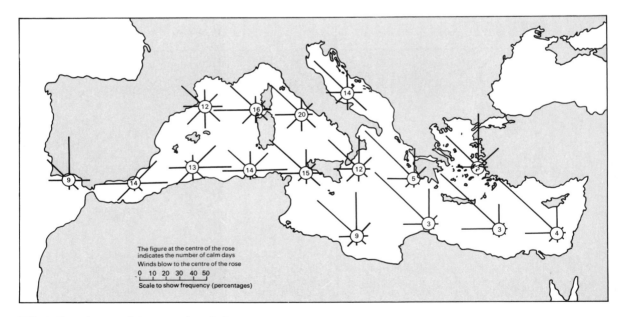

Wind directions and frequencies. July

In the summer winds from the NW prevail over most of the Mediterranean with the proportion of winds from other sectors much reduced except along the North African coast between the Strait of Gibraltar and Tunisia.

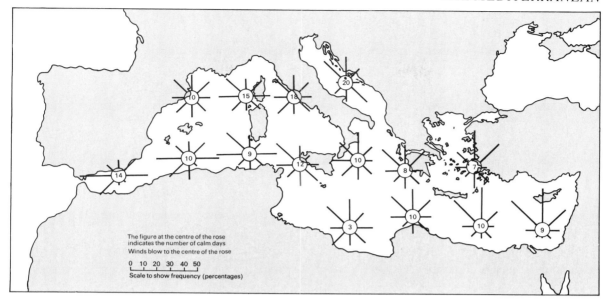

The figure at the centre of the rose indicates the number of calm days
Winds blow to the centre of the rose

0 10 20 30 40 50
Scale to show frequency (percentages)

Wind directions and frequencies. October
In the autumn winds from all sectors are more
equally represented. All of these wind charts show
the overall picture and it must be stressed that local
winds in an area can be radically different from this
picture.

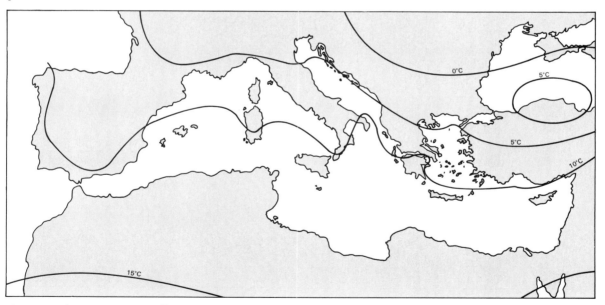

Average air temperatures. January
Note the low values for the northern Mediterranean when you are contemplating where to winter.
Again there can be protected local pockets where
the temperatures are considerably higher than the
average values for the region.

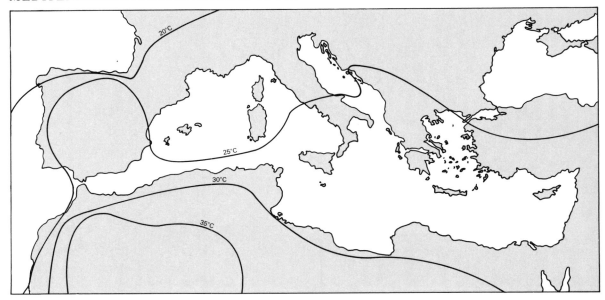

Average air temperatures. July
Note the high values across North Africa where it
can be just too hot in the height of summer. Temperatures tend to be lower on islands where the wind
blowing across the sea cools the land down.

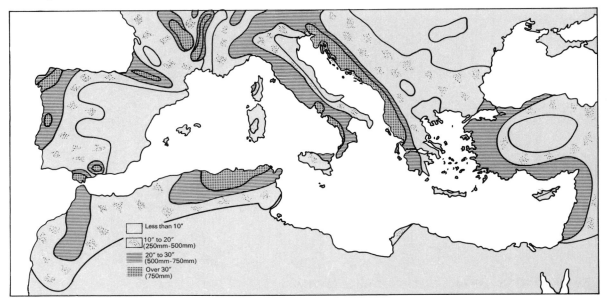

Less than 10"

10" to 20"
(250mm-500mm)

20" to 30"
(500mm-750mm)

Over 30"
(750mm)

Precipitation. Winter months: November to April
Moisture laden air moving in from the Atlantic
drops rain over the high land on the west side of a
country. It is worth studying this map when thinking about where to winter.

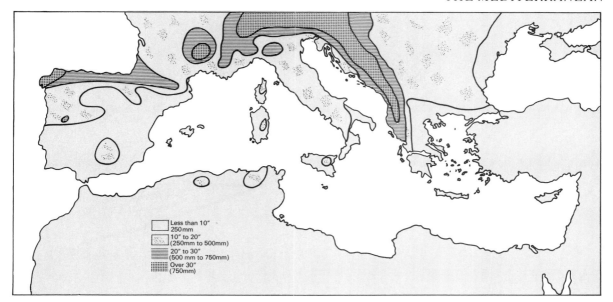

Precipitation. Summer months: May to October
Most of this rain falls in May and October with very
little or none falling in the summer proper.

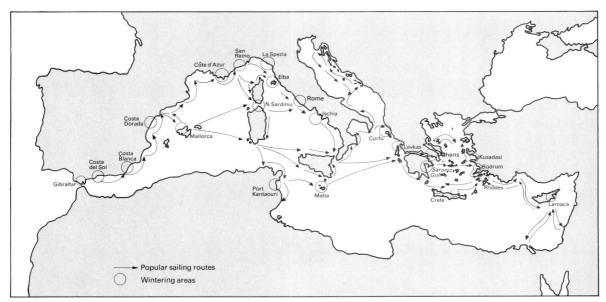

**Popular sailing routes and areas where yachts
winter**
Not all return routes from the E to the W are
shown, but are generally along the same route as
for W to E.

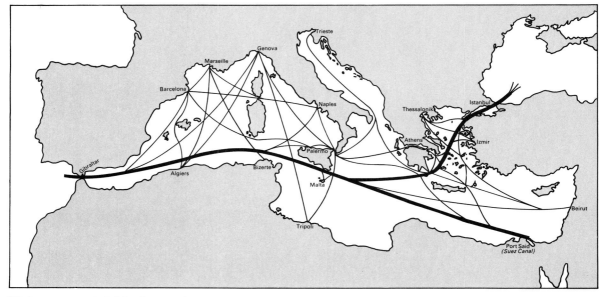

Main commercial shipping routes

Note the thick black snake forking east of Sicily that shows the popular route for most commercial shipping transiting the Mediterranean. Yachts should take care at the bottlenecks: Strait of Gibraltar, Sicilian Channel, Cape Malea, Dardanelles and the Bosphorus.

Historical maps

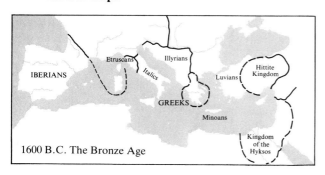

1600 B.C. The Bronze Age

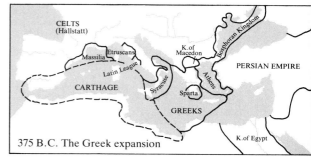

375 B.C. The Greek expansion

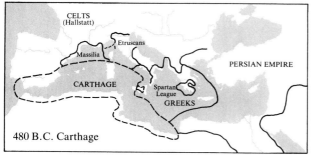

480 B.C. Carthage

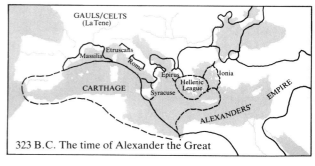

323 B.C. The time of Alexander the Great

145 B.C. Rome and Greece

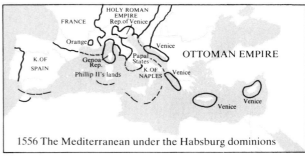

1556 The Mediterranean under the Habsburg dominions

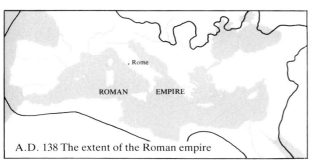

A.D. 138 The extent of the Roman empire

1812 At the time of Napoleon

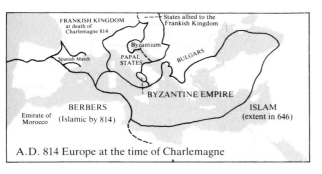

A.D. 814 Europe at the time of Charlemagne

1914 At the start of the Great War

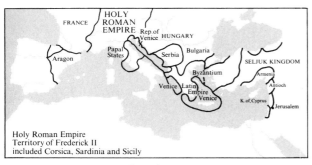

1230 At the time of the Crusades

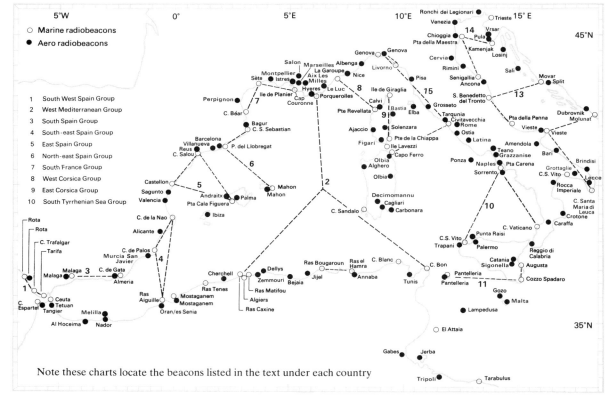

Note these charts locate the beacons listed in the text under each country

Radiobeacons

West Mediterranean group 313.5 kHz
    Cap Bon (Tunisia) BN 200M every 6 mins. Seq. 1, 2.
    Ras Caxine (Algeria) CX 200M every 6 mins. Seq. 3, 4.
    Porquerolles (France) PQ 200M every 6 mins. Seq. 5, 6.

Southwest Spain group 289.6 kHz
    Tarifa O 50M every 6 mins. Seq. 5, 6.
    Cabo Trafalgar B 50M every 6 mins. Seq. 3, 4.
    Rota D 80M every 6 mins. Seq. 1, 2.

South Spain group 298.8 kHz
    Málaga GA 50M every 6 mins. Seq. 1, 2.
    Cabo de Gata TA 50M every 6 mins. Seq. 5, 6.

Southeast Spain group 294.2 kHz
    Ras Aguille AG 100M every 6 mins. Seq. 1, 2.
    Cabo de Palos PA 50M every 6 mins. Seq. 3, 4.
    Cabo de la Nao NO 50M every 6 mins. Seq. 5, 6.

East Spain group 298.8 kHz
    Castellón AS 50M every 6 mins. Seq. 1, 2.
    Cabo Salou UD 50M every 6 mins. Seq. 3, 4.
    Punta de la Cala Figuera FI 50M every 6 mins. Seq. 5, 6.

Northeast Spain group 291.9 kHz
    Punta del Llobregat OR 50M every 6 mins. Seq. 1, 2.
    Mahón MH 100M every 6 mins. Seq. 3, 4.
    Cabo San Sebastián SN 50M every 6 mins. Seq. 5, 6.

Rota AOG 265 kHz 100M 36°39'.00N 6°19'W
Málaga RMA 330 kHz 60M 36°39'.55N 4°28'.9W
Almería AMR 310 kHz 60M 36°50'.92N 2°22'.67W

Murcia LCZ 381 kHz 40M 37°40'.67N 0°56'.32W
Alicante ALT 280 kHz 50M 38°17'.3N 0°33'.1W
Valencia VLC 340 kHz 50M 39°26'.3N 0°21'.0W
Sagunto/Cabo Canet SGO 356 kHz 50M 39°40'.4N 0°12'.4W
Reus RES 272 kHz 50M 41°08'.7N 01°09'E
Villanueva VNV 380 kHz 50M 41°12'.6N 1°42'.4E
Barcelona QU 325 kHz 80M 41°17'.2N 1°59'.1E
Bagur BGR 319 kHz 50M 41°57'N 3°13'E
Mahón MN 344 kHz 60M 39°50'.18N 4°12'.72E
Andraitx ADX 384 kHz 30M 39°32'.92N 2°23'.67E
Palma CST 351 kHz 50M 39°38'.47N 2°55'.27E
Ibiza IBZ 394 kHz 60M 38°54'.8N 1°28'.07E

South France group 287.3 kHz
    Cap Béar BR 50M every 6 mins. Seq. 1, 2.
    Sète SÉ 50M every 6 mins. Seq. 3, 4.
    Ile du Planier PN 100M every 6 mins. Seq. 5, 6.

West Corsica group 294.2 kHz
    Pointe Revellata RV 100M every 6 mins. Seq. 3, 4.
    La Garoupe GO 100M every 6 mins. Seq. 5, 6.

East Corsica group 308 kHz
    Ile de la Giraglia GL 60M every 4 mins. Seq. 1, 2.
    Pointe de Chiappa CP 100M every 4 mins. Seq. 3, 4.

Other stations
    Cap Couronne CR 305.7 kHz 50M 43°19'.58N 5°03'.25E

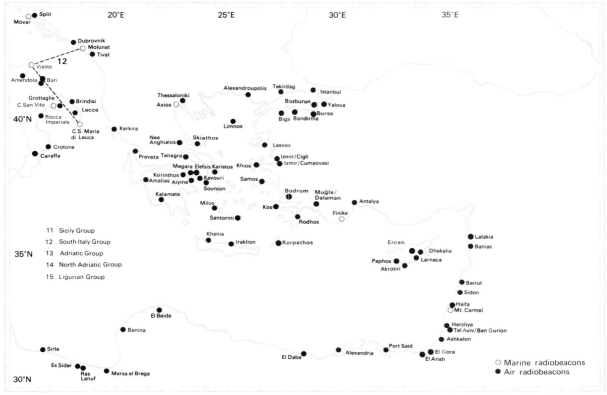

Istres ITR 390.5 kHz 43°31′.58N 4°55′.82E
Hyères HYE 322 kHz 70M 43°02′.02N 6°09′10E
Nice, Mont Leuza LEZ 398.5 kHz 75M 43°53′N 7°19′E
Ajaccio, Campo del'Oro IS 341 kHz 50M 41°53′.9N 8°36′.8E
Solenzara SZA 349.5 kHz 80M 41°55′.9N 9°23′.8E
Bastia, Poretta BP 369 kHz 50M 42°25′.7N 9°32′.2E
Calvi CV 404 kHz 42°34′.67N 8°48′.47E

Livorno LI 300 kHz 100M cont in fog. H + 28, 34, 58, 04 in clear weather. 43°32′.58N 10°17′.72E

Ligurian Sea group 301.1 kHz
 Civitavecchia CH 70M. Seq. 1, 2.[1]
 Genova GV 70M. Seq. 3, 4.[2]
 Capo Ferro CF 90M. Seq. 5, 6.[3]
 All continuous in fog and at [1]H + 06, 12, 36, 42. [2]H + 08, 14, 38, 44. [3]H + 10, 16, 40, 46 ev. 4 hours commencing at 0300 in clear weather.

South Tyrrhenian Sea group 296.5 kHz
 Pta Carena/Capis NP 100M. Seq. 1, 2.[1]
 C. S. Vito LC 100M. Seq. 3, 4.[3]
 Capo Vaticano VN 100M. Seq. 5, 6.[2]
 [1]Continuous in fog and at H + 12, 18, 42, 48 ev. 4 hours commencing 0300 in clear weather.
 [2]Continuous in fog and at H + 16, 22, 46, 52
 [3]Continuous in fog and at H + 14, 20, 44, 50 ev. 4 hours commencing at 0300 in clear weather.

Sicily group 287.3 kHz
 Pantelleria PT 90M. Seq. 1, 2.[1]
 Cozzo Spadaro PZ 100M. Seq. 3, 4.[2]
 Augusta AT 100M. Seq. 5, 6.[3]
 All continuous in fog and [1]H + 00, 06, 30, 36. [2]H + 02, 08, 32, 38. [3]H + 04, 10, 34, 40 in clear weather.

Capo San Vito/Taranto TN 291.9 KHz 70M. Seq. 1, 2.
 Continuous in fog and at H + 24, 30, 54, 00 ev. 4 hours from 0300 in clear weather.

South Italy group 305.7 kHz
 C. Sta Maria di Leuca MC 100M. Seq. 1, 2.[1]
 Vieste VS 70M. Seq. 3, 4.[2]
 Molunat YC 100M. Seq. 5, 6.[3]
 All continuous in fog and at [1]H + 06, 12, 36. 42. [2]H + 08, 14, 38, 44. [3]H + 10, 16, 40, 46 in clear weather.

Adriatic group 289.6 kHz
 Punta della Penna TL 80M. Seq. 1, 2.[1]
 S. Benedetto del Tronto CI 80M. Seq. 3, 4.[2]
 Movar (Yugoslavia) YV 100M. Seq. 5, 6.[3]
 All continuous in fog and at [1]H + 12, 18, 42, 48. [2] + 14, 20, 44, 50. [3]H + 16, 22, 46, 52 in clear weather.

North Adriatic group 298.8 kHz
 Senigallia SA 80M. Seq. 1, 2.[1]
 Kamenjak(Yugoslavia) YP 100M. Seq. 3, 4.[2]
 Pta da Maestra ME 80M. Seq. 5, 6.[3]
 All continuous in fog and at [2]H + 18, 24, 48, 54 [2]H + 20, 26, 50, 56 [3]H + 22, 28, 52, 58 in clear weather.

Vittoria/Trieste RD 311.5 kHz 70M. Continuous in fog and H + 00, 06, 30, 36 in clear weather. 45°40′.50N 13°45′.43E.

Albenga ABN 268 kHz 50M 44°03′.3N 8°13′.3E
Genoa GEN 318 kHz 50M 44°25′.38N 9°04′.9E
Genoa CMO 389 kHz 70M 44°20′.7N 9°10′.3E
Pisa PIS 379 kHz 25M 43°35′.3N 10°17′.8E
Elba ELB 360 kHz 100M 42°43′.9N 10°23′.7E
Grosseto GRO 406 kHz 50M 42°45′.3N 11°04′.6E
Tarquinia TAQ 312 kHz 50M 42°12′.8N 11°44′.1E

Teano TEA 316 kHz 50M 41°17'.7N 13°58'.2E
Ostia OST 321 kHz 50M 41°48'.2N 12°14'.2E
Ponza PNZ 367.5 kHz 50M 40°54'.6N 12°57'.4E
Sorrento SOR 426 kHz 100M 40°35'N 14°20.1E
Carbonara CAR 402 kHz 100M 39°06'.2N 9°30'.9E
Olbia SME 357 kHz 50M 40°54'N 9°30'.8E
Alghero ALG 382 kHz 50M 40°35'.1N 8°15'.8E
Cagliari CAG 371 kHz 25M 39°12'.8N 9°05'.8E
Palermo PAL 355.5 kHz 150M 38°02'N 13°10'.6N
Punta Raisi PRS 329 kHz 25M 38°11'.33N 13°06'.5E
Trapani TRP 317.5 kHz 50M 37°54'.8N 12°29'.9E
Catania CAT 345 kHz 80M 37°27'.4N 14°58'E

Pantelleria PAN 335 kHz 100M 36°48'.63N 11°57'.6E

Lampedusa LPD 373 kHz 50M 35°29'.9N 12°36'.7E
Reggio Calabria RCA 325 kHz 50M 38°01'N 15°38'.1E
Caraffa/Catanzaro CDC 376 kHz 150M 38°45'.2N 16°22'.2E
Crotone CRO 337 kHz 25M 38°59'.9N 17°04'.5E
Rocca Imperiale RMP 383.5 kHz 40°06'N 16°37'E
Grottaglie GRT 331 kHz 25M 40°26'.7N 17°25'.3E
Brindisi/Casale BRD 363.5 kHz 78M 40°36'.3N 18°00'.5E
Bari BPL 401 kHz 41°06'.5N 16°39'.6E
Amendola AME 381 kHz 50M 41°29'.9N 15°50'.3E
Vieste VIE 405 kHz 100M 41°54'.7N 16°03'.7E
Ancona ANC 374.5 kHz 100M 43°35'.1N 13°28'.3E
Cervia CEV 387 kHz 25M 44°16'.02N 12°10'.8E
Rimini/Miramare RIM 335 kHz 75M 44°04'.6N 12°30'.3E
Chioggia CHI 408 kHz 50M 45°04'.3N 12°16'.9E
Venezia/Tesséra VEN 379 kHz 25M 46°26'.8N 12°16'.7E
Ronchi dei Legionari RON 396 kHz 25M 45°49'.7N 13°21'.5E

Malta MTA 416 kHz 35°53'.5N 14°32'.3E
Gozo MLG 320 kHz 36°02'.3N 14°12'.5E

Pula PLA 351.1 kHz 50M 44°53'.4N 13°45'.2E
Pula/Kavran KAV 265 kHz 50M 44°53'.7N 14°00'.6E
Lošinj LOS 432 kHz 50M 44°31'N 14°28'E
Sali SAL 298 kHz 50M 43°56'N 15°10'E
Split DVN 392 kHz 50M 43°26'.6N 16°08'.9E
Dubrovnik KLP 318 kHz 25M 42°39'.9N 18°01'.5E
Tivat TAZ 345 kHz 50M 42°16'.9N 18°48'.4E

Kérkira KEK 403 kHz 25M 39°35'.3N 19°55'E
Prevéza PRV 353 kHz 50M 38'54'.8N 20°46'E
Korinthos KOR 392 kHz 50M 37°56'N 22°56'.1E
Amalias/Andravida AML 367 kHz 100M 37°46'.5N 21°20'.8E
Kalamáta KTA 348 kHz 45M 37°04'N 22°01'.2E (daytime)
Khania/Soúdha (Crete) SUD 289 kHz 200M 35°31'.3N 24°09'.2E (daytime only).

Iráklion (Crete) HER 259 kHz 150M 35°20'.1N 25°10'.7E
Ródhos/Paradisi ROS 339 kHz 150M 36°25'.2N 28°07'.1E
Milos MLO 378 kHz 36°42'.7N 28°07'.1E
Aiyina EGN 382 kHz 50M 37°45'.7N 23°25'.4E
Megara MGR 405 kHz 38°00'N 23°23'N
Elefsis ELF 252 kHz 50M 38°04'N 23°33'.6E
Kavouri KVR 357 kHz 200M 37°48'.9N 23°45'.6E
Sounion SUN 319 kHz 50M 37°40.2N 24°02'.7E
Karistos KRS 285 kHz 50M 38°00'.8N 24°25'.1E
Lesvos LVO 397 kHz 100M 39°03'.5N 26°36'.4E
Limnos LIO 270 kHz 150M 39°55'.5N 25°14'.9E
Alexandroupolis ALP 351 kHz 100M 40°51'.4N 25°56'.6E
Santorini THR 307 kHz 36°24'.1N 25°28'.8E
Kos KOS 311 kHz 50M 36°47'.8N 27°05'.5E
Samos SAM 375 kHz 80M 37°42'N 26°54'E
Khios HIO 299 kHz 80M 38°20'.4N 26°08'.5E
Tanagra TNG 303 kHz 80M 38°20'N 23°43'.8N

Nea Anghialos ANL 335 kHz 39°13'.1N 22°48'E
Thessaloniki TSL 345 kHz 80M 40°35'.6N 22°56'.9E

Antalya YT 302 kHz 50M 36°53'N 30°47'.5E
Tekirdag EKI 360 kHz 50M 40°57'.13N 27°25'.57E
Istanbul/Ataturk TOP 370 kHz 50M 41°01'.1N 28°54'.5E
Yalova YAA 305 kHz 75M 41°35'N 29°22'.3E
Bozburun BOZ 412 kHz 40°31'.3N 28°50'E
Bandirma BDM 450 kHz 75M 40°18'N 27°58'E
Biga BIG 428 kHz 40°16'.5N 27°21'.5E
Izmir CIG 363 kHz 75M 38°31'.5N 27°01'.1E
Izmir/Cumaovasi KAD 330 kHz 70M 38°24'.9N 27°08'.8E
Muğla/Dalaman DAL 346 kHz 36°42'.7N 28°46'.7E
Finike FR 303.4 seq. 3, 4 300M 36°16'.8N 30°09'.5E

Paphos PHA 328 kHz 100M 34°43'.1N 32°28'.6E
Akrotiri AK 363 kHz 120M 34°34'.6N 32°58'.3E
Dhekelia DKA 343 kHz 50M 34°59'N 33°44'E
Larnaca LCA 267 kHz 150M 34°49'.3N 33°33'.3E

Herzliya HRZ 250 kHz 15M 32°10'.8N 34°49'.7E
Beirut BOD 351 kHz 250M 33°54'N 35°28'.8E
Sidon SAD 296.5 kHz 100M 33°30'N 35°21'.6E
Haifa HFA 317 kHz 50M 32°48'.6N 35°02'.3E
Tel Aviv BGN 380 kHz 100M 32°01'.6N 34°57'.2E

El Gora GOR 309 kHz 100M 31°05'N 34°08'E
Port Said PSD 352 kHz 31°17'N 32°14'E
Alexandria AXD 403 kHz 31°11'N 29°57'E
El Daba DBA 415 kHz 31°02'N 28°28'.7E

El Attaia KR 308 kHz 100M. Seq. 3, 4.[1].
Cap Blanc BC 310.3 kHz 100M. Seq. 3, 4.[2].
Pantelleria PT 287.3 kHz 90M. Seq. 1, 2[3]
[1]Continuous in fog and ev. H + 02, 08, 32, 38.
[2]Occasionally inoperative.
[3]Continuous in fog and ev. H + 00, 06, 30, 36. Grouped with Cozzo Spadaro and Augusta

Gabes GAB 267 kHz 33°53'N 10°06'E
Jerba/Zarzes JER 371 kHz 33°52'.5N 10°44'.8E.
Tunis KDN 385.5 kHz 36°49'.4N 10°18'.5E

Grouped on 298.8 kHz.
    Ras el Hamra GD 50M Seq. 1, 2.
    Ras Bougaroun CB 50M Seq. 5, 6.
Ras Matifou MF 296.5 kHz 30M.
Ras Tenes TS 296.5 kHz 30M. Seq. 3, 4.
Mostaganem MN 305.7 kHz 5M.

Jijel/Taher DJI 340 kHz 50M 36°48'.8N 5°52.'4E
Dellys DEL 370 kHz 50M 36°55'N 3°54'E
Cherchell CHE 397 kHz 50M 36°37'N 2°12'E
Mostaganem MOS 334 kHz 100M 35°54'.5N 0°08'.2E
Annaba ANB 366 kHz 60M 36°50'.4N 07°47'.2E
Oran OLN 265 kHz 200M 35°39'.3N 00°37'.6W
Bejaia BJA 423 kHz 36°42'.3N 05°01'.5E
Zemmouri ZEM 359 kHz 36°48'.1N 03°37'.1E

Melilla MLL 292 kHz 50M 35°18'.5N 2°57'.3W

II THE MEDITERRANEAN COUNTRIES

The countries around the Mediterranean are described in a clockwise order beginning at Gibraltar and going on to Spain, France, Italy, Malta, Yugoslavia, Albania, Greece, Turkey, Cyprus, Syria, Lebanon, Israel, Egypt, Libya, Tunisia, Algeria and Morocco. As far as possible I have described them in a standard format so that the reader can easily find the information wanted but it cannot apply equally to all for the simple reason that they are not all equally accessible (Albania and Libya), do not have equal cruising grounds whether because of size (Gibraltar and Malta) or a paucity of harbours and anchorages (Cyprus, Israel, Egypt, Morocco), and in the case of the countries in the Middle East are at war. Full treatment is given to Spain, France, Italy, Yugoslavia, Greece, Turkey and Tunisia. A slightly abbreviated treatment is given to Gibraltar, Malta, Cyprus, Israel, Egypt, Algeria and Morocco. A brief mention is made of Albania, Syria, Lebanon and Libya.

Details of coast radio services, radiobeacons and weather forecasting are subject to frequent alteration, changes being promulgated in Admiralty *Notices to Mariners*. The lists are complete only for those countries where the facilities are of use to yachtsmen. For the North African countries these details are only listed where English or French is spoken as an alternative to Arabic.

The standard format is as follows:

Geography   Coast and islands, cruising areas.
Climate and weather   Winds, local names of winds, gales, thunderstorms, tides and currents, weather forecasts.
Harbours and anchorages   What to expect, security, wintering afloat.
Passage planning
Navigation aids   Buoyage, lights, radiobeacons, coast radio stations.
Formalities   Entry, documents, taxes.
Facilities   Everyday, boat repairs, duty free spares.
  Provisioning   General, specific, eating out.
  Charts and pilots
  Useful books

Gibraltar

Area 2¼ square miles

Population 30,000

Language English and Spanish

Religion Mostly Roman Catholic

Time Zone G.M.T. + 1 D.S.T. April-Sept.

Currency Gibraltar pound (£) or sterling which is legal tender.

Electricity 240V AC

Banks Open 0900-1530 Monday to Thursday and 0900-1530/1630-1800 Friday. All major cheque cards, credit cards, and travellers' cheques accepted.

Mail Reliable. Send to *poste restante* or one of the marinas.

Medical Good. U.K. nationals are treated free of charge within 30 days of having left England. E.C. nationals treated on production of *Form E.111*.

Internal travel Walk, bus or taxi.

International travel Flights to the U.K. Flights and ferries to Morocco. The frontier with Spain is now open.

Public Holidays
January 1 New Year's Day
Last weekend in May: Spring holiday
Last weekend in August: Summer holiday
December 25, 26 Christmas
Moveable:
Good Friday
Easter Monday
Commonwealth Day
Queen's birthday

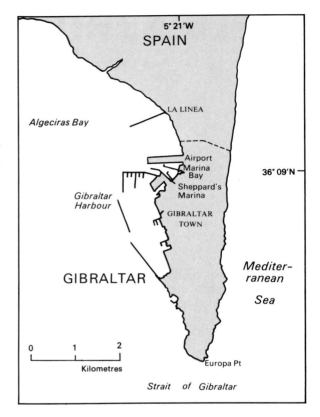

THE STRAIT OF GIBRALTAR

Getting through the Strait of Gibraltar from the Atlantic is not as difficult as getting out of the Mediterranean. Keep the following in mind as you approach the Strait:

i. A traffic separation zone operates. West-bound traffic uses the north lane and east-bound traffic the south lane. A yacht can normally keep in deep water outside of the shipping lanes.

ii. There is a permanent east-going current of 2 knots through the Strait. The current is strongest in the centre of the Strait and weak at the edges. In 40m depth or less it is very weak and easily reversed by contrary winds. The current is altered by the tidal stream so that there can be a maximum east-going current of nearly 5 knots and a west-going current of 2 knots. A yacht entering the Strait from the Atlantic can count on at least six hours of favourable current and because the tide turns earlier closer in, can work it so that as much as nine hours of favourable current can be obtained.

iii. Off the promontories and over any shallow banks there are overfalls with the strong current. Special care should be taken of these when the wind is against the tide.

iv. Winds blow either from the west *(poniente)* or the east *(levanter)*. The *levanter* is heralded by the appearance of cirrus cloud over Gibraltar. It is said to blow for three days at a time and then die off for three days before it blows again. With the *levanter* it is reported that you can get more useful slants of wind closer inshore to the European side.

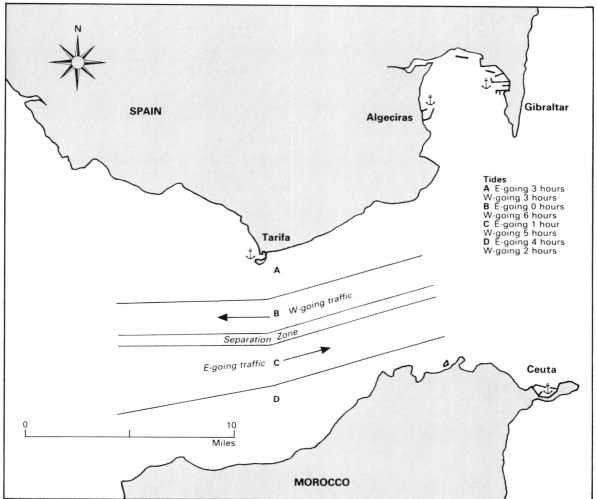

Strait of Gibraltar

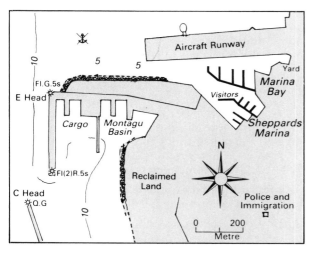

Gibraltar. Approach to Marina Bay and Sheppards Marina

GEOGRAPHY

Gibraltar is a conspicuous, mountainous promontory on the north side of the Strait of Gibraltar. From the distance it looks like an island but it is joined to mainland Spain by a low isthmus. In ancient times the promontory was known as one of the Pillars of Hercules guarding the entrance to the Mediterranean. It has been a British colony since 1713 and remains staunchly loyal to Britain despite claims by Spain for its return. The land border between Spain and Gibraltar is now open. The Rock has traditionally been a stopping-off point for yachts entering or leaving the Mediterranean.

CLIMATE AND WEATHER

Close to the Atlantic Ocean, Gibraltar does not have a strictly Mediterranean climate. Summers are warm and often mild. Winters are cool although frosts are rare.

WINDS About 80% of the winds in the Strait are funnelled into an ENE or W direction.

Levanter The predominant easterly wind. It is stronger in the narrow part of the Strait compared to its strength on either side. It is usually caused by an approaching Atlantic low and is most frequent in the spring and late summer and autumn. It often blows at gale force for several days or more.

Poniente The W wind. Although often strong it is usually less strong to the E of the Strait. It often lasts for five days or a week.

TIDES AND CURRENTS Tides are substantial enough to take into account:

MHWS 1.0m (3.2ft)   MHWN 0.7m (2.4ft)
MLWS 0.1m (0.3ft)   MLWN 0.3m (1.1ft)

Off Europa Point there is a strong E-going current. In the Strait of Gibraltar there is a permanent E-going current of 2 knots which is modified by the tidal stream. The W-going tide commences at local HW + 0200 and the E-going tide at local HW — 0200 or 0700. The maximum E-going current (permanent E-going current plus E-going tide) is nearly 5 knots. The maximum W-going (W-going tide minus E-going current) is 2 knots. Consequently the tides should be worked out when crossing the Strait, especially when trying to get out of the Mediterranean into the Atlantic.

WEATHER FORECASTS Weather forecasts for a 50 mile radius of Gibraltar are broadcast on:

British Forces Broadcasting Service (BFBS) VHF 89.4, 93.5, 97.8, 99.5 mHz at 0745, 0845, 1302, 1755 hours local time.* In English.

Gibraltar 1458 kHz (206m) at 0445, 0530, 0630, 0830, 1030 and 2157 hours local time. In English. Telephone: RAF 53416 for the Met. officer. Open 24 hours. A weather forecast with synoptic and local charts is also given on GBC television channels 6, 11, 53 at 2120 local time.

*GMT + 1 hour in winter; +2 hours in summer.

HARBOURS

There are two marinas in Gibraltar: Sheppard's which has pontoons and stern-to moorings or the newer Marina Bay which has stern-to moorings. Gibraltar is a popular place to winter where most facilities can be found and there are regular flights back to England.

NAVIGATION AIDS

Buoyage I.A.L.A. System 'A'. The approaches to Gibraltar are well buoyed.

Lights The approaches are well lit.

Coast radio stations

Tarifa (EAC) Transmits on **1678,** 2182, 2191, 2610 kHz. Receives on 2083, 2182, 3290 kHz. Traffic lists on 1678 kHz at ev. odd H + 33 (0333-1933) 2333 G.M.T. VHF Ch 16, 23, 24, 26, **27**

Gibraltar (ZDK) VHF Channels 1, 2, 3, 4, 16, 23, 24, 25, 27, 28, 86 and 87. Mon-Sat 0700-1900. Sun and holidays 0700-1300.

Rescue Service The Royal Navy operate a rescue service.

FORMALITIES

A yacht should be flying a 'Q' flag on entering Gibraltar where it should head for the customs quay on the south side of the yacht basin before proceeding to either marina. You are required to report to customs, immigration and harbour officials and a number of forms must be filled out. A list of crew and passengers is required in triplicate. The following regulations should be noted:

i. Any crew member or passenger intending to reside ashore during the time the vessel is in port, shall report to the immigration control post at Waterport police station and there give the address of intended stay.

ii. Immigration control should be advised of any guests residing aboard.

iii. If any person has employment in Gibraltar, it must be reported to the immigration office.

iv. Crew must not be paid off or enrolled (regardless of nationality) without permission of the principal immigration officer.

v. Before leaving report to the immigration control post at Waterport the time and date of departure.

DOCUMENTS The Small Ship's Register papers issued by the R.Y.A. or full registration papers are necessary.

TAXES Marina fees only are payable.

FACILITIES

EVERYDAY
Water At every berth in the marinas.
Ice Can be supplied.
Fuel Fuel berth.
Electricity At every berth.
Gas *Camping gaz* is available. Calor cylinders can be filled.
Paraffin Available at the fuel berth.

BOAT REPAIRS
Engines Most spares for well known makes of marine engines can be found or obtained. There are several well equipped and competent marine engine workshops.
Electrics and electronics Good facilities exist for the repair of electrical and electronic equipment.
Navigation instruments Spares and some new gear can be obtained.
Paints and antifouling Good quality paints and antifoulings available. Epoxy and other two-part paints can be obtained.
Hauling A 44 ton travel-hoist and hard standing. Two slipways for yachts up to 45 tons and 120 tons.
Engineering Good engineering shops that can take on all types of specialist yacht work.
Wood and GRP Good boat carpenters can be found for major hull work and fine interior work. Facilities exist for major GRP repairs including osmosis treatment.

DUTY FREE SPARES Duty free spares can be brought into Gibraltar but such items should be clearly marked 'yacht spare in transit to . . .' This will facilitate customs clearance of items. Yacht equipment being sent out of Gibraltar for repair or replacement should be taken to customs with a written statement describing the item, the nature of the repair and the servicing agents, the return address and the name of the owner and the yacht. This procedure will avoid delays and explanations on the return of items sent out of Gibraltar. There is a duty free store at Sheppards which stocks navigation equipment, autopilots, life-rafts, etc.

PROVISIONING

GENERAL Gibraltar is an excellent place to stock up in. Most provisions can be found including many hard-to-get imported goods from England. Prices are not cheap but nor are they overly expensive. There are a number of Liptons supermarkets and other familiar establishments in the town. Fresh fruit and vegetables are not the best although things have got better since the border re-opened.

Shopping hours are 0930-1300 and 1500-1900 Monday to Friday and 0930-1300 Saturday although some shops are closed all day Saturday.

EATING OUT There are a variety of restaurants of all types and categories. As a little bit of 'Blighty' in the sun most restaurants cater for English tastes so that you can find excellent English breakfasts, steak and kidney pie and apple pie and cream. You will also find Indian restaurants, pizzerias and bistros. In the back streets local restaurants cater for the Spanish population in Gibraltar. All in all there is a wide variety of good restaurants here.

CHARTS AND PILOTS

Admiralty *Mediterranean Sea Pilot* Vol. 1 (NP45).
Admiralty *Lists of Lights and Fog Signals* Volumes D (NP77) and E (NP78).
The Atlantic Coasts of Spain and Portugal. RCC Pilotage Foundation. Imray.
East Spain Pilot. Costa del Sol and Blanca. Robin Brandon. Imray. Covers Gibraltar and the approach from Mediterranean Spain.

Admiralty charts and other publications are available from the chandlers and bookshops.

Spain

Area   504,747 square kilometres (194,883 square miles)

Population   38,200,000

Capital   Madrid (3,100,000)

Language   Spanish. English fairly widely spoken.

Religion   Roman Catholic

Time Zone   G.M.T. +1; D.S.T. (April-September)

Currency   Spanish peseta (pta)

Electricity   125/220V 50Hz AC

Banks   Open 0900-1400 Monday to Friday, 0900-1300 Saturday. Eurocheques, credit cards and travellers' cheques widely accepted.

Mail   Reliable. Mail can be sent to *poste restante (lista de correos)* or perhaps best to a marina where it will be kept in the office.

Medical   On the whole treatment is good and fees moderate to high.

Internal travel   Numerous internal flights to all major cities. Trains are good (except the *expres* which is the slow train) and inexpensive. Local bus and taxi services are good. Hire cars can be found in most of the larger centres and charges are moderate.

International travel   Madrid is the centre for international flights but there are many others into Barcelona, Bilbao, Málaga, Palma de Mallorca and others. Ferries to Morocco.

Public Holidays
January 1 New Year's Day
January 6 Epiphany
March 19 St Joseph's Day
May 1 Labour Day
July 18 National Day
July 25 St James' Day
August 15 Festival of the Assumption
October 12 Columbus' Day
November 1 All Saints' Day
December 8 Festival of the Immaculate Conception
December 24 and 25 Christmas
Moveable:
Maundy Thursday
Good Friday.

GEOGRAPHY

COAST AND ISLANDS   The Mediterranean Spanish coast stretches from the Strait of Gibraltar to the border with France in the Gulf of Lions. The coastline is approximately 750 miles long. There is one major group of offshore islands, the Balearics (Islas Baleares), lying about 50 miles off the Spanish coast. The mainland coast has traditionally been divided into five *costas* which conveniently slice up the coast into: Costa del Sol, Costa Blanca, Costa del Azahar, Costa Dorada and the Costa Brava.

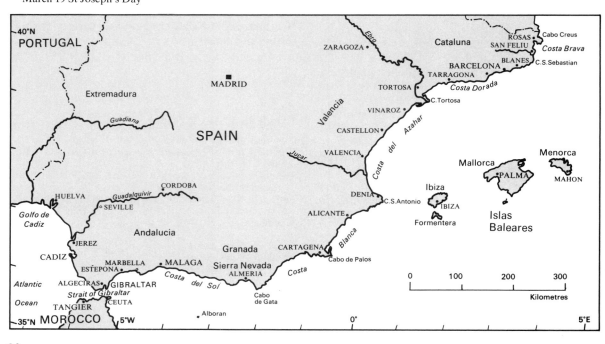

Costa del Sol   The sunny coast. Extends from the Strait of Gibraltar for 155 miles to Cabo de Gata. It is mostly flat near the coast although high mountains follow the coast a short distance inland. The coast is much developed for tourism.

Costa Blanca   The white coast. Extends nearly 200 miles from Cabo de Gata to just beyond Cabo de San Antonío. The coast is bordered by high white cliffs for part of its length from which it takes its name. Tourist development is moderate.

Costa del Azahar   Extends from Cabo de San Antonío for 115 miles to Cabo Tortosa. The coast is known as the orange blossom coast from the numerous citrus orchards along the coast. Tourist development is moderate.

Costa Dorada   The golden coast. Extends from Cabo Tortosa for 140 miles to Río Tordera. It takes its name from the many fine golden sand beaches along its length. The coast is much developed for tourism and has been dubbed the great wall of Spain.

Costa Brava   Extends from Río Tordera for 67 miles to the French border. This is a more mountainous coastline than the others. Tourist development is considerable but does not intrude too much upon the coast.

Balearics   This group of four major islands and several smaller ones lie about 50 miles off the coast. Ibiza, Formentera, Mallorca and Menorca are the four main islands. They are heavily developed for tourism with about 3 million tourists arriving annually.

CRUISING AREAS   The Spanish coast and the Balearics have long been a popular cruising area and many people base their yachts here. Consequently many new marinas have been built to accommodate this new aquatic population and associated boating facilities are well developed. Although there are numerous marina developments and more planned, there are still many attractive anchorages and small fishing harbours away from it all. In this it does not resemble the French Mediterranean coast where your choice is virtually between a marina or a marina. In many of the fishing harbours there is a quay allotted to yachts where a charge is made according to the facilities offered. For those wanting to get away from it all the two areas offering a good blend of marinas and anchorages are the Costa Brava and the Balearics.

CLIMATE AND WEATHER

The climate is of the Mediterranean type with hot dry summers and mild wet winters. Winters are particularly mild on the Costa del Sol and in the Balearics making these two areas popular for those wintering aboard. Winter temperatures are in the range of 10°-16°C and summer temperatures in the range of 25°-30°C. The relative humidity is moderate at 60-90%. Most of the rainfall occurs in the winter and autumn and varies between 20-30 inches (560-762mm). Characteristically rainfall occurs in heavy downpours of short duration.

WINDS   The winds in this area are considerably altered by the local topography. Thus a wind which is an easterly along one part of the coast can be a southerly along another part quite close to it. The prevailing wind, the *brisa de mar,* is a sea breeze blowing onto the coast. It generally gets up in the early morning, blows strongest in the early afternoon, and dies in the evening. This wind may increase or diminish the effect of other winds. Although it is usually described as blowing onto the coast, in combination with other winds or because of the local topography it can blow at a slant to the coast or even along it.

The wind most feared here is the *tramontana* or *mestrale.* It is strongest along the Costa Brava, Costa Dorada and in the Balearics. It blows from the N-NW-W and is most feared because it can reach gale force in a short time from a flat calm with few warning signs of its impending arrival. The *tramontana* is said to blow for three days but can last for a week and in the winter, when it is most frequent, it has been known to blow at Force 10-11.

LOCAL NAMES OF WINDS   Local names for the winds are as follows:
Tramontana, mestrale   Strong N-NW wind. Arrives without warning and can quickly reach gale force. The warning signs are a clear, glaring visibility, and a dry almost electric atmosphere. The barometer usually remains steady or rises slightly. It is rarely preceded by a swell.

Levante, llevantade, levanter   The E-NE wind frequent in the Strait of Gibraltar. It blows strongly in the sea area around Valencia where there are eight to nine gales from this direction on average. The warning signs are a heavy swell, a cold, damp atmosphere and low cloud and poor visibility.

Bagur, Gerona

Vendavales A strong SW-W wind that is most frequent along the southern coast. Most frequent in the spring and autumn.

Sirocco The hot humid wind blowing off the African coast. It is accompanied by bad visibility and low cloud. If it rains there will often be the red rain containing dust particles from the North African desert.

Brisa de mar The normal sea breeze blowing onto the land.

GALES The *tramontana* described above is the most feared source of gale force winds. The effects of the *tramontana* die off towards the south coast although a heavy swell may be felt. The east coast is effected by the *levante* which blows from the NE. It occurs when a depression travels through the Strait of Gibraltar and lodges between the Balearics and the North African coast. It can blow at gale force and is strongest to the north of Valencia and in the Strait of Gibraltar where the funnelling effect increases its force. In the south there are gales from the south, the *sirocco*, and from the SW-W, the *vendavales*.

In general the percentage frequency of gales in the winter dies off from N to S with 10-12% in the N, 6-8% in the Balearics, and 2% in the S.

THUNDERSTORMS These are most frequent in the autumn. They are often accompanied by strong winds of variable direction and often torrential rain or even hail. They are of short duration.

TIDES AND CURRENTS The tidal range at Gibraltar at springs is 0.9m (2.9ft) and at Málaga 0.5m (1.7ft). This is considerable enough to take into consideration when anchoring or berthing. Tidal streams are negligible. The tidal range drops to 0.15m (0.5ft) at Alicante and so for all intents and purposes tides can be ignored on the east coast.

The Atlantic pouring into the Mediterranean through the Strait of Gibraltar to replace the water lost by evaporation causes an E-going current of 1-2 knots along the S coast of Spain. On the E coast there is a SSW-going current of 1-1½ knots and around the Balearics a SE-E-going current of 1 knot.

Around some of the harbours in the Balearics a freak seiche, called the *resaca*, can occur, similar to the *marrobio* in Sicily. In the summer under certain meteorological conditions the water level can abruptly rise and fall as much as 1.5 metres (5 feet) every few minutes. The *resaca* has been known to occur when two major wave trains meet and the resonance set up causes the rapid 'tidal wave'. In 1984 a *resaca* at Ciudadela in Menorca was estimated to have a tidal wave of nearly 3 metres – 35 boats were sunk, 4 were missing, 42 sustained major damage, with total damage estimated at three million dollars. Fortunately most *resacas* are minor affairs and occur infrequently.

WEATHER FORECASTS   The south coast near Gibraltar is covered by VHF transmissions from Gibraltar. The Costa Brava and the Balearics are covered by the French weather forecasts. (See the weather forecast section in the chapter on France.) The sea area in between the Costa Brava and the coast near Gibraltar is covered by low power Spanish transmissions. These are read at dictation speed and after listening to a few you can understand the gist of them.

In many of the marinas a weather forecast will be posted or can be obtained. In some of the newspapers, *La Guardia* and *Levante* for instance, a synoptic chart is printed with the general weather forecast. On the national television channel a weather forecast with a synoptic chart is given at 2120 local time after the news. You can usually find a television in a café or bar.

Weather forecasts are transmitted as follows:

Gibraltar Radio 1458 kHz. 206m at 0445, 0530, 0630, 0830, 1030 and 2157 hours local time in English.

British Forces Broadcasting Service (BFBS) VHF 89.4, 93.5, 97.8 and 99.5 mHz at 0745, 0845, 1302 and 1755 (weekdays only) local time, in English.

Tarifa (EAC) 1678 kHz at 1103 and 1733 hours G.M.T., in Spanish.

Cabo de Gata 1866 kHz at 1103 and 1733 G.M.T.

Cabo de la Nao (EAV) 1690 kHz at 1103 and 1733 G.M.T.

Barcelona 1730 kHz at 1103 and 1733 G.M.T.

Bagur (EAB) 1740 kHz at 1103, 1733 G.M.T.

Marseille (FFM) 1906 kHz at 0103 (W of Ile d'Hyères only), 0705, 1220, 1615 G.M.T. on request. VHF Channels 26 and 28 at 0633 and 1133. Gives gale warnings, synopsis and 12 hour forecasts and outlook for further 12 hours in French for Mediterranean areas.

The Spanish television shows a very good meteorological situation chart with its land weather forecast every evening after the news at approximately 2120 hours except Saturday at 1520 and Sunday at 2020 hours. The BBC weather forecasts on 1500m can be received and do occasionally provide advance warning of the approach of a depression that could cause a *tramontana*.

The Spanish daily, *La Vanguardia*, published in Barcelona has a good weather section, particularly if you are heading up into the Gulf of Lions.

HARBOURS AND ANCHORAGES

WHAT TO EXPECT   Along the Spanish coast and in the Balearics there are numerous marinas with more to be built in the future. These marinas vary from huge conglomerates with every facility and an associated apartment complex to smaller and less fancy affairs. There are also a number of large commercial ports with quay space for yachts and numerous fishing harbours which may or may not have a special yacht quay. There are also a large number of anchorages, many offering good all-round shelter. The following list will give you some idea of what the *costas* are like:

Costa del Sol   Sixteen marinas and a number of anchorages. Marina development is likely to increase in the future.

Costa Blanca   Seven marinas and a few other harbours and a large number of anchorages.

Costa del Azahar   Five marinas and a few other harbours and anchorages.

Benidorm, Alicante

Spanish National Tourist Office

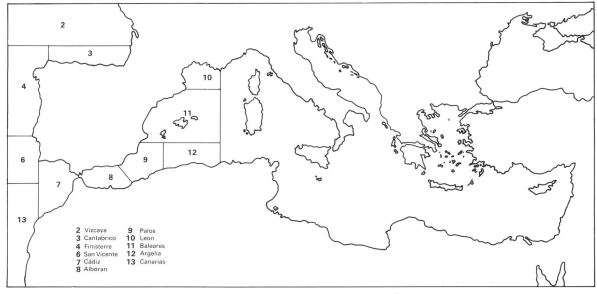

Spanish weather forecast areas

2	Vizcaya	**9**	Palos
3	Cantabrico	**10**	Leon
4	Finisterre	**11**	Baleares
6	San Vicente	**12**	Argelia
7	Cádiz	**13**	Canarias
8	Albóran		

Spanish National Tourist Office

Cabo Oropesa

Costa Dorada Four marinas, commercial and fishing harbours and numerous anchorages. Marina development is likely to increase.

Costa Brava Six marinas and a large number of anchorages.

Balearics Eight marinas, numerous other harbours and a large number of anchorages. Marina development is likely to increase.

SECURITY In recent years there has been an increase in petty crime in Spain. In the larger tourist centres and cities theft has become a real problem and the methods have become increasingly sophisticated. Much of it is carried out by non-Spanish nationals that come to Spain to prey on tourists. Thorough precautions should be taken.

WINTERING AFLOAT Spain is a popular place for wintering afloat with a mild climate and most facilities readily available. Most yachtsmen choose to winter in the Balearics (Palma is popular) or on the Costa Dorada or the Costa del Sol. Winter rates in many of the marinas are substantially below the summer rates making them an attractive proposition for many. Flights back to Britain are also cheap so that those who have to get back can do so easily leaving the yacht safely in a marina berth.

PASSAGE PLANNING

A yacht coming from the Strait of Gibraltar will usually follow the Spanish coast until Cabo San Antonío when they will either head for the Balearics or continue up the Spanish coast to France. Many yachts choose to cross from the Balearics to Sardinia and from there proceed east. Few yachts elect to cruise along the North African coast there being comparatively few harbours and little wind in the summer.

Specifically, yachts on passage to and from the Balearics to Sardinia will usually choose to leave from Menorca, usually Mahón and to make a landfall here when coming from Sardinia. The radiobeacon at Mahón with a range of 100 miles is useful when coming from Sardinia to Menorca.

NAVIGATION AIDS

Buoyage I.A.L.A. System 'A' was officially introduced in 1980. Buoyage is well developed and consistent.

Lights The coast is well lit and a yacht will have no problems navigating along the coast at night. In the more developed tourist areas it can be difficult to see low power harbour lights against the neon and other lights on the shore.

Radiobeacons There are numerous marine and aero radiobeacons along the mainland coast and around the Balearics. There are several sets of grouped beacons covering southern Spain, south east Spain, east Spain and northeast Spain. The Balearics are included in the east and northeast Spain group.

Times are G.M.T. Services are continuous unless otherwise stated.

Marine Radiobeacons

West Mediterranean group 313.5 kHz
Cap Bon (Tunisia) BN 200M every 6 mins. Seq. 1, 2.
Ras Caxine (Algeria) CX 200M every 6 mins. Seq. 3, 4.
Porquerolles (France) PQ 200M every 6 mins. Seq. 5, 6.

Southwest Spain group 289.6 kHz
Tarifa O 50M every 6 mins. Seq. 5, 6.
Cabo Trafalgar B 50M every 6 mins. Seq. 3, 4.
Rota D 80M every 6 mins. Seq. 1, 2.

South Spain group 298.8 kHz
Málaga GA 50M every 6 mins. Seq. 1, 2.
Cabo de Gata TA 50M every 6 mins. Seq. 5, 6.

Southeast Spain group 294.2 kHz
Ras Aguille AG 100M every 6 mins. Seq. 1, 2.
Cabo de Palos PA 50M every 6 mins. Seq. 3, 4.
Cabo de la Nao NO 50M every 6 mins. Seq. 5, 6.

East Spain group 298.8 kHz
Castellón AS 50M every 6 mins. Seq. 1, 2.
Cabo Salou UD 50M every 6 mins. Seq. 3, 4.
Punta de la Cala Figuera FI 50M every 6 mins. Seq. 5, 6.

Northeast Spain group 291.9 kHz
Punta del Llobregat OR 50M every 6 mins. Seq. 1, 2.
Mahón MH 100M every 6 mins. Seq. 3, 4.
Cabo San Sebastián SN 50M every 6 mins. Seq. 5, 6.

North Africa stations (misc.)
Cabo Espartel SP 312.6 kHz 200M
Ceuta CE 305.7 kHz 10M direction on Seq. 1, 2 158°

Air radiobeacons The following air radiobeacons operate but some do not operate continuously.

Rota AOG 265 kHz 100M 36°39'.00N 6°19'W
Málaga RMA 330 kHz 60M 36°39'.55N 4°28'.9W
Almería AMR 310 kHz 60M 36°50'.92N 2°22'.67W
Murcia LCZ 381 kHz 40M 37°40'.67N 0°56'.32W
Alicante ALT 280 kHz 50M 38°17'.3N 0°33'.1W
Valencia VLC 340 kHz 50M 39°26'.3N 0°21'.0W
Sagunto/Cabo Canet SGO 356 kHz 50M 39°40'.4N 0°12'.4W
Reus RES 272 kHz 50M 41°08'.7N 01°09'E
Villanueva VNV 380 kHz 50M 41°12'.6N 1°42'.4E
Barcelona QU 325 kHz 80M 41°17'.2N 1°59'.1E
Bagur BGR 319 kHz 50M 41°57'N 3°13'E

Mahón MN 344 kHz 60M 39°50'.18N 4°12'.72E
Andraitx ADX 384 kHz 30M 39°32'.92N 2°23'.67E
Palma CST 351 kHz 50M 39°38'.47N 2°55'.27E
Ibiza IBZ 394 kHz 60M 38°54'.8N 1°28'.07E

Coast radio stations   The following coast radio stations operate on this coast. In addition to the stations listed there is Pozuelo del Reyu (Madrid) (EHY) which operates a comprehensive commercial service on the HF band. Full details are contained in the Admiralty *List of Radio Signals Volume 1* as are morse code transmissions from some of the stations below.
Most commercial ports and marinas keep a continuous listening watch on VHF Channel 16.
Main operating frequencies are shown in bold type. 2191 kHz is used when 2182 kHz is engaged in distress working.
All times are G.M.T.
All stations offer a 24 hour service unless otherwise stated.

Station	Transmits (kHz or VHF Channel)	Listens (kHz or VHF Channel)	Traffic Lists (Frequ. & times)
Gibraltar (ZDK)	VHF Ch. 1, 2, 3, 4, 16, 23, 24, 25, 27, 28, 86, 87		Mon-Sat 0700-1900 Sun and holidays 0700-1300
Mijas	VHF Ch. 16, 24, 25, **26**, 27		Ch. 26 at 0233, 0633, 0833, 1033, 1233, 1633, 1833, 2233
Cabo de Gata	**1866**, 2182, 2191, 2679, VHF Ch. 16, 20, 25, 26, 27	2122, 2182, 2191, 3283	1866 at ev. odd H + 33 (0333-1933) 2333 Ch. 27 at 0233, 0633, 0833, 1033, 1233, 1633, 1833, 2233
Cartagena	VHF Ch. 16, 05, 25, 65		Ch. 05 at 0233, 0633, 0833, 1033, 1233, 1633, 1833, 2233
Alicante	VHF Ch. 16, **01**, 26, 88		Ch. 01 at 0233, 0633, 0833, 1033, 1233, 1633, 1833, 2233
Cabo de la Nao (EAV)	**1690**, 2182, 2191, 2799 VHF Ch. 16, **02**, 27, 61 66, 82, 86	2013, 2182, 2191, 3231	1690 at ev. odd H + 33 (0333-1933) and at 2333 Ch. 02 at 0233, 0633, 0833, 1033, 1233, 1633, 1833, 2233
Valencia	VHF Ch. 16, **26**, **27**		Ch. 26 at time above and 2303
Castellón	VHF Ch. 16, **07**, 28, 63		Ch. 07 at 0233, 0633, 0833, 1033, 1233, 1633, 1833, 2233
Marmella	VHF Ch. 16, **23**, 25, **26**,, 27		Ch. 26 at 0233, 0633, 0833, 1233, 1633, 1833, 2233
Barcelona	**1730**, 2182, 2191, 2707 VHF Ch. **4**, 16, 25, 26, **27**	2083, 2182, 2191 3290	1730 at ev. odd H + 33 (0333-1933) and 2333 Ch. 27 at 0233, 0633, 0833, 1033, 1233, 1633, 1833, 2233
Bagur (EAB)	**1740**, 2182, 2191, 2714, VHF Ch. 16, **23**, 26, 27, **28**	2122, 2192, 2182, 3283	1740 ev. odd H + 33 (0333-1933) 2333 Ch. 28 at time above
Palma de Mallorca	VHF Ch. 03, 16, **20**, 26, 27		Ch. 03 at 0233, 0633, 0833, 1033, 1233, 1633, 1833, 2233
Menorca	VHF Ch. 16, 23		As for Palma de Mallorca
Ibiza	VHF Ch. 16, **24**, 84		Ch. 24 as for Palma (Mallorca)

Radio navigation warnings are given in Spanish and English from the following coastal radio stations:

Tarifa (EAC) 1678 kHz at 0033, 0433, 0833, 1233, 1633 and 2033.
Mijas VHF Ch. 26 in Spanish at 0803 and 1503.
Cabo de Gata 1866 kHz at 0003, 0403, 0803, 1203, 1603 and 2003 and on VHF Ch. 27 at 0903 and 1603 in Spanish for local areas.
Cabo de Palos VHF Ch. 26 in Spanish at 0933 and 1633.
Cabo de la Nao (EAV) 1690 kHz at 0033, 0433, 0833, 1233, 1633 and 2033.
Barcelona 1730 kHz at 0003, 0403, 0803, 1203, 1603 and 2003. VHF Ch. 27 at 0803 and 1503.

Rescue services Lifeboats are stationed at the major ports. Many of the marinas also have an inshore rescue boat.

Spanish National Tourist Office

Calahonda, Costa del Sol

FORMALITIES

ENTRY FORMALITIES On entering Spanish waters a yacht should make for the nearest port with customs officials *(aduana)*. Here you will be boarded by the customs officials or by the *Guardia Civil*, the national police. There are two branches of the latter force, one dealing with the land and one with the sea. They will want your ship's papers (see note under Documents), passports and information about you and your yacht which will be noted down on a special form. You will be stamped into the country and in practice that is that. At the next harbour you visit where customs or *Guardia Civil* are stationed you will have to give all this information again. For this reason it is a good idea to have it already made out so that this procedure is simplified. (Imray's *Foreign Port Forms* or similar are useful for this.) In theory you should obtain a customs importation card from the customs for your yacht, but in practice it is extremely difficult to get one and it is almost never asked for at subsequent ports.

A yacht may be imported temporarily into Spain for six months of a calendar year. When you first arrive you will be given 90 days. For a yacht to remain longer than 90 days special permission must be obtained from customs. If you wish to leave your yacht in Spain it can be sealed by customs for a period of up to two years after which it must be exported. Alternatively you can clear out of Spain to Gibraltar or France and when you re-enter you will get another 90 days.

Holders of most foreign passports get 90 days on entering Spain without a visa. A visa for a stay longer than 90 days can easily be obtained at any Spanish consulate outside Spain. Holders of American passports automatically get 180 days without a special visa.

In practice the regulations governing yachts are not strictly enforced, especially in the summer and boats have been known to stay in Spanish waters for several years without problems. But it is as well to remember that they do exist and that heavy fines can be applied for contravening the regulations. The regulations governing entry are more strictly enforced.

Ports with the requisite officials for entry are:
Near to Gibraltar: Tarifa, Algeciras, José Banús and Málaga.
Near to the French border: Port Bou and Palamós.
In the Balearics: Ibiza, Palma, Alcudia, Cala Ratjada and Mahón.

DOCUMENTS You must have Small Ship's Register papers or full Part I Registration documents (the *Blue Book*). You should also have a certificate of competency for which the R.Y.A. *Helmsman's Certificate* is acceptable. In addition you should have insurance papers. Imray's *Foreign Port Forms*, or similar, simplify paperwork with the authorities. A ship's stamp is also useful.

TAXES Harbour dues are charged in most harbours. They vary from modest in municipal harbours to high in some marinas and yacht clubs. Marina charges vary from marina to marina but on the whole are reasonable, especially in the winter.

Import duty for a yacht imported permanently into Spain is around 40% of the value of the yacht.

For the exact details and scale of charges for importing a yacht into Spain contact the Spanish Tourist Office who will put you in touch with the relevant authority.

FACILITIES

EVERYDAY
Water Is potable from taps unless marked otherwise. Most harbours and all marinas have water laid on at the quay.

Ice Is available from most harbours and marinas in the summer. It should not be used for drinks unless it has been prepared from drinking water for that purpose.

Fuel Widely available in most harbours and marinas. A small tax is applied for its use in pleasure craft.

Electricity Is available in many harbours and all marinas.

Gas Camping gaz is widely available. Calor gas bottles can be refilled in the larger centres.

Paraffin (Petroleo) Not widely available and difficult to find in some places, the Balearics for instance. Sold in general stores, usually in the poorer quarter of a town. Here also methylated spirits will be found..

BOAT REPAIRS
Engines Most spares for the more well known makes of marine engines can be found. Competent mechanics can be found in most places but enquire amongst other yachtsmen for prices and about competence. Marine engines are manufactured in Spain.

Electrics and electronics Competent electrical and electronic repair shops can be found in the cities and large towns. Spares can be a problem.

Navigation instruments Some spares for well known makes of gear can be found but most spares will have to be imported.

Paints and antifouling Imported and locally manufactured paints and antifoulings are widely available.

Hauling There are a large number of yards, often associated with marinas, where a yacht can be hauled onto hard standing. Travel hoists and patent slips for larger yachts. On the whole costs are cheap for the Mediterranean.

Engineering Good engineering shops that can undertake all manner of work can be found in the cities or larger towns or associated with a marina. Specialist yacht fittings in stainless steel can be fabricated.

Wood and GRP Good wood and GRP work can be carried out. In many of the yards there are self-employed craftsmen but ask around to check on prices and skills. A number of GRP and wooden yachts are built to a good standard in Spain.

DUTY FREE SPARES Since the entry of Spain into the E.C. the requirements for importing spares on a duty free basis have changed. You must now lodge a cash deposit, equivalent to the imported goods value, with the local customs. The deposit is returned once the items have been seen to go onto your boat. A customs document, signed by the local civil guard, must be obtained to get the deposit back.

If you have a lot of things to bring in that are not overly bulky or heavy it can pay to fly to England and bring them back in your personal luggage. It depends on your audacity and luck as to what you can get through this way.

PROVISIONING

GENERAL Prices for most goods are moderate in Spain except for imported goods which are expensive. Prices for the same item may vary a great deal between say the smart mini-market on the waterfront and the local shop several blocks behind. Good fresh fruit and vegetables will be found in the markets at reasonable prices. Prices tend to increase quite dramatically in the resort areas for the summer.

Shopping hours vary but in general they are 0800/0900-1200 and 1400-1800/2000 Monday to Saturday.

SPECIFIC
Meat Is reasonably priced and good quality.

Fish Is plentiful and reasonably priced. In the smaller fishing harbours fresh fish can often be bought directly from the fishermen.

Fruit and vegetables Good selection at reasonable prices. The local markets are excellent and the produce of good quality.

Staples All the basics are widely available.

Cheese Local soft and hard cheeses are good value. Imported cheeses are expensive.

Canned goods Mostly confined to fish, fruit and vegetables unless imported.

Coffee and tea Instant coffee is available in most places and is moderately priced. Fresh coffee is good. English tea is available.

Wines, beer and spirits   Wine is cheap and eminently palatable. More expensive wines are of good quality. The local beer is good. In the tourist resorts you will often find English beer, sometimes on tap. Spirits manufactured under licence in Spain are good and much cheaper than the imported equivalent. Spain is of course the home of sherry and it is excellent value. *Fino* is dry and pale, *oloroso* is heavier and darker (brown and cream sherries). Spanish brandy, the better brands, is good and excellent value for money. *Sangria* is a popular summer drink made from red wine, brandy, mineral water, orange and lemon juices, with sliced fruit in it and served ice cold. Make it yourself on board.

Recommended   Good wines, brandy, sherry, spices (especially saffron), cheeses.

EATING OUT   A Spanish saying tells us that: 'In the south they fry, in the centre they roast, and in the north they stew.' That may have once been true but in most areas they do all three. Spanish food is both varied and good value — not at all the greasy fare it is often depicted as. Restaurant prices vary according to the category but even the impecunious can afford to eat out every now and again. One nice way to eat out is to go to a bar or restaurant that specialises in *tapas*. *Tapa* literally means lid and comes from the old custom of giving a small *meze* with a drink, the *meze* being served on a small plate that covered the top of the glass. This custom has largely died out but you can order *tapas* in some bars and restaurants — usually bits of roast meat, meatballs, fish, vegetable salads, olives, etc — and so sit down to an appetising selection of many small different dishes.

Restaurant prices vary considerably from the tourist areas to the local restaurants. In the popular tourist areas you can eat well and pay dearly for it but often as not you will be served a bland international cuisine revolving around steak and chips, mostly meagre overpriced portions. Eat in the local restaurants and you will find good food at reasonable prices.

Paella is probably the best known Spanish dish. Often it is prepared beforehand in bulk for the evening whereas a good *paella* will take at least half an hour to prepare. It combines seafood, chicken, pork and vegetables on a bed of saffron-flavoured rice. *Cocido* is a stew using whatever ingredients are available. *Zarzuela* is also a stew. *Calamares*, baby squid usually deep-fried, are invariably excellent. Cooked with tomatoes and garlic the dish is known as *calamares salteados*. *Lechona* is roast suckling pig. Spanish omelettes are also excellent, often having all manner of vegetables thrown into them.

CHARTS AND PILOTS

Admiralty*Mediterranean Pilot* Vol. 1 (NP45) Covers the south and east coast of Spain and the Balearics.
Admiralty *List of Lights and Fog Signals* Vol. I (NP 78)
East Spain Pilot. (In three volumes.) Robin Brandon. Imray. Covers the Spanish Mediterranean coast and the Balearics in detail.
Guia Nautica Turistica y Deportiva de España. Asambles de Capitanes de Yates. In Spanish but with harbour plans.

Charts   If you are used to Admiralty charts then it is best to stick to these for Spanish waters. Admiralty charts for Spain can be obtained in Gibraltar. Spanish charts for the area are probably the best. They can be obtained from the Commandancia Militar de Marina at major ports. Imray publish three medium-scale, folded charts of the Spanish Mediterranean.

USEFUL BOOKS

Blue Guide to Mainland Spain. Black. The best.
Nagel's *Guide to Spain and the Balearic Islands.*
Collins *Companion Guide to The South of Spain.*
Fabled Shore. Rose Macaulay. Hamish Hamilton. A classic.
Berlitz Guides to *Costa Blanca, Costa Brava, Costa Dorada and Barcelona, Costa del Sol and Andalusia, Ibiza and Formentera, Majorca and Minorca.* Up to date compact guides.
The Rough Guide to Spain. RKP.

France

Area   549,621 square kilometres (212,209 square miles)

Population   59,000,000

Capital   Paris (2,600,000)

Language   French

Religion   Roman Catholic

Time Zone   G.M.T. + 1; D.S.T. (April-September)

Currency   Franc (F)

Electricity   220V/50HzAC

Banks   Opening hours vary. Generally 0830-1300/1430-1630 Monday-Friday. Eurocheques, credit cards, and travellers' cheques accepted everywhere. Representatives of some of the major British banks on the Mediterranean coast.

Mail   Reliable. *Poste restante* or a marina address.

Medical   The standard of treatment is high. Medical fees vary from moderate to very high (for private doctors outside the French national health system). Reciprocal agreements exist with other E.C. countries for payment of fees. Alternatively take out private insurance or fly back to Britain for treatment.

Internal travel   Many internal flights. Bus and train travel is reliable and comfortable. Taxis are expensive. Hire car agencies are numerous and the cost reasonable.

International travel   There are regular flights to Marignane (Marseille) and Nice. In the summer there may be charter flights to Perpignan, Montpellier, Nimes, St Tropez, Cannes, Calvi, Ajaccio and Bastia. Trains and buses run to Paris where you can proceed on to other destinations.

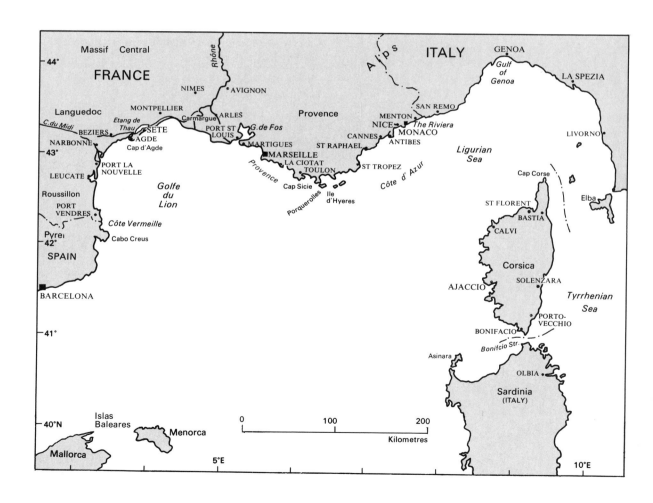

Public Holidays
    January 1 New Year's Day
    May 1 Labour Day
    July 14 Bastille Day
    August 15 Festival of the Assumption
    November 1 All Saints' Day
    November 11 Armistice Day
    December 25 Christmas Day
    Moveable:
    Good Friday
    Easter Monday
    Ascension Day
    White Monday.

GEOGRAPHY

COAST AND ISLANDS The coast stretches from the Spanish border and the Pyrénées to the Italian border at the junction of the Alps and the Apennines. This mainland coast is some 330 miles long with the large island of Corsica a hundred miles offshore adding a further 350 miles of coast. All of the coast is bordered by high mountains except for the Languedoc-Roussillon area west of the Rhône delta where it is marshy and flat. Corsica is often described as a mountain surrounded by sea, a description difficult to better.

The Mediterranean coast is very built up to provide accommodation and services for the large numbers of tourists, native and foreign, who arrive in this resort area in the summer. Many of the resorts, especially east of the Rhône which includes the Côte d'Azur and the French Riviera, have long been popular. The English aristocracy discovered Nice in the 18th century and flocked here in large numbers in the 19th century to escape the debilitating London winter fogs; the aristocracy of other nations soon followed so that the Côte d'Azur and the Riviera were booming tourist resorts fifty years before the notion of vacations and package holidays became popular.

The island of Corsica seems further than 100 miles from France; it is a majestic mountainous island, less crowded and dramatically more beautiful than the mainland and is a very un-Gallic part of France. The island has an Arabic flavour and the Corsican flag, a black Moor's head on a white background, reinforces the notion. In the early summer there is still snow on the high peaks and it is a strange feeling to be swimming in warm waters under snow capped mountains.

French Government Tourist Office

Cannes

CRUISING AREAS The south coast of France is the yachting Mecca of the Mediterranean. In the summer there are large numbers of yachts cruising the coast with many based permanently here and to accommodate them numerous marinas have been built so that it is not an exaggeration to say that one cruises from marina to marina. The facilities and services are the best offered anywhere in the Mediterranean but it is difficult to get away from it all to a quiet bay around the corner.

The coast is divided into regions:

Languedoc-Roussillon The low marshy coast west of the Rhône delta that extends almost to the Spanish border. (There is ten miles of rugged coast before the Spanish border called the *Côte Vermeille,* the vermillion coast, after the characteristic reddish rock bordering it.) Numerous new gargantuan marina developments have been built at intervals along the coast.

Provence Stretches from the Rhône to La Ciotat. There are numerous marinas, the *calanques* of Cassis, and some commercial and fishing harbours. Marseille is the principal commercial harbour.

Côte d'Azur The Azure coast that stretches from La Ciotat to Cap Ferrat; there are many marinas including of course St Tropez and Cannes. In the summer the more fashionable marinas are full to overflowing and it is difficult to find a berth.

The French Riviera Extends from Nice to the Italian border and Riviera. There are numerous marinas and the principality of Monaco along this stretch of coast.

Corsica There are fewer marinas but numerous picturesque anchorages. The island is popular in the summer but nothing like as crowded as the mainland coast.

CLIMATE AND WEATHER

The climate is typically Mediterranean being hot and dry in the summer and mild and wet in the winter, the mild winter climate of the Riviera being of course travel folklore. West of the Riviera it can be chilly in the winter with snow falling in some areas and when the *mistral* howls down the Rhône valley the temperature drops to a bone-chilling low. In the summer the *sirocco* occasionally reaches the south coast of France and brings with it an uncomfortable humidity.

January and February have a mean average temperature of 1°C to 11°C (34°F to 54°F) and are the coldest months. July and August are the hottest: average temperature 17°C to 29°C (63°F to 84°F).

Humidity is moderate at around 75% (80% in winter and 53% in summer). These figures are reduced by offshore and increased by onshore winds.

Mean sea temperatures vary from 12°C (54°F) in February to 23°C (73°) in August.

WINDS The prevailing summer winds are from the northwest and southeast. In the Gulf of Lions the winds in the winter and summer are almost entirely from the northwest while further east the direction of wind is altered by the local topography so that it blows from the southwest and southeast. The normal daybreeze (*vent du Midi, vent solaire*) blowing onto the land normally begins in the mid-morning and dies off by dusk, it can occasionally reach gale force but is more often Force 4-5.

The *mistral* is the wind most feared along this coast, in the winter it blows from the northwest down into the Gulf of Lions and for over 10% of observations blows at Force 8 or more. It normally blows for three days but can last up to a week and it blows out of a clear sky and can reach gale force in half an hour from a flat calm. Warning signs are a very dry almost electric atmosphere, a clear sky with no clouds and very clear visibility. The barometer provides little help in detecting an approaching *mistral* but it often develops when a depression is crossing central France and if this occurs it is wise to seek out a safe harbour in case a *mistral* blows.

LOCAL NAMES OF WINDS Local names for the winds are as follows:

Mistral The northwest wind that blows over the Gulf of Lions and spreads out fan-wise as far as the Balearics and Sardinia. The *mistral* blows out of a clear blue sky with an electric dry atmosphere and a stationary or slightly rising barometer and, it is said, if a *mistral* has not arrived by 1000 in the summer (1200 in the winter) then it will not come that day. A moderate northwest wind in the Gulf of Lions may create a secondary depression in the Gulf of Genoa which after 4-6 hours reinforces the wind in the Gulf of Lions to produce a strong *mistral*.

Tramontane The N-NW wind that blows through the Toulouse Gap between the Pyrénées and the Massif Centrale. It affects the coast from Spain to Sète. Like the *mistral* it can blow out of a clear blue sky with little warning. At times it may blow up to Force 10, though in the summer it rarely blows above Force 7.

Levante   A strong easterly wind accompanied by wet weather.

Ceruse   A strong southeasterly similar to the *levante*. Both may be heralded by low clouds forming on the hills and the air becoming damp.

Marin   A strong southerly wind (SE-S-SW) with a warm humidity.

Vent du Midi, vent solaire   The normal daybreeze blowing onto the land.

Southerly winds are sometimes preceded by a rise in the water level, hazy visibility and a swell.

GALES   As well as the *mistral* and *tramontane* which can raise a steep nasty sea, gale force winds also blow from the south causing a heavy sea to pile up on the coast. It should be noted that in the Gulf of Lions, there is a 12% frequency of gales in the winter, the highest frequency in the Mediterranean. However the percentage frequency in the summer (1->1%) is much the same as for other parts of the Mediterranean. If you are on passage in the French Mediterranean during the winter the area must be treated with the caution it deserves and a listening watch kept on the radio for gale warnings. In February 1983 a twenty-eight foot yacht on passage in the Gulf of Lions was rolled in a gale losing its mast and putting the engine out of action, the yacht drifted helpless for two weeks and was carried by the current to a position near Malta where a fishing boat helped it into harbour.

THUNDERSTORMS   May occur in the summer but are most frequent in the autumn. They can be spotted as a ragged line of black cloud moving rapidly and are accompanied by heavy rain and a strong squall but seldom last longer than three hours. Water spouts occasionally occur in the Gulf of Lions and off Corsica.

TIDES AND CURRENTS   The tidal range can be ignored for all intents and purposes (range: 0.15m/0.5ft at springs), but the sea level can rise as much as one metre with onshore winds and decrease as much as 0.5 metre with offshore winds. Along the Riviera the current follows the coast in a westerly direction. In the Gulf of Lions the current flows out of the gulf in a southwesterly direction with a slight easterly counter-current close to the coast.

WEATHER FORECASTS   These are transmitted in French at regular times, the forecasts are read at dictation speed twice and then repeated at normal speed, with a little practice and a garnish of schoolboy French they can be understood after a little time.

The main weather forecasts in French are transmitted as follows:

Times are G.M.T.
Marseille (FFM) 1906 kHz at 0103, 0705, 1220, 1615 and on request. VHF Chs. 26 and 28 (Fos) at 0633, 1133*
Grasse (TKM) 2649 kHz, 113m at 0733, 1233, 1645* and on request. VHF Ch. 02 at 0633 and 1133*
Perpignan, VHF Ch. 02 at 0633, 1133
Sète VHF Ch. 25 at 0633, 1133*
Radio France-Marseille 1241 kHz 150M at 0615, 1127*
France Inter 164 kHz (1829m) at 0555 and 1905*
Nice 1554 kHz at 0615, 0630, 0655 and 1100
Monte Carlo 1466 and 218 kHz 0800 and 1900*
Monaco (3AC and 3AF). 4363.6, 8728.2, 8743.7, 13172.1, 17251.5, 22651.8 kHz 0715, 1300 and 1800. Storm warnings on receipt. VHF Ch. 23.* Continuous. 0600 to 2300 and Ch. 28* at 0803, 0903, 1303, 1715 and 2033 with storm warnings on receipt.

At every marina a weather forecast, often with an English translation, is posted daily and sometimes twice daily. In some marinas the new *Antiope* video-text system has been installed with the general and local forecast continuously updated.

*Transmits one hour earlier during summertime (D.S.T.).

French Government Tourist Office

Agde, Languedoc-Roussillon.

Weather forecasts are also available by telephone from meteorological offices.

Corsica
This island has three French forecast areas: No. 33 Golfe de Gênes to N; No. 34 Ouest Corse to W and No. 35 Est Corse to E. The best forecasts are from Grasse (TKM) and Monte Carlo-Monaco, though the latter cannot always be received on the south coast of the island.

HARBOURS AND ANCHORAGES

WHAT TO EXPECT There must be more marinas per mile of coast than anywhere else in the world, certainly more than anywhere else in the Mediterranean. There are also commercial and fishing harbours in which there is usually a basin or section of the quay allotted to yachts but where a charge, often on a par with marina charges, is made. There are few anchorages and a few small islands close offshore which afford some shelter.

SECURITY Theft is not a major problem but occurs frequently enough for a need to take adequate precaution. Lock your boat securely and remove tempting items from the deck.

WINTERING AFLOAT Many of the marinas offer large reductions in berthing fees during the winter making the area an attractive place to winter afloat. The ease of getting back to Britain for a visit and the availability of spares and boat gear means that many yachts choose to winter here.

PASSAGE PLANNING

Most yachts follow the coast in either direction without there being any real guiding principles for route planning.

Port Vendres near the Spanish border is the usual jumping off place for the Balearics or the Spanish coast.

Yachts leaving for Corsica usually depart from somewhere between the Isles Porquerolles and St Tropez. A yacht leaving St Tropez in the late afternoon should arrive in Calvi about twenty-four hours later.

La Grande Motte, Languedoc-Roussillon.

French Government Tourist Office

CHARTER

There are numerous bare-boat charter companies along the coast, particularly along the Côte d'Azur. Many large charter boats winter over here or come for refits. A small flotilla operates around the Côte d'Azur. Around southern Corsica bare-boats and flotillas operate, often doing a Corsica-Sardinia cruise in the Strait of Bonifacio.

NAVIGATION AIDS

Buoyage The I.A.L.A. Buoyage System 'A' was introduced in 1980 and is well developed and consistent.

Lights The coast is well lit and a yacht will have no difficulty navigating along this coast at night.

Radiobeacons There are numerous radiobeacons along the coast and around Corsica. There are five sets of grouped marine radiobeacons and three air radiobeacons that are useful.

Marine radiobeacons. The following radiobeacons operate continuously in the area in groups or singly:

South France group 287.3 kHz
    Cap Béar BR 50M every 6 mins. Seq. 1, 2.
    Sète SÉ 50M every 6 mins. Seq. 3, 4.
    Ile du Planier PN 100M every 6 mins. Seq. 5, 6.

West Corsica group 294.2 kHz
    Pointe Revellata RV 100M every 6 mins. Seq. 3, 4.
    La Garoupe GO 100M every 6 mins. Seq. 5, 6.

East Corsica group 308 kHz
    Ile de la Giraglia GL 60M every 4 mins. Seq. 1, 2.
    Pointe de Chiappa CP 100M every 4 mins. Seq. 3, 4.

Other stations
    Cap Couronne CR 305.7 kHz 50M 43°19′.58N 5°03′.25E

West Mediterranean group 313.5 kHz
    Cap Bon (Tunisia) BN 200M every 6 mins. Seq. 1, 2.
    Ras Caxine (Algeria) CX 200M every 6 mins. Seq. 3, 4.
    Porquerolles (France) PQ 200M every 6 mins. Seq. 5, 6.

Air radiobeacons. The following air radiobeacons operate in the area but may not transmit continuously:

Istres ITR 390.5 kHz 43°31′.58N 4°55′.82E
Hyères HYE 322 kHz 70M 43°02′.02N 6°09′10E
Nice, Mont Leuza LEZ 398.5 kHz 75M 43°53′N 7°19′E
Ajaccio, Campo del'Oro IS 341 kHz 50M 41°53′.9N 8°36′.8E
Solenzara SZA 349.5 kHz 80M 41°55′.9N 9°23′.8E
Bastia, Poretta BP 369 kHz 50M 42°25′.7N 9°32′.2E
Calvi CV 404 kHz 42°34′.67N 8°48′.47E

Coast Radio Stations All commercial ports and most of the marinas listen on VHF Channels 9 and 16 and offer 24 hour service unless otherwise marked. VHF Ch 16 and 2182 kHz are reserved for emergency calls. Vessels wishing to contact on VHF should call directly on a working channel.
    Main operating frequencies are shown in bold type.
    All times are G.M.T.
    All stations offer a 24 hour service unless otherwise stated.

Station	*Transmits* *(kHz or VHF Channel)*	*Listens* *(kHz or VHF Channel)*	*Traffic Lists* *(Freq. & times)*
St Lys (FFL) (FFS) (FFT)	4366.7, 8808.8, 13178.3, 17316.6, 22673.5	4072.3, 8284.9, 12407.5, 16543.7	Continuous watch on 4072.3, 8284.9, 12407.5, 16543.7 (0700-2230). Watch from H+03 to H+10 4072.3, 8284.9, 12407.5, 16543.7, 22077.5 (0603-2010), 4072.3, 8284.9, 12407.5, 16543.7 (2103-0510). Traffic lists on 4366.7, 8808.8, 13178.3, 17316.6 and 22673.5 at ev. H + 03 and when nec. on H + 30 (0700-2230)
Marseille (FFM)	**1906**, 1939, 2182, 2628 3722, 3795	2182	Traffic lists on 1906 at ev. odd H + 10.
	VHF Ch. 16, **24, 26, 27, 28, 62**	24, 26, 27, 28, 62	
Grasse (TKM)	1834, 2182, **2649**, 3722	2182	Traffic lists on 2649 at ev. even H + 33 (0633-2033) 0630-2200*
	VHF Ch. 2, **4, 5,** 16	2, 4, 5	
Monaco (3AC) (3AF)	4363.6, 8728.2, 13172.1, 17251.5, 22651.8	4125, 8257, 12392, 16522, 22062	Traffic lists on 8728.2 at ev. H + 00 (0700-2300)
	VHF Ch. 16,28,26	16,28,86	Traffic lists on Ch. 16 at ev. H + 03 (0700-2300)*

*One hour earlier in summer time (D.S.T.) main frequencies only.

Corsica			
Ajacco	VHF Ch. 16, **24**	24	
Porto-Vecchio	VHF Ch. 16, **25**	25	0630-2200*

Radio navigational warnings are transmitted from the coast radio stations as follows, some are in English.

>   **Marseille**   1906 kHz at 0933, 2133
>   **Grasse**   2649 kHz at 0633, 1833
>   **Monaco**   8728.2 kHz at 0715, 1300. VHF Ch. 28 at 0903, 2033.* *1 hour earlier when D.S.T. is in force.

Rescue Services   Lifeboats *(sauvetage)* are stationed at all major ports and many of the smaller harbours as part of the CROSS-MED service. In addition many of the marinas have their own inshore rescue craft. An emergency call on 2182 kHz or VHF channel 16, or the report of distress flares, will be promptly answered. All-weather lifeboats are stationed at Port Vendres, Sète, Carro, La Ciotat, St Tropez, Cannes, Bastia, Macinaggio and Bonifacio.

FORMALITIES

ENTRY FORMALITIES When entering France it is no longer necessary to fly a 'Q' flag requesting customs clearance unless you have goods to declare. In practice you simply enter French waters and that is that. In 1986 the *Titre de Séjour*, a provisional resident permit, was introduced along the French Mediterranean coast. The permit is issued by customs and is ratified by them. It is issued free of charge. If you are laying up a boat in France, the *Titre de Séjour* is issued in place of the old *Passeport du Navire Etranger*. The *Titre de Séjour* considerably simplifies matters, absolving the owner from checking with customs every time the yacht is visited or used.

A yacht that is registered in a country that does not have a special financial arrangement with France (most do but amongst those that do not are Australia, New Zealand, South Africa and flags of convenience such as Panama, Liberia, Honduras and the Maldives) must pay an additional 3 Francs per registered ton per day while in French harbours. When it was introduced this additional tax caused a mass exodus from France, which left many marinas nearly empty in the winter and many out of work, so that an unofficial edict from Paris cancelled it; however, the tax still remains law.

An owner is allowed to use a yacht for six months in any 12 month period without being liable for T.V.A. (French V.A.T.). However you may not use the boat for any commercial purpose including chartering it. Although a co-owner or immediate family may use the boat, relatives and friends cannot. In the past there have been too many 'friends' and 'relatives' using boats in disguised charters. The new *Titre de Séjour* means you can actually keep your boat in France as long as the *Titre de Séjour* is renewed with the relevant customs office every year. I quote from the information pamphlet issued: 'If usually your boat stays in France, show your resident permit to the office which ratified it in order to have it renewed.' And further: 'Any modification relative to either the boat, the owner or the user will imply a new provisional resident permit.'

In practice the regulations are interpreted with typical Gallic common sense by the authorities. Spot checks are regularly carried out through the summer, though in a friendly fashion. The marine branch of the *Gendarmerie* also make spot checks and will apprehend anyone exceeding speed regulations or behaving recklessly in a boat. Anyone infringing customs regulations or entering prohibited areas should not expect the normal Gallic charm to be turned on them – customs and the *Gendarmerie Maritime* take their work seriously.

DOCUMENTS A yacht must have the Small Ship's Register papers or full (Part I) registration papers. Photocopies of registration papers will not be accepted. A radio licence, certificate of competency (the R.Y.A. *Helmsman's Certificate* is acceptable) and insurance documents should be carried but again photocopies are not acceptable.

TAXES Harbour and marina dues can be quite high in the summer but are substantially less in other seasons. If a yacht is to be imported into France then the French luxury tax, T.V.A. (as in V.A.T.), at around 18% must be paid. Owners of yachts registered in countries that do not have a special financial arrangement with France (see above) must pay an additional 3 Francs per registered ton per day spent in French harbours.

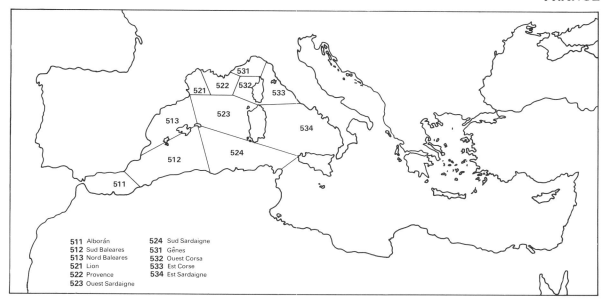

French weather forecast areas.

511	Alborán	**524**	Sud Sardaigne
512	Sud Baleares	**531**	Gênes
513	Nord Baleares	**532**	Ouest Corsa
521	Lion	**533**	Est Corse
522	Provence	**534**	Est Sardaigne
523	Ouest Sardaigne		

French Government Tourist Office

Mandelieu-la Napoule on the French Riviera

FACILITIES

EVERYDAY

Water   Is potable from taps unless marked otherwise. In the marinas there is water at or near every berth.

Ice   Obtainable in many of the harbours and marinas as large blocks and as ice cubes (suitable for drinks) in some of the marinas.

Fuel   Available in nearly all harbours from a fuel quay. Untaxed fuel for fishing boats cannot be purchased by yachts.

Electricity   Available in every marina.

Gas   Calor type gas bottles cannot be refilled but an adaptor that mates the threaded union of Calor gas equipment to a *Camping gaz* bottle can be obtained in England. *Camping gaz* is available everywhere.

Paraffin   Is difficult to obtain. Ask for *petrole kerdane*. Wood alcohol, methylated spirits without the blue dye commonly used elsewhere, can be purchased in supermarkets and grocery shops – ask for *alcool à bruler*.

BOAT REPAIRS

Engines   Most spares for the more well known makes of marine engines can be found. Spares are relatively easily obtained from England. Competent mechanics are on hand nearly everywhere but shop around for prices.

Electrics and electronics   Competent electric and electronic repair shops versed in the care and repair of marine gear are easily found everywhere.

Navigation instruments   Spares for the better known makes of gear can be found. Locally manufactured equipment is good and only slightly more expensive than the British equivalent.

Paints and antifouling   Imported and locally manufactured paints and antifouling are widely available but are more expensive than in England.

Hauling   There are a large number of yards, often within a marina, with patent slipways and travel hoists that can haul yachts of all types and sizes. Costs vary considerably.

Engineering   Good engineering shops that can undertake all types of work can be found near to most harbours.

Wood and GRP   Accomplished boat chippies can be found in many of the harbours. GRP skills are also good. In many of the harbours there are self-employed craftsmen who will undertake work but take advice from the locals and long-term yachtsmen first as skills and prices vary enormously. In the summer the demand on services is high and prices rise accordingly.

DUTY FREE SPARES   Small items sent from Britain can be posted with a green label customs declaration and should arrive quickly. Large items

French Government Tourist Office

Bonifacio in Corsica.

Les Calanques just past Marseille.

Sète.

St Louis du Rhône. Yachts lock through here to get to the Mediterranean.

take longer and may be inspected by customs before you can collect them. Take your registration papers and passport when you go to collect items from customs.

PROVISIONING

GENERAL In general prices are higher in France but so is the quality of goods. Costs vary considerably in the small shops between the winter and summer so it is best to do your shopping in one of the large supermarkets such as Monoprix. Imported goods are expensive and in any case often inferior to equivalent French brands.

Shopping hours in general are 0830-1200 and 1400-1800 Monday to Saturday but many shops also open on Sundays. Fresh produce can be obtained from local markets which are cheaper and the produce is often fresher.

SPECIFIC

Meat Is expensive but the quality is excellent. Remember that the cuts of meat do not usually contain fat and bone so that what you are buying is all lean.

Fish A good selection but again it is not cheap.

Fruit and vegetables Good selection all through the year at reasonable prices.

Staples All the basics are widely available.

Cheese Imported cheeses are expensive and in any case it is a nonsense to buy them when so many reasonably priced French cheeses of excellent quality are available. A camembert or brie with good French butter and a *baguette*, a bottle of *vin ordinaire* and you have an excellent and cheap lunch.

Canned goods A good selection at reasonable prices.

Coffee and tea Instant coffee is moderately priced. Fresh coffee is excellent but not as cheap as Italy. French tea is for 'infusions' and not the British cuppa.

Wines, beer and spirits Wine is of course excellent and even a *vin ordinaire* may bring a smile to your lips. French beer is of the lager type and quite palatable. Spirits are moderately priced. Stock up on cognac here if you prefer the true French cognac to imitations.

Recommended Good wines — white and red, cheeses, patés, tinned food, staples.

EATING OUT To experience the food and wine of France is as good a reason as any to go to France. The French take their food and wine seriously, sometimes a little pompously, but the national attitude means that you can eat better for less than anywhere else in Europe. Finding a good restaurant is an art which relies as much on your intuition as anything else. In places the quality of the food declines in the summer with the annual arrival of thousands of tourists, both foreign and French, but overall you are unlikely to be disappointed.

The south is famous for its fish dishes including the fabled *bouillabaisse* but otherwise almost anything that takes your fancy or fits your budget will be good. The French can even make the ubiquitous steak and chips stand apart from the depressing soggy mess that arrives under this name in other countries.

CHARTS AND PILOTS

Admiralty *Mediterranean Pilot* Vol. II (NP47) Covers the French Mediterranean coast and Corsica.

Admiralty *List of Lights and Fog Signals* Vol. E (NP78)

South France Pilot. Robin Brandon. Imray. Covers the Mediterranean coast and Corsica in detail.

Mediterranean France and Corsica – A Sea Guide. Rod Heikell. Imray. Covers the Mediterranean coast, Corsica and southern inland waterways.

Annuaire de Nautisme (Les Editions de Chabassol) Annual directory to French harbours and services.

Votre Livre de Bord — Méditerranée Bloc Marine. An annual directory published in French.

If you are used to the Admiralty charts it is best to stick to these. Admiralty charts are available in France from Lt. Commander M. Healy, 10, rue Jeanne-Bracco, 66310 Beaulieu. Tel (93) 01 15 72. French charts are more up to date but do not have wind roses on them necessitating the use of a Portland plotter, Douglas protractor, or similar. They are widely available from the Librairie Maritime and chandlers and bookshops in the larger ports. The Navicarte Carte-Guide charts that fold up like road maps are also widely available.

USEFUL BOOKS

Collins Companion Guide to the South of France. Archibald Lyall. Collins. Excellent guide.

Michelin green guides to Provençe and the Riviera.

Berlitz Guide to the French Riviera. Good compact guide.

Monaco

Monaco is a miniature quasi-independent principality on the French coast between Nice and Menton. It is ruled by the Grimaldi family whose Prince Rainer married Grace Kelly tragically killed in a car accident. The principality is divided into four parts: the port area of Fontvielle and La Condamine, Monte Carlo, and the old city of Monaco on top of the Rock. Except for Monte Carlo with its famous casino, opera house, and very, very fashionable and expensive boutiques and restaurants, prices in Monaco are roughly equivalent to the rest of France.

A yacht should make for the marina at Fontvielle and not for the old harbour which is entirely open to the east and at times positively dangerous. At least one yacht I know of has wintered at Fontvielle and thoroughly enjoyed it. The marina offers excellent shelter, water, electricity and a cable TV outlet included in a price comparable to French marinas. Ashore there is much to see and do with touring opera, ballet, and dance companies passing through, a resident symphony orchestra, cinemas, a gymnasium and swimming pool, and the ski resorts of France, Italy and Austria a short distance away. And if you feel lucky you can have a flutter in the casino.

Monaco ... often described as a little Manhattan.

Port de Monaco looking E.

Italy

Area 301,191 square kilometre (116,290 square miles)

Population 56,828,500

Capital Rome (2,914,640)

Language Italian. English and French commonly spoken

Religion Roman Catholic

Time Zone G.M.T. + 1; D.S.T. (April-September)

Currency Lira (L)

Electricity 220V 50Hz AC

Banks 0830-1330 Monday-Friday. Eurocheques, credit cards and travellers' cheques widely accepted.

Mail Not always reliable. It is better to use a private address or that of a marina than to rely on *poste restante*.

Medical Generally good. Private medical treatment is expensive but reciprocal agreements with the U.K. exist.

Internal travel Internal flights link major cities. Train and coach travel is fast and relatively inexpensive. Ferries serve the smaller islands and Sardinia and Sicily. Car rental agencies operate throughout the country.

International travel Rome and Milan are the principal centres although there are flights from major European cities to other centres in the summer.

Public holidays
January 1 New Year's Day
April 25 Liberation Day
May 1 Labour Day
August 15 Festival of the Assumption
November 1 All Saints' Day
December 8 Festival of the Immaculate Conception
December 25 Christmas
December 26 St Stephen's Day
Moveable: Easter Monday

GEOGRAPHY

COAST AND ISLANDS Italy consists of a peninsula jutting southeast into the Mediterranean for some 500 miles from the Alps and so closely resembles a leg with a boot on it that it is common to talk of the toe and heel of Italy. On the west side south of Elba lies the Tyrrhenian Sea and on the eastern coast the Adriatic. Between the French border and the Tuscan archipelago lies the Ligurian Sea and along the south between Sicily and the heel and toe of Italy, the Ionian Sea. On the western side the Republic of Italy encompasses Sardinia and Sicily, two of the largest islands in the Mediterranean, as well as numerous small archipelagos lying close to the coast.

The backbone of the Italian peninsula is the Apennine range of mountains which terminates in the Calabrian massif and the mountains of Sicily.

Around Naples and extending southwards there is an extensive volcanic area with several volcanoes still active, amongst them Vesuvius, Stromboli, Vulcano, and Etna in Sicily. A fault line runs through this area along the west coast of Italy to Sicily.

The coast varies dramatically from region to region, much is mountainous close to the coast where depths are considerable a short distance off the coast. In other places, most notably along much of the eastern seaboard, the coast is low-lying with shallows extending some distance seawards. The climate and vegetation vary from the north down to the south. Vegetation in the north is of the Mediterranean type near the coast but tends to be greener and more diverse than the south which in the summer takes on a burnt brown aspect under the hot sun.

CRUISING AREAS In effect all the coastal regions of Italy are cruised extensively by local and foreign yachts, but several areas are more popular than others:

The Italian Riviera between the French border and Tuscany. Here there are numerous marinas providing every facility. This is geographically and architecturally a beautiful coast providing much high class cruising. Crowded in the summer.

The Tuscan archipelago and adjacent coast A delightful mix of anchorages, harbours and marinas. Also crowded in the summer.

The Tyrrhenian seaboard to Sicily The harbours close to Rome are perennially full with local yachts but south of Naples the coast is comparatively little frequented. The off-lying Pontine Islands, the islands in the Bay of Naples and the Aeolian Islands are crowded in the summer.

Sardinia The north is popular but otherwise it is comparatively uncrowded. An exquisite cruising ground.

Sicily The north is popular but the south is not.

From the toe to the boot. Not so much a cruising ground as a stepping stone to Yugoslavia and Greece.

The east coast. Not a popular cruising ground. There are few attractive harbours and anchorages and most yachtsmen choose to cruise in Yugoslavian waters.

SWITZERLAND

Dolomites

0   100   200   300
Kilometres

A l p s

Friuli

FRANCE

Piemont

MILAN

TURIN

45°N

Lombardia

VENICE

TRIESTE

RIJEKA

YUGOSLAVIA

Po

Liguria

FERRARA

BOLOGNA

GENOA

RAPALLO

RAVENNA

LA SPEZIA

Gulf of
Genoa

Adriatic

NICE
MONACO
CANNES

SAN REMO

Arno
FLORENCE
LIVORNO

SAN MARINO

ANCONA

Sea

SPLIT

Ligurian

Sea

Capraia

Tuscany

Appennino

DUBROVNIK

Cap Corse

Elba
Pianosa

PORTO
FERRAIRO

Tiber

Corsica
(FRANCE)

BASTIA

Monte
Cristo

Giglio

PORT ERCOLE

ITALY

PESCARA

Pianoza

Pelagosa

AJACCIO

CIVITAVECCHIA

ROME

Abruzzi

Caprara

Campania

Pugia

Bonifacio Strait

Asinara

I.Maddalena

PORTO
CERVO

OLBIA

Tyrrhenian

Ponza
Ventotene
Ischia

BARI

NAPLES
SALERNO
AMALFI

Bay of Naples

Capri

TARANTO

BRINDISI

OTRANTO

40°N

Sardinia

Sea

Lucania

Gulf of
Taranto

LEUCA
C.Sta Maria
di Leuca

ORISTANO

CAGLIARI

Calabria

CROTONE

Cap Carbonara

Cap
Spartivento

Lipari
or
Aeolian Is

Stromboli

Gulf of
Squillace

Ionian Sea

Ustica

Lipari

MESSINA

REGGIO DI
CALABRIA

Egadi Is

PALERMO

C.Spartivento
Cap dell'Armi

TRAPANI

Strait of
Messina

CATANIA

Sicily

Sicilian

SIRACUSA

BIZERTE

Cap Bon

Pantelleria

Cape Passero

TUNIS

Strait

Gozo

VALLETTA

TUNISIA

G.de
Hammamet

Pelagi Is

Linosa

MALTA

35°N

Lampedusa

10°E

15°E

Acireale harbour, Sicily

The north coast between Venice and Trieste. Many marinas catering for the Italians and also for the many German and Austrian yachts kept permanently here.

CLIMATE AND WEATHER

Summers are of the Mediterranean type but the winters vary according to the area. The head of the Adriatic around Venice and Trieste can be very wet and cold in the winter (average temperature in February is 7°C (44°F)). The south of Italy and Sicily have mild winters (January average 13°C (59°F) and very hot summers (August average 29°C (84°F)). As a general rule it is a good idea to be south of Rome in the spring and autumn and further north in the summer as temperatures in the south, particularly in Sicily, can be uncomfortably hot in July and August.

WINDS In the summer winds are predominantly from the northwest and west although in some areas (the west coast of Italy) land and sea breezes are well developed. As in many parts of the Mediterranean the complex topography of the area significantly alters winds close to the coast and the wind in one area may be quite different from the wind 20 miles down the coast or out to sea.

LOCAL NAMES OF WINDS
Maestrale A corruption of *magistralis* (the masterful one), describing the predominant northwest winds. It gets its name from the fact that gales frequently blow from the northwest but it has been generalised to most winds from that direction.
Libeccio The south westerly and westerly wind that blows over Corsica and in the central and northern Tyrrhenian.
Tramontana A north or northeast wind which mostly blows in the winter along the west coast of Italy. It blows with some strength and off high ground there are violent gusts. Often associated with a depression in the Adriatic and an anticyclone further west.
Gregale A strong northeast wind blowing in the central Mediterranean. It normally blows for three days but can last longer.

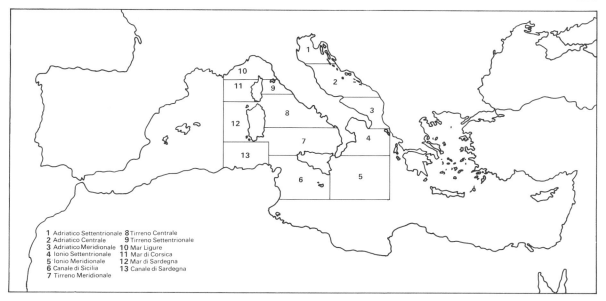

1 Adriatico Settentrionale 8 Tirreno Centrale
2 Adriatico Centrale 9 Tirreno Settentrionale
3 Adriatico Meridionale 10 Mar Ligure
4 Ionio Settentrionale 11 Mar di Corsica
5 Ionio Meridionale 12 Mar di Sardegna
6 Canale di Sicilia 13 Canale di Sardegna
7 Tirreno Meridionale

Italian weather forecast areas.

Cala dei Genovesi SpA.

Lavagna Marina

Sirocco A southerly wind blowing off North Africa. It can reach gale force and although more frequent in the winter, it does blow in the summer. It originates as a warm dry wind but picks up moisture over the sea thus bringing high humidity and often deposits of fine sand from the North African deserts (the red rain).

Bora Chiefly blows in the northern Adriatic. In the winter is a violent wind similar to the *mistral*.

GALES Depressions originate in the Mediterranean or can enter from the Atlantic through the Strait of Gibraltar or through the Toulouse gap across the border between Spain and France, into the Gulf of Lions and south eastwards across Sardinia or Sicily. The latter frequently stop and deepen in the Gulf of Genoa before moving on and although not big by Atlantic standards, they can nonetheless give rise to violent winds, especially in the winter.

Sardinian fishing boats.

THUNDERSTORMS These are most frequent in the summer and autumn and may be associated with a cold front or result from the particular properties of a thermal air mass (a heat thunderstorm) and occur on successive evenings in some areas depending on thermal conditions. Thunderstorms are more common near the coast than out to sea and although they may be accompanied by a squall, the wind does not usually last for long.

TIDES For all intents and purposes tidal differences can be ignored. At spring the maximum difference is 0.3 metre, a difference which can easily be cancelled out by strong winds. The *marrobio*, a form of fluctuation in water level or *seiche*, occasionally affects southern Sicily, especially Mazara del Vallo and Marsala.

WEATHER FORECASTS Despite the complex topography with high mountains close to the coast, Italian weather forecasts are probably the best in the Mediterranean. In my experience they have been correct for 60% to 70% of the occasions I have noted them. Weather forecasts *(bolletini del mare)* are transmitted on RaI 2° (Radiotelevisione Italiana/Radio Due) at the following local times*: 0715, 1515 (1640 on Sundays), 2315.

It is transmitted on the following frequencies:
846 kHz *Rome*
1035 kHz *Genoa, Firenza, Milan, Naples, Oristano, Pescara, Venice.*
1116 kHz *Bari, Palermo, Pisa, Trieste*
1143 kHz *Messina*
1188 kHz *San Remo*
1314 kHz *Ancona, Catanzaro*
1413 kHz *Pescaro, Taranto*
1449 kHz *Agrigento, Cagliari, Catania, La Spezia, Salerno, Sassari.*
1485 kHz *Cosenza, Lecce, Nuoro, Savona.*

The weather forecast on 1035 kHz is the best bet, it can usually be picked up anywhere.

The weather forecasts are broadcast in Italian only, but at dictation speed and after listening to a few their gist can be picked up. The forecasts follow a standard pattern:

Gale warnings *(avviso)*, general situation *(situazione)*, and then a forecast for each sea area or group of sea areas. The forecast for each area is given as follows: wind direction and strength, sea state, sky, visibility, weather (sunny, rainy, etc.).

The forecast concludes with the further outlook and notices to mariners.

*Local time = G.M.T. + 1, G.M.T. + 2 in the summer.

Sta Maria di Leuca on the heel of Italy.

HARBOURS AND ANCHORAGES

WHAT TO EXPECT The sort of harbours encountered in Italy vary from fashionable and expensive marinas catering for the yachtsman's every need to small fishing harbours where your yacht will be in stark contrast to the local fishing boats. As a general rule the number of marinas decrease the further south you go. Along the Italian Riviera as far as La Spezia there is literally a chain of yacht marinas except where a large commercial harbour interrupts the line, the same holds true between Venice and Trieste at the far north of the Adriatic. South of Rome, where yacht marinas are less evident, small fishing harbours become the rule and facilities for yachts become few and far between. In Sardinia there is a cluster of yacht marinas on the north and east coast around fashionable Porto Cervo, but otherwise there are commercial and fishing harbours and many wonderful sheltered bays and coves. Around the Sicilian coast there are commercial and fishing harbours with some attractive anchorages in the off-lying Aeolian and Egadi Islands. Along the south coast of the mainland from toe to boot there are few harbours or anchorages and up the east coast as far as Venice there are fishing harbours and commercial ports.

SECURITY The amount of theft varies from place to place. On the whole yachtsmen experience fewer problems than land-based tourists but precautions are in order, especially in the larger towns and cities where theft from yachts is a real problem. Most marinas have night watchmen and here security is good. In many of the commercial and fishing harbours you will encounter that Italian institution: the *ormeggiatori*. Literally translated this means the person who ties up your yacht for you and if necessary fuels, waters and cleans it. Many of the harbours in Italy have a section of the quay or a basin run by a co-operative of *ormeggiatori* who will charge you for a berth. The co-operative leases the quay or basin and so carries out a legal business; however many self-styled *ormeggiatori* do not have the lease of a section of quay and in the words of a friend of mine are simply little *mafiosi*. The problem confronting the yachtsman is whether to pay up or not to self-styled

Weaving fish traps at Carloforte, Sardinia.

ormeggiatori who usually control the water supply so if you refuse to pay the berthing fee (usually reasonable) you may end up simply paying more for water and to this extent the situation must be played by ear.

WINTERING AFLOAT   Italy is a popular country for wintering afloat offering a good climate, good facilities and good travel connections for trips back home.

For those intending to winter in Italy and live aboard there are a number of popular harbours. They are: San Remo, Santa Margherita Ligure, Cala Galera, Portoferraio on Elba, Fiumocino near Rome, Porto d'Ischia, Porto Cervo in Sardinia and Sibaris Marina. Occasionally yachts winter in Venice or one of the marinas along the north coast. My choice would be Portoferraio or Porto d'Ischia.

PASSAGE PLANNING

IN GENERAL   The variable winds in the summer make for few logical routes, these being determined by your choice of cruising area and the time you have available.

In late July and August the Italians are on holiday en-masse, and these holiday-makers include large numbers of Italian yachtsmen so that most of the marinas and fishing harbours are often crammed to over and above what would seem to be a reasonable capacity. To add to the problem there is the annual influx of French yachts, also on holiday at this time, seeking accommodation along the Italian Riviera, in the Tyrrhenian Sea and around northern Sicily and northern Sardinia.

At such a time when harbours are filled to alarming proportions, it makes sense to avoid the more popular areas, but often this will not be possible in which case it is wise to get into a harbour as early as possible. It is rare to be turned away from a harbour, the Italian yachtsman being an expert at fitting the ubiquitous *motoscafi* with a 5 metre beam into what appears to be a one metre gap. You too will become something of an expert at this coarse art.

SPECIFIC ROUTES   From France there are two principal routes through Italy; the first follows the mainland coast around the Italian Riviera and on down the west coast with perhaps visits to the offlying islands (the Tuscan archipelago, the Pontine Islands, the islands in the Bay of Naples, and the Aeolian Islands) and then through the Strait of Messina. Alternatively many yachts cross to Corsica, follow its west coast to the Bonifacio Strait and then run down the east coast of Sardinia before crossing to the north of Sicily. Yachts on passage to Malta will often make for the south coast of Sicily and then cross to Malta. Yachts crossing from the Balearics often make for the south of Sardinia and then proceed to Sicily or Tunisia.

Yachts going eastwards from Sicily or the toe of Italy can follow the southern coast crossing the Gulf of Taranto from Crotone to Gallipoli or Sta Maria di Leuca but this is a long lee shore should the wind blow from the southeast, with few safe ports of refuge. In addition the Gulf of Squillace is noted for its bad weather even in the summer. Yachts crossing to Greece may be better off avoiding the south coast altogether and crossing directly to Preveza, Argostoli or Pylos. Going northwards up the Adriatic most often cross to Yugoslavia which is attractive and offers more anchorages than the east coast of Italy; likewise southwards down the Adriatic it is preferable to cross to Yugoslavia and cruise down the offshore islands.

CHARTERING   There are a number of Italian based companies offering yachts or bareboats but many people hire a yacht in the south of France and visit Italy from there. A number of companies also operate from between Venice and Trieste catering mostly for yachtsmen wishing to visit the Yugoslavian islands. Several flotilla companies offer cruises around the north coast of Sardinia and the La Maddalena archipelago, the latter cruising ground is recommended.

NAVIGATION AIDS

Buoyage I.A.L.A. System 'A' was introduced between 1981 and 1983. In general the buoyage is consistent and good although small fishing harbours may not conform.

Lights The Italian coast is well lit and the lights well maintained and rarely out of action. In general night passages pose no problems as far as lights are concerned.

Radiobeacons There are numerous marine and aero radiobeacons which provide an excellent network useful to yachtsmen. However remember that the characteristics and frequencies of air radiobeacons may be changed without notice to mariners.

Marine Radiobeacons

Livorno LI 300 kHz 100M cont in fog. H + 28, 34, 58, 04 in clear weather. 43°32′.58N 10°17′.72E

Ligurian Sea group 301.1 kHz
Civitavecchia CH 70M. Seq. 1, 2.[1]
Genova GV 70M. Seq. 3, 4.[2]
Capo Ferro CF 90M. Seq. 5, 6.[3]
All continuous in fog and at [1]H + 06, 12, 36, 42. [2]H + 08, 14, 38, 44. [3]H + 10, 16, 40, 46 ev. 4 hours commencing at 0300 in clear weather.

South Tyrrhenian Sea group 296.5 kHz
Pta Carena/Capis NP 100M. Seq. 1, 2.[1]
C. S. Vito LC 100M. Seq. 3, 4.[3]
Capo Vaticano VN 100M. Seq. 5, 6.[2]
[1]Continuous in fog and at H + 12, 18, 42, 48 ev. 4 hours commencing 0300 in clear weather.
[2]Continuous in fog and at H + 16, 22, 46, 52
[3]Continuous in fog and at H + 14, 20, 44, 50 ev. 4 hours commencing at 0300 in clear weather.

Sicily group 287.3 kHz
Pantelleria PT 90M. Seq. 1, 2.[1]
Cozzo Spadaro PZ 100M. Seq. 3, 4.[2]
Augusta AT 100M. Seq. 5, 6.[3]
All continuous in fog and [1]H + 00, 06, 30, 36. [2]H + 02, 08, 32, 38. [3]H + 04, 10, 34, 40 in clear weather.

Capo San Vito/Taranto TN 291.9 KHz 70M. Seq. 1, 2.
Continuous in fog and at H + 24, 30, 54, 00 ev. 4 hours from 0300 in clear weather.

South Italy group 305.7 kHz
C. Sta Maria di Leuca MC 100M. Seq. 1, 2.[1]
Vieste VS 70M. Seq. 3, 4.[2]
Molunat YC 100M. Seq. 5, 6.[3]
All continuous in fog and at [1]H + 06, 12, 36, 42. [2]H + 08, 14, 38, 44. [3]H + 10, 16, 40, 46 in clear weather.

Adriatic group 289.6 kHz
Punta della Penna TL 80M. Seq. 1, 2.[1]
S. Benedetto del Tronto CI 80M. Seq. 3, 4.[2]
Movar (Yugoslavia) YV 100M. Seq. 5, 6.[3]
All continuous in fog and at [1]H + 12, 18, 42, 48. [2] + 14, 20, 44, 50. [3]H + 16, 22, 46, 52 in clear weather.

North Adriatic group 298.8 kHz
Senigallia SA 80M. Seq. 1, 2.[1]
Kamenjak (Yugoslavia) YP 100M. Seq. 3, 4.[2]
Pta da Maestra ME 80M. Seq. 5, 6.[3]
All continuous in fog and at [2]H + 18, 24, 48, 54 [2]H + 20, 26, 50, 56 [3]H + 22, 28, 52, 58 in clear weather.

Vittoria/Trieste RD 311.5 kHz 70M. Continuous in fog and H + 00, 06, 30, 36 in clear weather. 45°40′.50N 13°45′.43E.

Air radiobeacons. Some of these are liable to be temporarily inoperative and should be used with caution.

Albenga ABN 268 kHz 50M 44°03′.3N 8°13′.3E
Genoa GEN 318 kHz 50M 44°25′.38N 9°04′.9E
Genoa CMO 389 kHz 70M 44°20′.7N 9°10′.3E
Pisa PIS 379 kHz 25M 43°35′.3N 10°17′.8E
Elba ELB 360 kHz 100M 42°43′.9N 10°23′.7E
Grosseto GRO 406 kHz 50M 42°45′.3N 11°04′.6E
Tarquinia TAQ 312 kHz 50M 42°12′.8N 11°44′.1E
Teano TEA 316 kHz 50M 41°17′.7N 13°58′.2E
Ostia OST 321 kHz 50M 41°48′.2N 12°14′.2E
Ponza PNZ 367.5 kHz 50M 40°54′.6N 12°57′.4E
Sorrento SOR 426 kHz 100M 40°35′N 14°20.1E
Carbonara CAR 402 kHz 100M 39°06′.2N 9°30′.9E
Olbia SME 357 kHz 50M 40°54′N 9°30′.8E
Alghero ALG 382 kHz 50M 40°35′.1N 8°15′.8E
Cagliari CAG 371 kHz 25M 39°12′.8N 9°05′.8E
Palermo PAL 355.5 kHz 150M 38°02′N 13°10′.6N
Punta Raisi PRS 329 kHz 25M 38°11′.33N 13°06′.5E
Trapani TRP 317.5 kHz 50M 37°54′.8N 12°29′.9E
Catania CAT 345 kHz 80M 37°27′.4N 14°58′E

Pantelleria PAN 335 kHz 100M 36°48′.63N 11°57′.6E

Lampedusa LPD 373 kHz 50M 35°29′.9N 12°36′.7E
Reggio Calabria RCA 325 kHz 50M 38°01′N 15°38′.1E
Caraffa/Catanzaro CDC 376 kHz 150M 38°45′.2N 16°22′.2E
Crotone CRO 337 kHz 25M 38°59′.9N 17°04′.5E
Rocca Imperiale RMP 383.5 kHz 40°06′N 16°37′E
Grottaglie GRT 331 kHz 25M 40°26′.7N 17°25′.3E
Brindisi/Casale BRD 363.5 kHz 78M 40°36′.3N 18°00′.5E
Bari BPL 401 kHz 41°06′.5N 16°39′.6E
Amendola AME 381 kHz 50M 41°29′.9N 15°50′.3E
Vieste VIE 405 kHz 100M 41°54′.7N 16°03′.7E
Ancona ANC 374.5 kHz 100M 43°35′.1N 13°28′.3E
Cervia CEV 387 kHz 25M 44°16′.02N 12°10′.8E
Rimini/Miramare RIM 335 kHz 75M 44°04′.6N 12°30′.3E
Chioggia CHI 408 kHz 50M 45°04′.3N 12°16′.9E
Venezia/Tesséra VEN 379 kHz 25M 46°26′.8N 12°16′.7E
Ronchi dei Legionari RON 396 kHz 25M 45°49′.7N 13°21′.5E

Coast Radio Stations

All the commercial ports and some of the marinas keep a continuous listening watch on 2182 kHz and VHF Channel 16. Many of the larger harbours and marinas also listen out on VHF Channel 12, 25, 26, 27.

Main operating frequencies are shown in bold type.

All times are G.M.T.

All stations offer a 24 hour service unless otherwise stated.

Station	Transmits (kHz or VHF Channel)	Listens (kHz or VHF Channel)	Traffic Lists (Freq. & times)
Cagliari (Sardinia) (IDC)	**1722**, 2182, 2683 VHF Ch. 16, 25, **26**, **27**	2182, 2023	1722 at 0535, 1035, 1435, 1835, 2235. Ch. 26, 27 ev. H + 15
Porto Cervo (Sardinia) (Remotely controlled from Porto Torres)	VHF Ch. 16, 25, **26**, 27, 28, 88		Ch. 26 ev. H + 15
Porto Torres (IZN) (Sardinia)	**1806**, 2182 VHF Ch. 16, 25, **26**, **27**, 84, 87	2023, 2182	1806 at 0510, 0810, 1210, 1610, 2010. Ch. 26 ev. H + 15
Genova (ICB)	1667, 2182, 2642 **2722** VHF Ch. 7, 16, **25**, **26**, **27**, 28, 83	2023, 2182	2722 at 0405, 0905, 1305, 1705, 2105. Ch. 25 ev H + 15
Livorno	1925, 2182, **2591** VHF Ch. 16, 25, **26**, 27, 61, 84	2023, 2182	2591 at 0415, 0915, 1315, 1715, 2115. Ch. 26 ev. H + 15
Civitavecchia	**1888**, 2182, 2710, 3747 VHF Ch. 16, 25, 26, **27**	2023, 2182	1888 at 0545, 1045, 1445, 1845 2245. Ch. 27 ev. H + 15
Roma (IAR)	VHF Ch. 16, **25**, 26, 27		Ch. 25 ev. H + 15
Napoli (IQH)	1675, 2182, **2635**	2023, 2182	2635 at 0425, 0925, 1325, 1725, 2125
Monte Tuoro	VHF Ch. 16, 25, 26, **27**		Ch. 27 ev. H + 15
Maratea	VHF Ch. 16, **25**, 26, 27		Ch. 25 ev. H + 15
Messina (Sicily)	2182, **2789** VHF Ch. 16, **25**, 26, 27	2023, 2182	2789 at 0605, 1105, 1505, 1905 2305. Ch. 25 ev. H + 15
Palermo (Sicily)	1705, 2182 VHF Ch. 16, 25, 26, **27**	2023, 2182	1705 at 0435, 0935, 1335, 1735, 2135. Ch. 27 ev. H + 15
Trapani (Sicily)	1737, 1848, 2182 VHF Ch. 16, 25, 26, 27, 84, 85, 88	2023, 2182	1848 at 0150, 0810, 1210, 1610, 2010. Ch. 25 ev. H + 15
Mazara del Vallo (Sicily)	1883, 2182, **2211**, **2600** VHF Ch. 16, 25, 26, 27	2023, 2182	2211, 2600 at 0521, 1521, 1821, 2321. Ch. 25 H + 15
Augusta (Sicily)	1643, 2182, **2628** VHF Ch. 16, 25, **26**, 27	2023, 2182	2628 at 0505, 1005, 1405, 1805, 2205. Ch. 26 ev. H + 15
Lampedusa (Pelagie Is)	1876, 2182 VHF Ch. 16, 25, **26**, 27, 84, 85	2023, 2132, 2182	1876 at 0513, 0818, 1343, 1713, 2018. 24 hour watch only on 2182. Ch. 26 ev. H+15 (0515-2115)
Crotone	1715, 2182, **2663** VHF Ch. 16, **25**, 26, 27	2023, 2182	2663 at 0525, 1025, 1425, 1825 2225. Ch. 25 ev. H + 15
Bari (IPB)	1771, 2182, **2579**	2023, 2182	2579 at 0445, 0945, 1345, 1745, 2145
Selva di Fasano	VHF Ch. 16, 25, 26, **27**		Ch. 27 ev. H + 15
Monte Parano	VHF Ch. 16, 25, **26**, 27		Ch. 26 ev. H + 15
Pescara	VHF Ch. 16, 25, **26**, 27		Ch. 26 ev. H + 15 0700-2100 hrs
San Benedetto del Tronto	**1855**, 2182	2023, 2182	1855 at 0518, 0918, 1518, 1818,

Ancona (IPA)	2182, **2656**	2023, 2182	2656 at 0505, 1005, 1405, 1805, 2205
	VHF Ch. 16, **25**, 26, 27		Ch. 25 ev. H + 15
Ravenna	VHF Ch. 16, 25, 26, **27**		Ch. 27 ev. H + 15
Venezia	1680, **2698**, 2182	2023, 2182	2698 at 0515, 1015, 1415, 1815, 2215
	VHF Ch. 16, **25**, 26, 27		Ch. 26 ev. H + 15
Trieste (IQX)	2182, **2624**	2023, 2182	2624 at 0535, 1035, 1435, 1835, 2235
	VHF Ch. 16, **25**, 26, 27		Ch. 25 ev. H + 15

Weather Forecasts are also transmitted from coast radio stations as follows:

Times are G.M.T.
Storm warnings in Italian and English.

Cagliari (Sardinia) (IDC) 1722 kHz and VHF Ch. 26 (P. Campu Spina), 27 (Mte Serpeddi) at 0135, 0735, 1335, 1935. Storm warnings on receipt and at 0303, 0803, 1203, 1603, 2003 and on VHF at the next two H + 15.

Porto Cervo VHF Ch. 26 at 0150, 0750, 1350, 1950. Storm warnings on receipt and at the next two H + 15.

Porto Torres 1806 kHz and VHF Ch. 26 at 0150, 0750, 1350, 1950. Storm warnings on receipt and at 0433, 0833, 1433, 1833, 2333 and on VHF at next two H + 15.

Genova (ICB) 2642, 2722 kHz and VHF Ch. 27 (Mte Bignone and Zoagli), Ch. 25 (Genova) at 0135, 0735, 1335, 1935. Storm warnings on receipt and at next two H + 15.

Livorno 2591 kHz and VHF Ch. 26 at 0135, 0735, 1335, 1935. Storm warnings on receipt and at 0433, 0933, 1533, 1833, 2333 and VHF at next two H + 15.

Civitavecchia (Mte Argentario) 1888 kHz and VHF Ch. 27 at 0135, 0735, 1335, 1935. Storm warnings on receipt and at 0433, 0833, 1233, 1633, 2033 and VHF at next two H + 15.

Roma (Mte Cavo) (IAR) VHF Ch. 25 at 0135, 0735, 1335, 1935. Storm warnings on receipt and at next two H + 15.

Napoli (IQH) 2635 kHz and VHF Ch. 27 (Mte Tuoro), Ch. 25 (Maratea) at 0135, 0735, 1335, 1935. Storm warnings on receipt and at 0403, 0903, 1303, 1703, 2103 and VHF at next two H + 15.

Messina (Sicily) 2789 kHz and VHF Ch. 25 at 0135, 0735, 1335, 1935. Storm warnings on receipt and at 0233, 0633, 1133, 1533, 1933 and VHF at next two H + 15

Palermo (Sicily) 1705 kHz and VHF Ch. 27 at 0135, 0735, 1335, 1935. Storm warnings on receipt and at 0333, 0833, 1233, 1633, 2033 and VHF at next two H + 15

Trapani (Sicily) 1848 kHz and VHF Ch. 25 at 0150, 0750, 1350, 1950. Storm warnings on receipt and at 0503, 0903, 1203, 1503, 2003 and VHF at next two H + 15.

Mazara del Vallo (Sicily) 2211 kHz and VHF Ch. 25 (Gela) at 0150, 0750, 1350, 1950. Storm warnings on receipt and at 0533, 0933, 1533, 1833, 2333 and VHF at next two H + 15

Augusta (Sicily) 2628 kHz and VHF channel 26 at 0150, 0750, 1350, 1950. Storm warnings on receipt and at 0303, 0803, 1203, 1603, 2003 and VHF at next two H + 15.

Lampedusa 1876 kHz and VHF Ch. 26 at 0150, 0750, 1350, 1950. Storm warnings on receipt and at 0503, 0803, 1203, 1603, 2003.

Crotone 2663 kHz and VHF Ch. 25 at 0150, 0750, 1350, 1950. Storm warnings on receipt and at 0503, 0803, 1203, 1603, 2003 and VHF at next two H + 15

Bari (IPB) 2579 kHz and VHF Ch. 27 (Selva di Fasano) Ch. 26 (Mte Parano) at 0135, 0735, 1335, 1935. Storm warnings on receipt and at 0333, 0833, 1233, 1633, 2033 and VHF at next two H + 15

Pescara VHF Ch. 26 at 0750, 1350, 1950. Storm warnings on receipt and at next two H + 15.

San Benedetto del Tronto 1855 kHz at 0150, 0750, 1350, 1950. Storm warnings on receipt and at 0433, 0833, 1433, 1833, 2333.

Ancona (IPA) 2656 kHz and VHF Ch. 25 at 0135, 0735, 1335, 1935. Storm warnings on receipt and at 0303, 0803, 1203, 1603, 2003 and VHF at next two H + 15.

Ravenna VHF Ch. 27 at 0150, 0750, 1350, 1950. Storm warnings on receipt and at next two H + 15

Venezia 2698 kHz and VHF channel 26 at 0150, 0750, 1350, 1950. Storm warnings on receipt and at 0403, 0903, 1303, 1703, 2103 and VHF at next two H + 15.

Trieste (IQX) 2624 kHz and VHF Ch. 25 at 0135, 0735, 1335, 1935. Storm warnings on receipt and at 0433, 0933, 1333, 1733, 21333 and VHF at next two H + 15.

Rescue service In all of the larger harbours there are specialised inshore rescue craft. Some of the marinas also maintain an inshore rescue boat. There are numerous tugs equipped for salvage work around the coast which will answer a distress call.

FORMALITIES

ENTRY FORMALITIES Formalities are straight forward and simple in theory if somewhat casually carried out in practice. On entering the first major Italian port a yacht should be issued with a *Constituto in arrivo per il naviglio da diporto*, usually shortened to simply *Constituto*, which details a yacht's particulars and members of crew. The *Constituto* is valid for one year and may be examined at subsequent ports of call. It should be surrendered at the final port of call. This is the theory but often the yacht will have to call at several ports before a harbour master ready and able to issue a *Constituto* can be found. Generally no difficulties result from not having a *Constituto*, indeed in early 1988 I came through Italy without obtaining one, but there have been stories of yachts which have encountered problems with officials because they had not obtained a *Constituto*, so it would be wise to obtain one on entry to Italy.

Valid passports or identity cards are required for all persons arriving on a yacht. Evidence of insurance for craft with engines exceeding three horsepower will be asked for.

DOCUMENTS The Small Ship's Register Papers, or full registration papers (the *Blue Book*) are accepted. A certificate of competency for the captain of a yacht may be asked for but in practice very rarely is. The R.Y.A. *Helmsman's Certificate* is sufficient if asked. Evidence of third party insurance is required and will be asked for in most harbours. Moreover the documents must have an Italian translation, something your insurance company will do for you given adequate notice. If you do not have proof of valid third party insurance you will be prevented from leaving harbour and can be fined. Much misunderstanding has arisen over this requirement so take note.

TAXES In 1976 a circulation tax *(Tassa di stazzionamento)* was introduced for foreign flag yachts in Italy, the tax is not high which may explain the haphazard way in which it is enforced.

The charge is L60 per ton per day for sailing yachts up to 50 registered tons and L75 per ton per day over 50 registered tons. For motor yachts it is double the above rates (i.e. L120 per ton per day for motor yachts up to 50 registered tons and L150 over 50 registered tons). The fee is normally paid at the post office and the receipt obtained then produced for the port police. The levy is reduced by one third for a two month subscription, by half for a four months' subscription, and by two thirds for a one year subscription. Once the tax has been paid a yacht can use any *Porto Communale* free of charge, apart from any charge made by the local *ormeggiatori*.

Normally a yacht can stay in Italy for up to one year before customs duties must be paid, however in practice many stay longer with few difficulties. If a yacht leaves Italy and then returns after a reasonable period then in practice it can stay in Italy for up to one year again.

FACILITIES
EVERYDAY
Water In nearly all harbours and in all marinas water is available on the quay but in some of the off-lying islands there may be shortages in the summer. It is everywhere potable unless otherwise specified.

Ice Is available in most of the larger fishing harbours and in some of the marinas.

Fuel Widely available. Most marinas and many of the larger harbours have a fuel quay. Elsewhere there is often a fuel station a short distance away.

Gas Calor type gas and *Camping gaz*.

Paraffin Not readily available. Try in the large towns or fishing harbours where the fishermen use it for their lamps.

BOAT REPAIRS
Engine Spares for the major marine engines are readily available and the larger manufacturers such as Volvo Penta and Perkins have an extensive repair and spares network throughout the country. As a general rule the main distributor and the majority of the distribution outlets are in the north, often in Milan, as are the major Italian manufacturers of marine equipment. There are numerous competent and well-equipped workshops throughout Italy capable of dealing with all types of engine repairs.

Electrics and electronics Good marine electric and electronic repair shops in the larger centres. Spares and repairs to most electronic gear can be carried out although satnavs and the like are best returned to the manufacturers.

Navigation instruments Most spares can be obtained, repairs carried out. Local and imported gear can be obtained, the locally manufactured gear has a good reputation.

Paint and antifoulings Most foreign manufactured paints and antifoulings can be obtained although they are more expensive than locally manufactured counterparts which are of excellent quality, indeed often superior to imported paints. *Veneziani*, two-component paints, (epoxies and polyurethane) and antifouling have a good reputation.

Hauling In the large marinas there is often a yard within the marina complex solely for hauling yachts, usually by travel hoist or at least a yard close to the marina specialising in hauling yachts. Away from the yacht marinas there are boatyards which can haul yachts on a slip or by a crane to haul a small to medium sized yacht onto the quay in even quite small fishing harbours. The following list of yards are those frequented by foreign cruising yachtsmen, they are not necessarily the best nor the cheapest, simply the most popular.

San Remo: 40 ton travel hoist and slipway for larger craft up to 400 tons.

Santa Margherita Ligure: Small and medium sized yachts craned onto the hard and slipway for larger craft up to 120 tons.

Lavagna: 50 ton travel hoist and slipway for larger craft up to 300 tons.

Punta Ala: 50 ton travel hoist.

Porto Santo Stefano: Cantiere dell'Argentario can haul craft up to 400 tons. Open and covered storage and extensive workshops carrying out repairs to a high standard.

Cala Galera: 40 ton travel hoist.

Porto Ferraio: Small and medium sized yachts hauled and stored on the hard in two boatyards around the bay.

Fiumocino: Small and medium sized yachts craned onto the hard.

Porto d'Ischia: Small and medium sized yachts hauled.

Pozzuoli: 50 ton travel hoist. Covered storage.

Salerno: Craft up to 500 tons hauled on a slipway. Open and covered storage.

Porto Cervo: Travel hoist. Craft up to 350 tons hauled on a slipway. Open and covered storage.

Brindisi: Yachts craned onto the hard at the yacht club.

Sibaris Marina: Travel hoist up to 40 tons and hard standing.

Cesenatico: Travel hoist up to 50 tons and hard standing.

Engineering Well equipped workshops which can carry out all types of engineering to a high standard can be found all over Italy. Charges are reasonable.

Wood and GRP Skills in both wood and GRP are among the highest in the Mediterranean. Quality boat joinery to a very high standard is carried out in some yards — such quality work is not of course cheap. A number of yards handle osmosis problems in a professional manner.

DUTY FREE SPARES Spares and new items can be imported without paying duty and in practice this is straightforward.

PROVISIONING

GENERAL In all but the smallest hamlet adequate provisions can be found. In the cities and large towns there will often be a Standa or Upim or other large supermarket offering a wide range of goods (groceries, fruit and vegetables, frozen meat and fish, toiletries and kitchen utensils) with clearly marked prices. In the smaller towns and villages there are well-stocked grocery and fruit and vegetable shops. Local brand products are generally of a high quality and not expensive, indeed many processed foodstuffs are less expensive than equivalent U.K. brands. Meat is of good quality, and fresh fish and shellfish are excellent value, especially in the fishing harbours where there will often be an open-air market or a fish shop close to the quay selling fish from the day's catch. You should not hesitate to try some species of fish you rarely see in home waters.

Shopping hours are generally 0900-1230 and 1500-1930 Monday-Saturday. Shops close on a morning or afternoon once a week, usually a Monday morning or a Wednesday afternoon.

SPECIFIC

Meat Plentiful and of good quality. It is usually butchered in recognisable cuts. Hams (*prosciutto*), sausages and salamis are superb and reasonably priced.

Fish Is plentiful and comparatively cheap.

Fruit and vegetables Plentiful and not subject to seasonable variations. In the larger centres there is usually an open air market with a large selection of fresh fruit and vegetables.

Staples Easily obtained everywhere. Pasta is obviously a mainstay, if you can, try to get fresh pasta from one of the shops specialising in it.

Cheese Local cheeses may not always be to your taste but there are generally one or two which will appeal. Local and imported cheeses are reasonably priced. Parmesan should be bought in a block and grated only when you need it.

Canned goods Good selection of everything although there is not a wide variety of canned meat.

Coffee and tea Italian coffee blends are among the world's best and reasonably priced; instant coffee is more expensive. Tea is good and cheap.

Wines, beers and spirits Italian wine varies from very cheap and good to higher priced superb wines. Local beer is excellent. Spirits are reasonably priced.

Recommended Hams, sausages, salamis, cheese, pasta (of course), coffee (filter), wines and spirits. Italy is a good place to stock up in before heading east.

EATING OUT Italy offers the gastronome good food on a par with French cuisine. Historically the cross-roads of medieval food fads and foibles, it has taken all of the best that found its way to Europe and refined it to produce a rich cuisine with regional variations. Only later did the French refine European cuisine and elevate it to the gastronomic art it is today.

The prices shown on a menu do not include the *coperto* (cover charge) or the service charge, both of which will be added at the end of the bill. Many restaurants offer a *menu turistico*: usually three courses from a limited choice at a fixed price; these are normally good value. In recent years the cost of eating out in Italy has risen dramatically and it is now one of the most expensive countries in the Mediterranean to dine out in. Nonetheless the cuisine warrants the occasional splurge on a good meal even if you are on a shoestring budget.

Pizzas are popular and excellent throughout Italy and in quite out of the way places there will often be a *pizzeria*. Other cheaper eating places are the *rosticceria* and *tavola calda*. A little higher up the scale is the *trattoria* followed by restaurants and luxury restaurants. However these categories may be confused somewhat by, for example, a restaurant that calls itself a *trattoria* to impart a homely atmosphere.

The standard *antipasto* will include cold meats, sausages, salami, fish and shellfish, fish salads, pies and pasties and many mouth-watering salads.

Soups include minestrone, broths and consommés and excellent fish soups with many regional variations which are a meal in themselves.

Pasta has many variations with my favourites being *spaghetti alle vongole* (with shellfish) and *spaghetti carbonara* (with cheese and egg). If a homemade pasta is available it must be tried.

Main courses. Veal *(vitello)* is the principal me. and is excellent throughout Italy. Veal and chicken, less commonly lamb, beef and pork may be grilled or cooked in casseroles. Fish also may be grilled or cooked in a casserole, some of which are novel and delicious combinations of fish with other ingredients (in Lipari a swordfish steak stuffed with cheese, tomato and green pepper and cooked in a tomato and fennel sauce for instance). The vegetables for a main course are ordered separately.

Desserts are excellent everywhere.

Wines. Always good, sometimes excellent, often cheap.

CHARTS AND PILOTS

Admiralty *Mediterranean Pilot* Vol I (NP45). Covers Sardinia, Sicily.

Admiralty *Mediterranean Pilot* Vol. II (NP46). Covers the west coast.

Admiralty *Mediterranean Pilot* Vol. III (NP47). Covers the east coast.

Admiralty *List of Lights and Fog Signals* Vol. E (NP78).

Italian Waters Pilot. Rod Heikell. Imray. Covers the west and south coasts of Italy, offshore islands and Sardinia and Sicily.

Adriatic Pilot. T & D Thompson. Imray. Covers the east coast of Italy, as well as Yugoslavia.

The Tyrrhenian Sea. H. M. Denham. John Murray. Covers the area bordered by the Tyrrhenian Sea.

Porticcioli d'Italia. Bruno Ziravello. The best of the Italian pilots. In Italian only.

156 Porti d'Italia. Instituto Geografico de Agostini. Good colour photographs but covers a limited number of ports. In Italian only.

Admiralty charts cover the area well. Italian charts are available and also the excellent Nauticard International (plastic coated) charts in most of the larger centres.

USEFUL BOOKS

Blue Guides to *Northern Italy*. *Rome and Environs*. *Southern Italy*. *Sicily*. Black. The guide-books *par excellence*.

Collins *Companion Guides to Tuscany*. Archibald Lyall. *Southern Italy*. Peter Gunn. Collins. Good readable guides.

A Concise History of Italy. Vincent Cronin. Cassell.

Sardinia. Virginia Waite. Batsford.

Sea and Sardinia. D. H. Lawrence. Penguin.

Italian Food. Elizabeth David. Penguin.

Sardinia:
Local St Francis feeding the strays.

Malta

Area 316 square kilometres (122 square miles)

Population 350,000

Capital Valletta (14,500)

Language English and Maltese. Italian also fairly common.

Religion Roman Catholic

Time zone G.M.T.+ 1; D.S.T. (April-September)

Currency Maltese pound (£M) = 100 cents

Electricity 240V 50Hz AC

Banks Open 0800-1200 Monday-Saturday. Eurocheques, credit cards, and travellers' cheques accepted.

Mail Reliable. Use *Poste restante*, Yacht Marina, Gzira, Malta; or Manoel Island Yacht Yard, Gzira, Malta.

Medical Good. Medical fees are low to moderate. Reciprocal agreement with the U.K.

Internal travel Buses are very cheap (and delightfully antiquated) and run everywhere regularly. Hire cars are cheap. Taxis are expensive. Ferries to Gozo.

International travel Regular international flights to many destinations.

Public holidays
January 1 New Year's Day
March 31 National Day
May 1 May Day
August 15 Festival of the Assumption
December 13 Republic Day
December 25 Christmas Day
Moveable: Good Friday

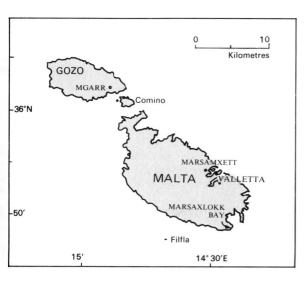

GEOGRAPHY

ISLANDS The Republic of Malta consists of two islands, Malta and Gozo, and two smaller islands, Comino and Filfla. They lie approximately 60 miles south of Sicily and 220 miles north of the deserts of Libya, in the middle of the narrow channel joining the western and eastern areas of the Mediterranean. Their strategic position between Africa and Europe has meant that these small arid islands have been coveted by many different nations as a stepping stone between the two continents and the two halves of the Mediterranean sea. The navies and armies of the world have trampled back and forth across Malta but two great sieges stand apart from the rest: the Great Siege of Suliman the Magnificent against the Knights of St John in 1565; and the siege of Malta by the Italian and German air forces in 1941 and 1942.

CRUISING AREAS The regulations which restricted cruising around Malta until 1986 have now been totally lifted and it is possible to freely cruise around the islands. Around Malta and Gozo there are a number of attractive harbours and anchorages: Marsaxlokk, St Pauls Bay, Selmun Bay, Blue Lagoon on Comino, and Mgarr on Gozo; but the real attraction of Malta is as a base or somewhere to winter over for cruising yachts rather than a cruising area.

CLIMATE AND WEATHER

Malta's climate is more akin to North Africa than to the typically Mediterranean type. Summers can be excessively hot and may be oppressive when a *sirocco* blows bringing a stifling humidity. Winters are warm with little rain, although when it does rain it buckets down. The very mild winters make Malta a popular place to winter afloat.

In both winter and summer the prevailing wind is from the northwest although there are also winds from north and northeast. In the winter winds from the northeast *(gregale)* are the worst as Marsamxett is open to this direction and a considerable surge is set up in the harbour. In the spring and autumn the *sirocco* blows frequently but its effects are more unpleasant in the autumn when the sea has warmed up and the wind is not cooled on its passage from North Africa. With the *sirocco,* visibility is much reduced because of the dust in the air.

Weather forecasts are posted daily at the yachting centre and Manoel Island Yacht Yard. Valletta Radio transmits a weather forecast on VHF channel 12 at 0803, 1203, 1803 and 2303 local time in the summer, and 0703, 1103, 1703 and 2203 local time in the winter. A preliminary announcement is made on channel 16. The meteorological office is open 24 hours a day and can be contacted (Tel. 65032 or 65008) for local and long range forecasts.

PASSAGE PLANNING

Yachts usually arrive in Malta from Sicily. Popular spots in Sicily in which to wait for good weather to make the crossing are Porto Palo on the southeast corner and Port Empedocle or Licata on the south coast. Most yachts going to Greece either cross directly to Argostoli or Pylos, or go to Siracusa and then around the south coast of Italy. Yachts bound for Tunisia often break the trip by stopping at the Italian island of Lampedusa.

HARBOURS AND ANCHORAGES

There are numerous delightful harbours and anchorages including Marsaxlokk, the 'Blue Lagoon' on Comino, Mgarr and several other anchorages dependent on wind direction. Marsamxett offers numerous advantages as a place to winter and a number of yachts are permanently based here, strategically placed in the middle of the Mediterranean. The new marina in Msida Creek offers better shelter than Lazaretto or Ta' Xbiex quays. The latter suffer from a heavy surge when a *gregale* blows and a yacht should not be left unattended in these conditions. It is planned to build a breakwater across the entrance to Marsamxett harbour at some future date and this will give the whole harbour excellent all-round shelter.

Manoel Island Yacht Yard is a good place to haul out and the rates are very reasonable in the long term; there are good repair facilities and some spares are available. Malta is a good place to provision; flights to the U.K. are relatively in-

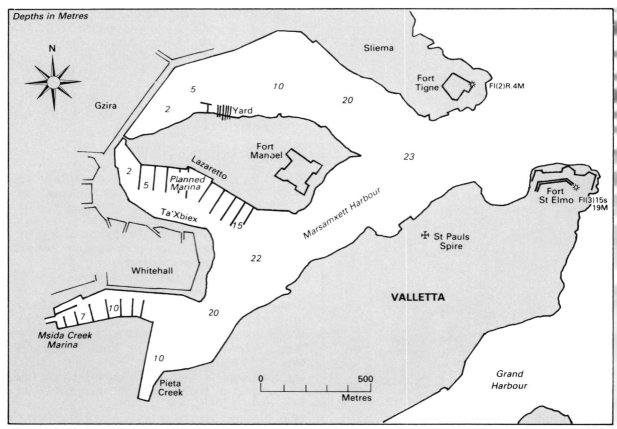

Marsamxett Harbour 35°54′.46N 14°29′.56E (Fort Tigne)

expensive; there are many excellent bars and restaurants; there are a number of cinemas showing quite recent movies in English; and you can even get a British newspaper on the same day it is printed!

NAVIGATION AIDS

The principal islands, Gozo and Malta, are low-lying and difficult to see from a distance. There are no mountains or peaks to make identification easy: Gozo is a slightly undulating island reaching 194 metres (638ft) at its western end; Malta is a wedge sloping from the southwest (240m/786ft) to the east. Many of the marks described in the Admiralty Pilot have been obscured by modern developments but the spire and dome of St Pauls in Valletta is still conspicuous. Two air radiobeacons have a good range and are useful:

Malta MTA 416 kHz 35°53′.5N 14°32′.3E
Gozo MLG 320 kHz 36°02′.3N 14°12′.5E
Malta Radio is open on 2182 kHz and VHF channel 16 on a 24 hour watch.

The Maltese Government runs a fleet of patrol boats, the Task Force, and you will probably be buzzed by one of these as you enter Maltese waters, especially if you do so near sunset. The Task Force boats also double as rescue boats for craft in trouble in Maltese waters, you will be charged on a time basis if you avail yourself of their services.

FORMALITIES

ENTRY FORMALITIES A foreign yacht entering Malta for the first time should go straight to Marsamxett, here customs will clear you in, but paradoxically you are not stamped in by the immigration authorities although they will want to see passports. (If you are keeping your yacht in Malta and leaving the country by some other means then you must go to the immigration authorities with your ticket and they will then stamp your passport.) A berth will then be allotted to you by the Yachting Centre. Valletta Radio can be contacted on VHF channels 16 or 12 to advise of your arrival. The Yachting Centre can be contacted on VHF channel 37 or, if not available, on channels 8 or 9.

When approaching Malta you should not anchor off the coast anywhere but should proceed straight to Marsamxett without delay. A yacht can be fined for breaking this regulation and will almost certainly be escorted in by one of the Task Force patrol boats.

Note that it is illegal to bring animals into Malta and a cat or dog on a yacht may be destroyed by the authorities.

DOCUMENTS The Small Ship's Register papers issued by the R.Y.A. or full registration papers are necessary. Other certificates are rarely asked for but it would be wise to have your insurance documents and a certificate of competency.

TAXES Marina fees only are payable.

FACILITIES

(These refer to those in or near the marina and the yard).
Water Near every berth in the marina. Water used to be scarce in the summer months and tasted brackish, but is reported to be improved with the installation of new desalinators.
Fuel Can be carried from the station near Manoel Island bridge by jerry cans or a tanker can be ordered to deliver it. It is planned to build a fuel quay in Msida Creek.
Electricity Can be connected at most berths. A deposit must be paid.
Gas Gas bottles of most types can be refilled in 24 hours.
Paraffin Small tankers come around Gzira regularly. Cheap but not the best quality. Methylated spirits also available from the tankers.

BOAT REPAIRS

Engines Spares for the major makes of marine engines are available. First class mechanics can be found.
Electrics and electronics Good electricians and electronic repairs can be carried out. Some spares available.
Navigation instruments Some spares available and a limited range of new gear but it is expensive (about 50 per cent more than U.K. prices).
Paints and antifoulings Hempels' range of paints and antifoulings are made in Malta under licence. Imported paints and antifoulings are more expensive.
Hauling Manoel Island Yacht Yard operates seven slipways capable of slipping vessels up to 60 metres and 500 tons. A 25 ton travel hoist also operates and about 250 yachts can be stored on the hard in the yard boat park. The yard offers a wide range of services. Several small yards can also haul yachts.
Engineering All manner of engineering work can be carried out inside and outside the yard by competent engineers.
Wood and GRP There are some first class boat carpenters in Malta. GRP skills are also good.

DUTY FREE SPARES   Duty free goods can be sent to Malta and are then loaded aboard the boat under customs supervision. Extracting goods from customs can be a time-consuming business and it may be worth your while to employ an agent to do it. It is better to have goods air-freighted than brought by ship as customs clearance of air cargo is more easily facilitated. A tip: have the goods addressed to your yacht with these three simple but all-important words on the label: 'Yacht in Transit'.

PROVISIONING

GENERAL   Although goods in Maltese shops cannot be described as cheap, they are not overly expensive. The delight is that you can stock up here on many old favourites from the U.K. such as Marmite, Rose's Lime juice, custard powder and digestive biscuits at quite reasonable prices.

There are several good supermarkets close to the marina. Fruit and vegetable vans also ply their trade close by. Shops are open 0800-1200 and 1600-1900.

SPECIFIC

Meat   Is quite expensive and quality can vary so it is advisable to look around until you find a good butcher and stick with him; frozen beef and lamb are good value. Small vans or carts come around selling live chickens and rabbits which they will kill and prepare for you on the spot.

Fish   Reasonably priced, dorado *(lampuki)* is cheap and delicious in season.

Fruit and vegetables   are expensive and the quality and choice is poor.

Staples   Widely available and reasonably priced.

Cheese   Locally made cheddar is cheap and good, imported cheeses are reasonably priced.

Canned goods   Wide range of imported canned food-stuffs (including ham, bacon, cheeses, salmon, soups etc) available at reasonable prices.

Coffee and tea   Instant coffee here is cheap. Tea is good and cheap.

Wines, beer and spirits   Local wines are mediocre but cheap, local beer is excellent and cheap. Imported spirits are moderately priced and are available duty free.

Recommended   Stock up on stores here, particularly packet and canned items. Nescafé is particularly good value.

EATING OUT   The local cuisine is much subordinated to English tastes, partly because of the British presence here until 1979 and partly because of the large numbers of British tourists arriving in Malta in the summer. You can eat well for a modest sum and eat very well with attentive service for not a lot more. Local dishes are not much in evidence but some seafood dishes are usually offered as well as *timpani* (a macaroni pie) and *fragioli* (beef olives). For a snack try the delicious local meat pies.

PILOTS AND CHARTS

Admiralty *Mediterranean Pilot* Vol I. (NP45).
Admiralty *List of Lights and Fog Signals* Volume E (NP78).
Italian Waters Pilot. Rod Heikell. Imray. Covers Malta as well.
The Tyrrhenian Sea H. M. Denham. John Murray. Covers Malta but is out of date.
North Africa Pilot. RCC Pilotage Foundation. Imray.

Admiralty charts cover the islands, harbours and anchorages well.

USEFUL BOOKS

Blue Guide to Malta. Black. Excellent.
The Great Siege of Malta 1565. Ernle Bradford. Penguin.
The Kapillan of Malta. Nicholas Monsarrat. Penguin. Monsarrat spent his last years living and writing on Gozo.

National Tourist Organisation of Malta

Marsaxlokk, Malta

Yugoslavia

Area   255,804 square kilometres (98,766 square miles)

Population   22,800,000

Capital   Belgrade (Beograd) (1,300,000)

Language   Serbo-Croat. Latin script in the north and cyrillic in the south. Italian and German are spoken along the coast as well as some English.

Religion   Eastern Orthodox, Roman Catholic, small percentage of Islam in the south.

Time zone   G.M.T. + 1

Currency   Yugoslav dinar (din)

Electricity   220V 50Hz AC

Banks   Open 0700-1900 Monday-Friday and 0700-1300 Saturday. May occasionally close earlier. Eurocheques, most credit cards and travellers' cheques are accepted.

Mail   Reliable. *Poste restante* service is good.

Medical   Ranges from good to just adequate. You may have to queue for attention if it is not urgently required and again for medication. Fees are very reasonable. Reciprocal agreements for health care exist with Austria, Belgium, Netherlands, U.K. and West Germany. Almost free treatment for holders of these passports.

Internal travel   Trains and coaches to many destinations but they are often crowded. Internal flights to major cities by JAT (Yugoslavian Airlines). Car hire in the large centres only.

International travel   Belgrade is the centre for international flights but in the summer there are scheduled and charter flights to Split and Dubrovnik. Ferries from Bar, Dubrovnik, Split and Zadar to Italy. Bus and train to Italy.

Public holidays
January 1, 2 New Year
May 1, 2 Labour Days
July 4 Day of National Liberation
November 29, 30 Republic Days

GEOGRAPHY

COAST AND ISLANDS   From the Albanian border to the Italian border the Yugoslav coastline is mountainous, rising abruptly from the sea, often spectacularly so in places. Although the country is only 370 miles long, the much indented coastline and numerous islands give a total length of more than ten times this figure. Apart from a sixty mile stretch of coast northward from the Albanian bor-

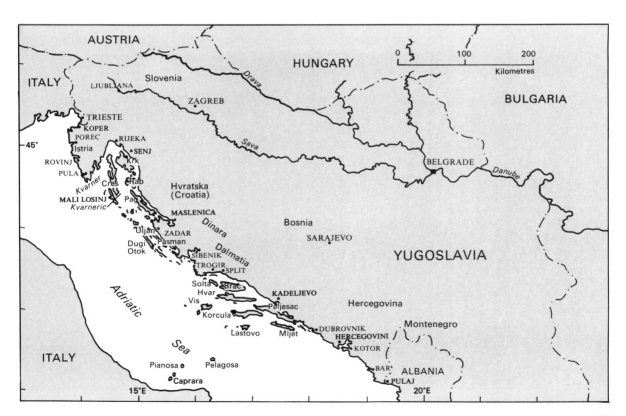

der, the remainder is bordered by three chains of islands which form attractive and sheltered cruising areas.

Although there is nearly always vegetation in the valleys, the coastal mountain slopes and some of the islands are often bare. This absence of vegetation has been attributed to the Venetians who stripped the forests in search of timber for their fleets. Some reafforestation has been attempted but with little success owing to the lack of topsoil. Viewed from the air the Venetian's devastation of the coast forests can be fully seen and in fact the islands are most attractive viewed from seaward.

CRUISING AREAS   The area can be roughly broken down into four parts.

From Bar to Dubrovnik   There are no offshore islands along this stretch of coast but there are numerous harbours and anchorages including the spectacular Gulf of Kotor.

From Dubrovnik to Split.   There are numerous harbours and anchorages along the mainland coast and the off-lying islands are much indented offering a superb cruising ground. The principal islands are Mljet, Korcula, Hvar and Brač which are all quite large (Hvar is 43 miles long) with numerous safe harbours and anchorages. There are also many smaller islands.

From Split to Zadar   The mainland coast is much indented with bays and fjords. At Šibenik you can navigate up the Krka river into Lake Prokljan and from here take a boat to see the famous Krka Falls. The Zadar Channel cuts off a chain of islands to form another large cruising area with many safe harbours and anchorages around the coast and islands — the largest of which are Kornat, Dugi, Pašman and Uljan. This group of islands actually extends somewhat north of Zadar.

From Zadar to Pula   The off-lying islands enclose a huge inland sea east of Pag, Cres and Krk Islands; this northern area is peppered with islands which in turn are so indented as to form a very large number of anchorages. The mainland mountains are mostly bare but some of the islands are green and wooded.

Korcula

Yugoslav National Tourist Office

CLIMATE AND WEATHER

Summers are of the Mediterranean type with high temperatures and little if any rainfall. Most rain falls in early spring and late autumn (April and November). The winters are of the Balkan type, very cold and wet, and this makes Yugoslavia an unattractive place to winter.

Average air temperature in August 23°C (73°F) in the north, 26°C (78°F) in the south; in February 7°C (44°F) in the north, 10°C (50°F) in the south. Rainfall: averages range from 59 inches (1500mm) in the north to 20 inches (500mm) annually in the south.

WINDS   The prevailing wind in the summer is the west-northwest to southwest *maestral*. It gets up at midday, blows Force 4-5 at most, and dies in the evening. The nights are usually calm although in the early morning there may be a light land breeze. In the spring and autumn, when a depression is passing across the northern tip of the Adriatic, there may be southerlies for a few days.

In the spring and autumn, and sometimes in the summer, a *sirocco* (or *yugo*, *jugo*) may blow. This happens when a high pressure zone sits over the southern Balkans, the wind sets in slowly from southeast and may reach Force 9-10 in 48 hours although this is rare. Its direction can vary from east-southeast to south-southeast depending on where you are. It is a warm and moist wind and because it may last for several days it can build up a large swell. It is most common in the southern Adriatic and affects the northern end little.

The wind to be feared most is the *bora (bura)*, a distant cousin of the *mistral*, which fortunately blows mostly in winter. It is a dry cold wind from north-northeast to east-northeast and often reaches Force 9-10 with stronger gusts. It is not to be underestimated. Some areas are notorious for

violent *boras:* the Bay of Trieste, Rijeka, Senj, Vir, Sibenik, Vrulja Gap and Makarska, and Peljesac. Like the *mistral*, the *bora* occurs when cold continental air manages to get over the hump of the mountains along the coast and tumbles down onto the sea. In summer there may be brief katabatic winds off the mountains lasting for 2-4 hours and although of some force, these summer squalls at night are not to be confused with the *bora*.

LOCAL NAMES OF WINDS
Maestral, maestro   West to northwest.
Yugo, jugo, sirocco   East-southeast to south-southeast. It can blow at gale force and is often accompanied by a heavy swell because of the long fetch up the Adriatic.
Bora, bura   North-northeast to east-northeast.

Decreasing visibility (haze) and low cloud on the southern slopes of the mountains is said to herald a *sirocco*. A southerly swell usually precedes a *sirocco* by a number of hours. Cloud sitting on the tops of mountains heralds northerly winds (not necessarily a *bora*) and a cold, almost electric atmosphere heralds a *bora*.

GALES   Gales are rare in the summer. In the winter gale force winds may be from the north or south but the wind most to be feared is the *bora*.

THUNDERSTORMS   In the summer there are often thunderstorms accompanied by violent squalls and heavy rain. They occur most often in the evening and come from nowhere out of a flat calm. They are usually over in 1-3 hours.

WEATHER FORECASTS
Weather forecasts are broadcast first in Serbo-Croat and then in English from the following coast radio stations. (Times are G.M.T.)

Rijeka 2771 kHz and VHF Ch 24 at 0535, 1435, 1935.
Split 2685 kHz and VHF Ch 07, 23, 28 at 0545, 1245, 1945.
Dubrovnik 2615 kHz and VHF Ch 04, 87 at 0625, 1320, 2120.
Bar 2752 kHz and VHF Ch 24 at 0850, 1420, 2050.

The forecast is in four parts:
i: gale warnings (including warnings of a *Bora*)
ii: reports from coastal stations
iii: general situation
iv: forecast for the next 24 hours

In practice if you are used to listening to the Italian weather forecast on Ra I 2° then this covers the Adriatic as well. Reception on 1035 kHz is good for most parts of the Adriatic.

TIDES   For most Yugoslavian waters these are negligible and can be ignored. The vertical interval at Dubrovnik at springs is 0.37m (14½″) whilst in

Yugoslav National Tourist Office

Zadar

the north it is 1.05m (3'5"). Only in the far north need you keep an eye on the depth under your keel. Currents are light, in general they follow the Yugoslavian coast north and return southwards along the Italian coast. The sea-level can also be altered by the barometric pressure and by strong northerly or southerly winds, northerlies reduce the level while southerlies increase it.

HARBOURS AND ANCHORAGES

WHAT TO EXPECT   In recent years the Yugoslavs have invested heavily in marina development and at present there are some thirty-two marinas completed with others in the pipeline. Sixteen of the marinas currently in operation are administered by the Adriatic Club Yugoslavia (ACY). Not all of these are purpose built marinas as we understand them, but are harbours or a part of a harbour provided with additional facilities and laid moorings.

Apart from these marinas there are numerous commercial ports and many small harbours suitable for yachts as well as very many anchorages along the mainland coast and around the islands (there are said to be 750 islands) offering excellent shelter. In recent years the Yugoslavs have started to charge for harbours and even some anchorages!

In the north you will come across considerable numbers of German and Austrian yachts in the summer. Many of them are kept permanently in Yugoslavia as it is a comparatively short drive from Austria or southern Germany to the northern Adriatic.

SECURITY   On the whole the Yugoslavs are an honest people and theft is very rare. An efficient police force keeps it that way.

WINTERING AFLOAT   Because the winters are rainy and cold Yugoslavia is not a popular place for wintering afloat. A few boats have wintered in Dubrovnik.

A yacht may be left for the winter in Yugoslavia without the owner aboard under the supervision of a marina or one of their sub-contractors. The vessel is bonded by customs for the period but an owner may leave a yacht for up to twenty days without it being bonded.

PASSAGE PLANNING

IN GENERAL   Yachts usually sail from the boot of Italy or from Brindisi to the Yugoslavian coast. Passages are then straightforward along the coast and between the islands going north and returning the same way.

CHARTERING   Flotilla and bareboat charter companies operate from the adjacent Italian coast (Trieste) to the northern islands (bareboat), between Zadar and Primosten (flotilla) and from Dubrovnik (flotilla).

Yugoslav National Tourist Office

Charter fleets are increasing and spreading to parts of Yugoslavia that previously saw only a few cruising yachts.

SPECIFIC ROUTES   None. A yacht may sometimes return to Corfu instead of Italy in which case a dog leg course must be followed to avoid Albanian waters.

NAVIGATION AIDS

Buoyage   I.A.L.A. System 'A' is being introduced between 1981 and 1985. In practice only those areas used by commercial shipping are buoyed, elsewhere buoyage is neither developed nor consistent.

Lights   Given the complicated sea area to be marked especially the channels between the numerous islands, then the area can only be described as being passably catered for with lights. However these are all well maintained and rarely out of action.

Radiobeacons   There are a few radiobeacons in Yugoslavia but these combined with those along the Italian coast provide a good network useful when crossing to Yugoslavia.

Marine radiobeacons

See page 119 for the Italian radiobeacons with which the following Yugoslavian beacons are grouped.
Molunat   YC 305.7 kHz 100M. Seq. 5, 6. Continuous in fog and at ev. H + 10, 16, 40, 46 in clear weather.
Movar   YV 289.6 kHz 100M. Seq. 5, 6. Continuous in fog and at ev. H + 16, 22, 46, 52 in clear weather.
Kamenjak YP 298.8 kHz 100M. Seq. 3, 4. Continuous in fog and at ev. H + 20, 26, 50, 56 in clear weather.

Air radiobeacons
The following beacons operate continuously.
Pula PLA 351.1 kHz 50M 44°53′.4N 13°45′.2E
Pula/Kavran KAV 265 kHz 50M 44°53′.7N 14°00′.6E
Lošinj LOS 432 kHz 50M 44°31′N 14°28′E
Sali SAL 298 kHz 50M 43°56′N 15°10′E
Split DVN 392 kHz 50M 43°26′.6N 16°08′.9E
Dubrovnik KLP 318 kHz 25M 42°39′.9N 18°01′.5E
Tivat TAZ 345 kHz 50M 42°16′.9N 18°48′.4E

Coast radio stations

Most commercial ports and marinas keep a listening watch on VHF Channel 16.
Main operating frequencies are shown in bold type.
All times are G.M.T.
All stations offer a 24 hour service unless otherwise stated.
Services are in Serbo-Croat and English.[1]

Station	Transmits (kHz and VHF channel)	Listens (kHz)	Traffic Lists (Freq. and times)
Rijeka	2182, 2191, 2585, **2771** VHF Ch. 04, 16, 20, 24	2182	2771 ev. odd H + 35. Ch. 24 ev. odd H + 35
Split	2182, 2191, 2221, **2685** VHF Ch. 16, 23, 28	2182	2685 ev. even H + 35. Ch. 23, 28 ev. H + 35.
Dubrovnik	2182, 2191, 2221, **2615** 2670, 2685, 2771, 3670 VHF Ch. 16, 4, 12, 14, 23, 24, 25, 26, 27, 28	2182	2615 ev. odd H + 20
Bar (YUW)	2182, 2191, 2615, **2752** VHF Ch. 16, 24, 87	2182	2752 ev. even H + 20 Ch. 24 ev. even H + 20.

Rescue Service   A salvage tug is based at Split and listens on 2182 kHz but not continuously. There are navy patrol boats which will answer distress calls but by and large you will have to rely on your own resources if you get into trouble.

FORMALITIES

ENTRY FORMALITIES   A yacht must enter at one of the designated ports of entry where a sailing permit (permit of navigation) will be issued and must be stamped by the customs. A triangular sticker with the year of issue will also be given to you and this must be displayed prominently on the mast or wheelhouse. A yacht must go first to a port of entry as heavy fines have been imposed on skippers who have entered elsewhere, even in good faith. You may be asked for the sailing permit in any other port you go to but in practice the sight of the triangular sticker seems sufficient.

At the port of entry you must produce passports for all crew members, registration papers for the boat, an insurance certificate, a R/T licence for radio transmitters on board, five crew lists and three lists of items liable to duty on board. The latter list should include navigation instruments, radio(s), cameras, tender and outboard engine, indeed anything on board you could conceivably sell. You may also be asked for a certificate of competency and the latest developments indicate it would be wise to get one.

Trailed boats have to get through the border but must still obtain a sailing permit when they are launched. The officials are used to large numbers of Germans and Austrians bringing trailed boats into Yugoslavia so there are no difficulties here. Ports of entry (north to south): Koper, Umag, Rovinj, Pula, Raša, Rijeka, Mali Losinj, Senj, Maslenica, Zadar, Šibenik, Split, Kadeljevo, , Korčula, Dubrovnik, Herceg-novi, Bar.

The following ports of entry are also open in the summer: Izola, Piran, Novigrad, Poreč, Opatija, Punat (Krk), Rab, Primošten, Hvar, Kotor, Tiuvat, Budva, Ulcinj.

DOCUMENTS   The Small Ship's Register papers issued by the R.Y.A. or full registration papers (Part 1 registration: the *Blue Book*) are both acceptable. A certificate indicating your competence (the R.Y.A. *Overseas Helmsman's Certificate* or other) should be taken as there are indications that the officials are tightening up on this requirement. Your insurance documents and a R/T certificate are also needed. Lack of the latter does not seem critical but be prepared just in case. A ship's stamp is useful.

TAXES   For the cost of a sailing permit you can stay for the year to 31st December and, if your boat is under customs supervision, until the 31st October of the following year. Apart from those harbours designated as marinas and where a charge is made, some of the smaller harbours also impose a daily charge.

FACILITIES

EVERYDAY

Water   In most harbours there is a tap nearby although you may often have to carry it by jerry cans. In the summer some of the smaller islands run short of water and it may be rationed. It is everywhere potable unless otherwise specified.

Ice   Available in the larger cities and towns only.

Fuel   Fairly widely available although you will often have to carry it by jerry cans. It is best to keep your tanks topped up because of the uncertainty of supply. In the marinas you can obtain duty free diesel but payment must be in hard currency.

Electricity   Available in the marinas and some harbours. Mostly you will have to rely on generating it yourself.

Gas   Calor type bottles can be filled at INA stations in the large centres: Dubrovnik, Split, Zadar, Rijeka. *Camping gaz* is available in the popular tourist resorts.

Paraffin   Freely available in litre bottles.

BOAT REPAIRS

Engines   Spares for marine engines are few and far between. You are advised to go to Italy for your requirements.

Electrics and electronics   Competent electricians can be recommended by the marinas and have been reported to do good work. Specialist repairs to electronic gear is best carried out in Italy.

Spares and repairs   Small repairs can be undertaken at various marinas but spare parts are almost impossible to obtain quickly.

Paints and antifoulings   Locally manufactured paints and antifoulings are available. Imported paints and antifoulings are expensive.

Hauling   There is a travel hoist in Dubrovnik and one planned for Zadar. Elsewhere yachts can be hauled on a sledge and runners or craned out although out of the way places may have trouble coping with extreme fin keel yachts. It is probably best to stick with the marina yards which are used to hauling and chocking yachts. Dubrovnik appears to be the favourite for hauling.

Engineering Skills are good in the larger centres and rates reasonable.

Wood and GRP Woodwork skills vary widely but in general most of the yards are not well-versed in quality repairs and joinery. The following places might be worth investigating: Tivat in the Kotor area, Dubrovnik, Losinj and Punat. GRP skills can be found in a number of places and there have been reports of good work carried out. GRP yachts are now manufactured in Yugoslavia. Ask around for competence.

DUTY FREE SPARES Spares and new items may be imported without paying duty, however it can be a complicated business and you will need a Yugoslav translator at the airport to extract the goods from customs. Duty free goods including some boat gear can be purchased in the marinas.

PROVISIONING

GENERAL While most goods are available, there can be sudden and inexplicable shortages so it is best to stock up when you can. In the summer there may be shortages of quite basic items like bread when demand exceeds supply with the influx of tourists. Often you will have to queue to get items in short supply and as the shops open at 0600 you will have to be up early with the local inhabitants. Shopping hours are 0600-1100 and 1730-2000. Some shops in the larger centres known as Nonstop are, as their name suggests, open all day. On some of the smaller islands the shops seem to open at the whim of the proprietor and have only limited stocks for the small local population.

In recent years Yugoslavia has experienced a spiralling inflation rate measured in hundreds of per cent. At the moment you get tens of thousands of *dinar* for the pound or dollar and it is difficult to know when it will stop. It is likely that the *dinar* will be drastically devalued in the near future, but until it is change hard currencies into *dinar* in small amounts on a weekly basis.

SPECIFIC

Meat Is plentiful only in the larger centres, it is not hung and it may be butchered in an odd fashion. Local salami and smoked hams are delicious but not cheap.

Fish Is scarce and expensive.

Fruit and vegetables There is a plentiful although seasonal supply and prices are reasonable. Markets in the larger centres.

Staples Can be obtained everywhere although as previously mentioned there can be shortages and you may have to queue. Stock up well when you can.

Cheese Local varieties are good and reasonably priced: *Trappist*, something like a gruyère; *baski sir* from Pağ is tangy; *travnicki sir* is a sheep's cheese; *belava,* a cottage cheese.

Canned goods Reasonable choice.

Coffee and tea Coffee is scarce and expensive. The tea is terrible.

Wines, beers and spirits Local wine is cheap and excellent. Some of the *reisling* from Herzegovina and the Neretva valley and the white from Korcula are excellent. Wine can be bought in bulk and many of these, both red and white, are good value but try them first. Local beer, including draught beer, is good. Local spirits, notably some fruit liqueurs such as *slivovitza* plum brandy, *kajsijevaca* (apricot brandy) and *maraskino* (cherry brandy), as well as *vinjak* (a reasonable cognac) are excellent value.

Recommended Dalmation smoked ham, *trappist* cheese, fruit juices and local wines and liqueurs.

EATING OUT Yugoslavia does not boast of a cuisine of international repute and the food is satisfying rather than exotic. Yugoslavian cuisine, along the coast is a combination of the more mundane aspects of Italian, Turkish and Balkan influences, while in the popular tourist resorts this has been subordinated to a rather bland international cuisine. With the increase in yacht tourism more private restaurants are being established around the coast and islands and fortunately many of these offer a better cuisine with more care and attention paid to the food compared to the bland and poorly cooked fare found in state run restaurants.

A service charge is not usually added to bills and it is customary to leave a small tip, about 5-10 per cent. Some restaurants have fixed price tourist menus usually offering three courses of a limited choice. Otherwise the price on the menu is the price you pay so it is straightforward to check your bill.

The following categories of restaurant exist but the category really has little to do with the quality of the food.

Bife A buffet bar serving sandwiches, cold meats and drinks.

Ekspres restoran A self-service café.

Gostiona A village inn often privately owned and serving home cooked meals. A restaurant may call itself a *gostiona* to attract custom but the original article can often serve good food in convivial surroundings.

Restoran   A restaurant from the simplest to the more sophisticated.

Mlecni restoran   A dairy shop selling light meals, pancakes, pastries and yoghurt.

For starters ask for *Istarski* or *dalmatinski prsut* (smoked ham), salami or *juha* (soup). Fish soup (often with paprika) is good.

For a main course you will be offered the ubiquitous kebab *(ražnjići),* meatballs *(ćevapčići,* the small ones, or *pljeskavica,* a larger hamburger), or *culbastija* (grilled pork). These are all grouped under *rostilj:* charcoal grilled meats. If you can try *djuveč* (a casserole of pork or lamb with vegetables), stuffed green peppers, *musaka* (like the Greek one) and *pasticada* (beef with noodles). Pasta may also be offered but it is not up to Italian standards.

Sweets can be pancakes with various fillings *(palacinke)* which are excellent and baklava similar to its more eastern namesake.

PILOTS AND CHARTS

Admiralty *Mediterranean Pilot* Vol. III (NP47). Covers the Adriatic.
Admiralty *List of Lights and Fog signals* Vol. E (NP78)
Adriatic Pilot. T. and D. Thompson. Imray. Covers the east coast of Italy and Yugoslavia.
The Adriatic H. M. Denham. John Murray.
National Guide to the Adriatic. Yugoslavian publication available in large bookshops here. Notes and plans of harbours.

The Admiralty charts are adequate. Yugoslavian charts may be obtained from the Yugoslav Academy of Sciences and Arts, Zagreb, Gunduliceva 24 or from the harbour master's office in Rijeka, Zadar, Korcula and Dubrovnik.

USEFUL BOOKS

The Yugoslav Coast. Yugoslav Lexicographical Institute. Available in Yugoslavia.
Berlitz Guides. *Split and Dalmatia. Dubrovnik and Southern Dalmatia.* Compact and quite comprehensive.
Yugoslavia. Tito. Eastern Approaches. Fitzroy Maclean. All fascinating reading although having little to do with modern Yugoslavia.
The Yugoslavian Coast. C. F. Edwards.

Šibenik.

Yugoslav National Tourist Office

Albania

Shqipëria

Area   28,749 square kilometres (11,100 square miles)

Population   2,800,000

Capital   Tirana (200,000)

Language   Albanian. Some Italian and English spoken (mostly by the older generation)

Religion   Officially atheist, but traditionally Islamic and Greek Orthodox

Time zone   G.M.T. + 1;   D.S.T. (May-September)

Currency   Lek (L) = 100 quintars

Electricity   220V 50Hz AC

Banks   Official Drejtbanka open 0700-1400 Monday-Saturday. Credit cards and cheque cards are not accepted. Cash in US dollars or pounds sterling is the most useful

Medical   Adequate to poor. Medical treatment is free. Few western drugs available

Internal travel   Restricted

International travel   Limited flights to Tirana

Prior to the Second World War British yachts used to visit Albania for cruising and to land shooting parties, however in 1946 two British destoyers, the *Volage* and the *Saumarez* were sunk by Albanian mines in the Corfu Channel and consequently Britain cut all diplomatic ties with the country. They have not been resumed. Since the war the government has been single party communist with a variety of allegiances. After the war the Russians supported the Albanians, but in 1961 they left to be replaced by the Chinese. Today even the Chinese appear out of favour and trade is carried out with a variety of partners including Yugoslavia, Czechoslovakia, West Germany, Italy and the Netherlands. In Albania it is wise not to praise any major foreign power and especially not the U.S.S.R., China or the U.S.A.

No yacht should attempt to visit Albania unless a visa has been obtained and since these are not issued to yachtsmen you simply do not visit the country. Reports from yachtsmen who have inadvertently strayed into Albanian waters and who have been apprehended by the Albanians vary widely. Almost certainly you will be escorted to a harbour by a patrol boat and you will have to stay one or two days until things have been sorted out. The only reliable reports I have indicate that after those one or two days, when it becomes apparent that you are not a Western spy and that you

entered Albanian waters inadvertently or by stress of weather, you will be escorted out of Albanian waters to continue on your way.

I have not been able to verify tales of fines (to the value of the yacht in question) imposed on yachtsmen as a penalty for entering Albanian waters and would not care to test the theory by intentionally entering Albania in my yacht.

If you should end up in Albania remember it is the only country in the world that still considers Stalin a hero, and his brand of repressive communism the proper way to run a country. Under the Russian cloak tourism was developed but after the two countries separated Albania turned in on itself. Over the last few years indications are that some restrictions will be lifted and tourism encouraged again to a limited extent although restrictions on what is 'suitable' have not yet been removed which means that long hair, long beards, flashy clothes and mini or maxi skirts are not allowed nor can subversive literature be introduced into the country, 'subversive' covering everything from *Playboy* to the Bible.

For more information see *Adriatic Pilot* by T. and D. Thompson or *Hafenhandbuch Mittelmeer Teil V* which gives harbour plans for Shengjini, Durres (the main port), and Sinikol (the *Hafenhandbuch* is in German only). H. M. Denham mentions Durres, Sazan, Vlorës, Palermo, Sarandes and Butrino (no plans).

Note There have recently been reports and rumours circulating to the effect that it is possible to cruise in Albanian waters. I must emphasise that there has been no official change of policy and to my knowledge, no change in practice. Any yacht entering Albanian waters will be intercepted by the Albanian authorities and questioned. If a satisfactory explanation is given the yacht will be allowed to return to Greek or Yugoslavian waters – I suggest those who value their yachts do not test Albanian laws in this matter.

Greece

Area   131,944 square kilometres (50,930 square miles).

Population   9,800,000.

Capital   Athens 3,000,000.

Language   Greek. English and German also spoken in some places.

Religion   Predominantly Greek Orthodox. Some Roman Catholicism.

Time zone   G.M.T. + 2;   D.S.T. (April-September).

Currency   Drachma.

Electricity   220V 50Hz AC.

Banks   Open 0800-1300 Monday-Friday. Eurocheques, credit cards and travellers' cheques widely accepted.

Mail   Reliable. *Poste restante* service is good in the winter but muddled in the summer.

Medical   Ranges from adequate to good depending on the area. Medical fees vary from moderate to high. Dentists are adequate to good, fees are moderate.

Internal travel   Coach travel is widespread and cheap. Ferries serve the islands and are cheap. Internal flights link the major cities and islands. Car rental agencies in the cities and tourist resorts.

International travel Athens is the principal airport with flights to many overseas destinations. In the summer there are regular international flights to Corfu, Preveza, Thessaloniki, Thira, Mykonos, Rhodes and Iraklion and less frequent flights to a number of other popular tourist resorts. Buses and trains to European destinations.

Public holidays
January 1 New Year's Day
January 6 Epiphany
March 25 Independence Day
May 1 Labour Day
August 15 Assumption Day
October 26 St Dimitrus Day
October 28 Ochi Day
December 25 Christmas Day
December 26 St Stephen's Day
Moveable:
1st day of Lent
Good Friday
Easter Monday
Ascension

GEOGRAPHY

COAST AND ISLANDS For the yachtsman Greece is not a single country but a thousand islands sown across the sea. Even a great chunk of mainland Greece, the Peloponnesus, has been chopped off by the Corinth Canal to become a sort of large island. From the beginning of written history the islands shaped the fate of ancient Greece and it is fitting that for the modern yachtsman the islands of Greece are what shapes our mental map of the country.

The islands vary dramatically in character from the green Ionian islands to the barren rocky Cyclades, from the snow-capped peaks of Crete to the pine-clad slopes of the northern Sporades. There are few sandy beaches except in the far north of the Aegean and in Crete.

Three major seas beat upon the shores of Greece: the Ionian on the west, the Mediterranean in the south and the Aegean in the east, the latter is peppered with islands from Crete in the south through the Cyclades, Dodecanese, the islands in the Saronic, to the eastern and northern Sporades. Nearly everywhere the mountains drop sheer into the sea and keep going down so that in most places you can sail close to the coast. Coastal settlements are invariably of modern origin, often not more than 100 years old, as not so long ago these coasts and islands were infested by pirates so the locals built their towns and villages far inland to avoid constantly being raided by pirates.

CRUISING AREAS Without exaggeration the whole area is superb for cruising, only the south coast of Crete poses real problems as in the summer violent squalls sweep down off the mountains and in the winter heavy seas batter the coast. There are numerous popular and consequently relatively crowded areas in the summer, to some extent because of the charter fleets that operate in these areas. The northern Ionian between Corfu and Cephalonia; the Saronic between Athens and

Greek *caique*

Spetsai; the Cyclades, particularly the northern islands closer to Athens; and the Dodecanese between Patmos and Rhodes are the parts most frequented; however, in the spring and autumn, my favourite times for cruising, these areas are not crowded.

Beyond those popular areas mentioned above, there are more and equally fine cruising grounds. Perhaps fifty per cent of Greece is little touched by yachtsmen and it is a constant amazement to me when I am told that there are too many yachts there. The yachtsman in search of idyllic places and solitude might try: the coast of the Peloponnesus: the Argolic Gulf; the northern Sporades; northern Greece; the eastern Sporades; and some of the more southerly Cyclades.

CLIMATE AND WEATHER

Summers are of the Mediterranean type, hot and dry, temperatures in July and August being very hot in places. Spring and autumn are mild almost everywhere except in northern Greece where it is cooler than the average. The winters are, without exception wet, although some areas, notably the Ionian and the northern Aegean (north of a line due east from Athens) are very wet. Crete and Rhodes have the mildest winters.

In the spring and early summer air temperatures are warm but the sea temperature lags behind, in the autumn when air temperatures have dropped from the summer highs, the sea temperature remains high until early winter.

WINDS In the summer months the winds in the Ionian and the Aegean are predominantly from the north. In the Aegean the constancy of the northerly winds in the summer has been noted from ancient times when they were called the *etesians* from *etos* (annual). Today they are commonly called by the Turkish name — the *meltemi*. This wind begins blowing in May and June, reaches full strength in July and August, and dies off in late September or early October. In the northern Aegean the *meltemi* blows from the northeast, in the middle Aegean from the north and in the southern Aegean from the northwest to west so that in effect the wind describes an arc from the northeast through to the northwest from the northern to the southern Aegean. In strength the *meltemi* varies from Force 3 to Force 7, however violent gusts can blow off the lee side of any high land in the vicinity (particulary off some of the islands in the Cyclades and Dodecanese) which must be guarded against.

The *meltemi* is a consequence of a pressure gradient between a low pressure area over Pakistan which extends its influence into the eastern Mediterranean and the high pressure area over the Azores which effects the western Mediterranean. The pressure gradient between these two stable areas produces the constant northerlies in the summer. In the winter the pressure gradients over the eastern Mediterranean are not pronounced and winds are not from any constant direction, thus almost equal proportions of northerly and southerly winds can be expected.

Gaios on Paxos in the Ionian.

Local names for the winds are as follows:

North winds   *Vorias, boreas, tramonata.*

Northeast winds   *Vorias anatolikos, gregorio, gregoa.*

East winds   *Anatolikos, levante, ageliotes.*

Southeast winds   *Notios anatolikos, sirocco, euros.*

South winds   *Notios, ostra.*

Southwest winds   *Notios ditikos, garbis.*

West winds   *Pounente, ditikos, zephyros.*

Northwest winds   *Vorias ditikos, maistro, schiron.*

Northerly winds   *Meltemi, etesians.*

A long cigar-shaped cloud over an island (particularly in the Cyclades) is said to herald a strong *meltemi*.

Southerly gales often turn around and blow with renewed force from the north. A swell often precedes southerly blows but not northerlies. See the Coptic calendar for winter gales in the eastern Mediterranean. (Appendix III)

GALES   There are few if any gales in the summer, those in the winter result from small depressions moving in an easterly direction either southeastward towards Cyprus or north-eastwards towards the Black Sea. Although these depressions are usually of small dimensions they can give rise to violent winds. (Very occasionally, hurricane force winds have been recorded.) The depressions can develop rapidly and are often difficult to trace as their movement is fast and erratic. Depressions often linger in the Ionian Sea and the southern Aegean.

THUNDERSTORMS   These occur in the spring and the autumn and are often accompanied by a squall, they are generally of short duration and over in one to three hours. The distribution of thunderstorms is reported to vary over the mainland and the islands: thunderstorms are more frequent over the mainland in the spring and autumn and over the islands in the winter.

WEATHER FORECASTS   Because of the high and large land masses close to all sea areas in Greece it is extremely difficult to predict what local winds and wind strength will be, the Greek Meteorological Service does its best but nonetheless cannot give accurate forecasts for many areas. Warnings of approaching depressions will be given but again their erratic progress makes forecasting difficult.

The view from a monastery in the Saronic Gulf.

The weather forecast is transmitted in Greek and English on the National Programmes at 0630 on the following frequencies:

Athens 729kHz
Zakinthos 927kHz
Kerkyra 1008 kHz
Thessaloniki 1044 kHz
Komotini 1404 kHz
Patrai 1485 kHz
Volos 1485 kHz
Rodos 1494 kHz
Khania (Crete) 1512 kHz
Samos 1602 kHz

On the national television channel, a weather forecast in Greek but with a synoptic chart is given after the news at 2130 local time. In almost any café you will find a television you can watch.

Coast radio stations also transmit forecasts in Greek and English.

HARBOURS AND ANCHORAGES

WHAT TO EXPECT   The few marinas there are in Greece are mostly concentrated in the area of Athens. Most are administered by the National Tourist Organization although charges do vary from one to the other for some inexplicable reason. Apart from the marinas in the Athens area

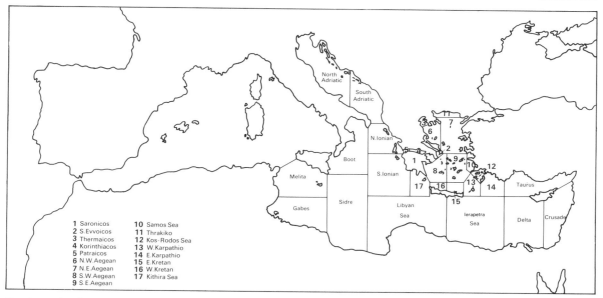

1	Saronicos	10	Samos Sea
2	S.Evvoicos	11	Thrakiko
3	Thermaicos	12	Kos-Rodos Sea
4	Korinthiacos	13	W.Karpathio
5	Patraicos	14	E.Karpathio
6	N.W.Aegean	15	E.Kretan
7	N.E.Aegean	16	W.Kretan
8	S.W.Aegean	17	Kithira Sea
9	S.E.Aegean		

Greek weather forecast areas

On VHF radio, weather messages are available on request with gale warnings and forecasts in Greek and English for all areas as follows:
Kerkyra Ch 23, 26; Kefallina Ch 25, 28; Kalamata Ch 03; Kalamata Ch 24, 27; Thessaloniki Ch 23, 26; Pilion Ch 25, 28; Kythira Ch 23, 26; Gerania Ch 24, 27; Poros Ch 25, 28; Parnis Ch 23, 26; Thásos Ch 25, 28; Knossos Ch 24, 27; Syros Ch 24, 27; Limnos Ch 24, 27; Faistos Ch 23, 26; Thira Ch 23, 26; Sitia Ch 25, 28; Ikaria Ch 25, 28; Mytilini Ch 23, 26; Rodos Ch 24, 27.

Windmills on Astipálaia (Cyclades).

(six in all and all of them crowded) there are marinas at Corfu (Gouvia), Thessaloniki, Porto Carras (privately owned) and Rhodes (nominally a marina as berths are reserved). There are plans to build a large marina complex close to Athens in the future.

There are numerous commercial ports (large and small) and many fishing harbours offering good shelter and often facilities of some sort nearby. There are also many many anchorages offering good shelter so that for the most part you can choose between a small fishing harbour or an attractive anchorage depending on your inclinations. Few countries offer so many harbours and anchorages within such short distances.

SECURITY   Except in the large cities, towns and popular tourist spots, the Greeks are an honest race and theft is rare. I very rarely lock up my boat in Greece although I cannot recommend the practice in case you are one of the unfortunate exceptions. In the large cities and the popular tourist spots the locals have learnt from the visitors and it is wise to lock your boat securely and remove loose items from the deck.

WINTERING AFLOAT   There are numerous spots where a yacht can winter afloat, the popular places are: Gouvia, Nidri (Levkas), Zea marina, Kalamaki (Alimos) marina, Aegina, Poros, Porto Kheli, Spetsai, Khania and Rhodes. If you are leaving your yacht for a period then I cannot recommend the native Greek boat-minders I have come across, in most cases they are not diligent at the task for which they have been paid (often dearly). There are exceptions, however, and the best policy is to ask other cruising folk what their experience of a particular boat-minder has been.

PASSAGE PLANNING

IN GENERAL   In the Aegean, yachts move north in the spring with the intention of going south when the *meltemi* begins to blow, in the autumn they again head north. Beating back against the *meltemi* is neither a pleasant nor a sensible plan. In the Ionian and those parts of the Aegean unaffected by the *meltemi* it is much easier to head north at any time of the year.

SPECIFIC ROUTES   A yacht arriving in Corfu will normally hop down the Ionian islands to the Gulf of Patras and Gulf of Corinth to go through the Corinth canal to the Saronic Gulf. Few yachts go around the Peloponnesus to enter the Aegean from the southwest corner although this route is quite straightforward. Yachts going to the northern Aegean should endeavour to get up there in the spring before the *meltemi* makes it difficult work. Route planning across the Aegean is straightforward with the prevailing northerlies and there are no obvious routes. Those returning from the southeast corner of the Aegean in the *meltemi* season are best advised to head up to Kos and then westward around the southern Cyclades until, at the fringe of the *meltemi* area (around Milos), they can head north towards Hydra or Poros.

CHARTERING   Flotilla and bareboat charter companies operate in the northern Ionian between Corfu and Cephalonia; from Athens, usually going south to the Saronic islands or to the Cyclades; in the Saronic Gulf, and in the northern Sporades.

Corfu, Athens and Rhodes are the major charter boat bases. Most of the companies advertise in the British yachting press and the best deals can usually be negotiated from Britain rather than going out to Greece on spec.

NAVIGATION AIDS

Buoyage   In general, buoyage is neither developed nor consistent and buoys may vary from those well maintained, lit and conforming to the I.A.L.A. System to rusty 44 gallon oil drums on an old bit of chain and a concrete block. Away from the large commercial harbours do not expect to find buoys always in place, often when they are being maintained buoys are withdrawn and not replaced until their maintenance is complete.

Lights   Given the complicated sea area and large numbers of islands, big and small, that must be marked, then Greek waters are well catered for in lights. At night shaping a passage through the islands I have encountered few problems although some of the smaller groups of islands off the well-trodden routes are not well lit. In general the lights are well maintained and it is rare for a major light to be out of action although harbour entrance lights may occasionally be out for a day or two.

Radiobeacons   There are few radiobeacons in Greece specifically for marine use although there are numerous air radio beacons. The latter may be changed without notice to mariners and not all of them operate on a 24 hour basis. In practice navigating around the coast and between islands little use is made of them, most of one's navigation being of the 'eyeball type'. Approaching Greece from the west the beacons at Corfu, Preveza, Araxos, Andravida and Kalamata are useful.

Air radiobeacons

Kérkira KEK 403 kHz 25M 39°35′.3N 19°55′E
Prevéza PRV 353 kHz 50M 38′54′.8N 20°46′E
Korinthos KOR 392 kHz 50M 37°56′N 22°56′.1E
Amalias/Andravida AML 367 kHz 100M 37°46′.5N 21°20′.8E
Kalamáta KTA 348 kHz 45M 37°04′N 22°01′.2E (daytime)
Khania/Soúdha (Crete) SUD 289 kHz 200M 35°31′.3N 24°09′.2E (daytime only).
Iráklion (Crete) HER 259 kHz 150M 35°20′.1N 25°10′.7E
Ródhos/Paradisi ROS 339 kHz 150M 36°25′.2N 28°07′.1E
Milos MLO 378 kHz 36°42′.7N 28°07′.1E
Aiyina EGN 382 kHz 50M 37°45′.7N 23°25′.4E
Megara MGR 405 kHz 38°00′N 23°23′N
Elefsis ELF 252 kHz 50M 38°04′N 23°33′.6E
Kavouri KVR 357 kHz 200M 37°48′.9N 23°45′.6E
Sounion SUN 319 kHz 50M 37°40.2N 24°02′.7E

Karistos KRS 285 kHz 50M 38°00′.8N 24°25′.1E
Lesvos LVO 397 kHz 100M 39°03′.5N 26°36′.4E
Limnos LIO 270 kHz 150M 39°55′.5N 25°14′.9E
Alexandroupolis ALP 351 kHz 100M 40°51′.4N 25°56′.6E
Santorini THR 307 kHz 36°24′.1N 25°28′.8E
Kos KOS 311 kHz 50M 36°47′.8N 27°05′.5E
Samos SAM 375 kHz 80M 37°42′N 26°54′E
Khios HIO 299 kHz 80M 38°20′.4N 26°08′.5E
Tanagra TNG 303 kHz 80M 38°20′N 23°43′.8N
Nea Anghialos ANL 335 kHz 39°13′.1N 22°48′E
Thessaloniki TSL 345 kHz 80M 40°35′.6N 22°56′.9E

Coast radio stations   By and large shore radio stations are for commercial shipping and a yacht can call forever without getting an answer (except in distress).

Main operating frequencies are shown in bold type.
All times are G.M.T.
All stations offer a 24 hour service unless otherwise stated.
H + commences at minutes past the hour.

All these stations operate on VHF Ch. 16. Call sign 'Hellas Radio'.
The following stations operate on VHF Ch. 16 only: Preveza, Argostoli, Kalamata, Sitia, Paros, Siros, Kithera, Thira, Ikaria, Thessaloniki, Thasos, Mitilini.
Corinth Canal authorities work on VHF Ch. 11.

Station	*Transmits* (kHz or VHF Channel)	*Listens* (kHz or VHF Channel)	*Traffic Lists* (Freq. & times)
Kerkira (SVK) **Corfu**	1696, 2182 **2607**, 2830, 3613	2182	2830 ev. odd H + 10
Iraklion (SVH) **(Crete)**	1742, 2182, **2799**, 3640	2182	2799 ev. H + 20
Rodos (SVR) **(Rhodes)**	1824, 2182, **2624**, 3630	2182	2624 ev. H + 03
Athens	1680, **1879**, 2182 2590, 2768, **3624.4**, 3660.9, 3772.9	2182	2590 ev. even H + 05
Chios (SVX)	**1820**, 2182, 3743	2182	1820 ev. H + 03
Limnos (SVL)	2182, **2730**, 3793	2182	2730 ev. H + 05

Rescue Services   Most of the larger harbours where there are port police or customs have vessels that are used as rescue boats although most of them would be of little use in even a moderate sea. A distress call might then be answered by a fishing boat who will of course place a salvage claim. Some harbours have all-weather craft but these are few and far between, so by and large do not rely on a rescue boat to get you out of trouble.

FORMALITIES

ENTRY FORMALITIES   A foreign yacht entering Greece for the first time is required to enter at a designated port of entry where a Transit Log will be issued. There are 29 such ports scattered around the perimeter of Greece (they are listed at the end of this section), these ports are those where there are police, customs, health and immigration authorities. The Transit Log thus obtained becomes the ship's papers while it is in Greece, it details particulars of the yacht, the engine or engines, including outboard engines, items such as

Astros harbour

binoculars, radios, cameras and the like and crew members. You will be asked for the Transit Log at any large port and sometimes at smaller harbours depending on the inclination of the port policeman, if there are no port police stationed at a small harbour the customs official or even the local policeman may want to look at the Log which may be taken and kept until your departure.

When leaving Greece the Transit Log should be handed in at one of the ports of entry and you will be stamped out of the country. If the yacht is going to be wintered in Greece without the owner or crew then the Transit Log should be left with the nearest customs authority or with the port police. If you are leaving the country by means other than your yacht take a photo-copy of the Log to show the immigration authorities when you leave. If you are having your yacht hauled out you must obtain permission from the port police before hauling out and again when you go back in the water.

A Transit Log is issued initially for six months, renewable for a further six months. After this a yacht should be taxed $US15 per annum per foot (see Taxes).

Ports of entry listed alphabetically: Ayios Nikolaos, Alexandroupolis, Argostoli, Chania, Corfu, Ermoupolis, Iraklion, Itea, Kalamata, Katakolon, Kavala, Khios, Kos, Lavrion, Levkas, Mirina, Mitilini, Navplion, Patras, Pylos, Pithagorion, Preveza, Rhodes, Thessaloniki, Volos, Vouliagmeni, Zante, Zea.

DOCUMENTS The Small Ship's Register papers issued by the R.Y.A. or full registration papers (Part I registration: the *Blue Book*) are both acceptable. A certificate indicating your competence may be useful although seldom if ever asked for. The R.Y.A. *Helmsman's Certificate* is sufficient if asked. A ship's stamp is useful.

TAXES In public harbours a yacht may be charged modest dues depending on the whims or otherwise of the port police, these harbour dues are negligible. Any foreign yacht in Greek waters for more than one year, where the owner is not resident, must pay a tax of 15 dollars (U.S.) per foot per annum for harbour and light maintenance. There is some confusion over whether or not this is a cumulative tax. Anyone who is resident in

Greece must pay customs duty on their yacht, a figure varying between 11% and 18% depending on length, tonnage and country of origin. The scale of customs duty can be obtained on application to the National Tourist Organisation in Athens.

In 1987 a form of VAT was introduced, but it is not a set amount, varying from 6% to 33% depending on what is being taxed. Luxury goods, and these include yacht spares and equipment, are taxed at the luxury category of 33%. No doubt the tax will be applied willy-nilly to all sorts of things such as boat repairs, eating out, drinks in bars, and so on, depending on how the government assesses items and how much the vendor thinks he can get away with.

IN PRACTICE A Transit Log normally costs a small sum for stamp duty, but in practice an additional fee (between 500 Dr and 1000 Dr) may be levied, a receipt will be issued and given the cost of cruising permits in some other countries it seems

Fiskardo on Cephalonia.

churlish to question where this additional sum goes to. The tax of fifteen dollars per foot per annum for a stay of over one year is not, in practice, levied on yachts spending say six months in Greece out of any one year, and the other six months in another country say Italy, Malta, Turkey and Cyprus as the obvious choices.

FACILITIES

EVERYDAY

Water   In most harbours a water tap can be found on the quay, but it may be some distance away and you will regularly have to carry water by jerry cans. In many places water is in short supply in the summer and its distribution may be regulated. Often there is a water-man who generally makes a good living charging exhorbitant amounts for water. In places where water is in short supply, you should not be a conspicuous consumer; it is saddening on occasion to observe the crass behaviour of a yachtsman washing down his yacht on an island where water is a precious commodity even if he is paying for it.

Ice   Large blocks of ice about a metre long can be bought in many places. In most fishing harbours there is a fish shop which buys the fish from local boats and which makes or stocks the ice used in the boats. It is not always suitable for consumption in drinks.

Fuel   There are a few places where there is a fuel station on the quay, but you generally will have to carry it by jerry cans for small amounts or order a mini-tanker (if there is one) for larger amounts.

Electricity   Electricity points are only available in a few places and by and large you will have to rely on generating it yourself.

Gas   Local gas and *Camping gaz* are widely available all over Greece. The local gas is of good quality and suitable for Calor type appliances.

Paraffin   Can be found in most villages and bought in bulk in the cities and larger towns. Ask for *petreleon katharon*. Methylated spirits is widely available in small plastic bottles in grocery or hardware shops.

BOAT REPAIRS

Engines   Spares for most marine engines are difficult to find although things may change (albeit slowly) in future now that Greece is a member of the E.E.C. The distributors are mostly concentrated in Athens and Piraeus but even they carry only a small stock of very basic spares. General repairs can be carried out in the cities, towns and larger villages although expertise will only be found in the larger centres.

Electrics and electronics Competent electricians can only be found in the larger centres with Athens being the obvious place to head for. Electronic repairs only in Athens and Rhodes.

Navigation instruments Spares are difficult to obtain and new gear is heavily taxed.

Paints and antifouling Imported paints and antifouling are heavily taxed and can cost twice as much as they do in the country of origin. Local antifouling is cheap and effective but it is all of the soft type. Local paints vary in quality but are generally acceptable. Two-part polyurethane and epoxy paints are manufactured locally as is polyester resin and gelcoat.

Hauling Two travel hoists operate, one in Lavrion and one in Rhodes, and it is likely others will be introduced in the future. Elsewhere yachts are hauled on a sledge and runners and although this method is primitive, it is quite safe and there is little to go wrong with it. Shop around for prices as they vary considerably. A number of places are popular for hauling: Corfu, Levkas, Nidri, Patras, Lavrion, Aegina, Spetsai, Chania, Salamis, around Athens, Volos and Rhodes.

Engineering In general if a Greek does not have it he will make it; local engineering skills are good even if the equipment is often antiquated. Costs are reasonable.

Wood and GRP Woodwork skills are not developed and caiques are generally built with a sharp adze (with which Greek craftsmen are skilled). Specialist boat joiners doing work to European standards are hard to find. GRP skills are not developed despite the fact that a number of factories build small numbers of GRP craft. The Olympic Boatyard in Lavrion will treat osmosis problems.

DUTY FREE SPARES Duty free spares can be imported into Greece for yachts in transit but expect problems extracting items from customs. Delays and frustrations will most likely be your lot getting duty free spares into Greece.

PROVISIONING

GENERAL In all but the smallest villages you will have few problems obtaining basic provisions. Fresh fruit and vegetables are seasonal but now that Greece has joined the E.C. there may be a better selection over a longer period, and of course prices will rise. Shopping hours vary but are 0800-1300 and usually 1630-2000.

SPECIFIC

Meat Is usually not hung for long if at all and is invariably butchered in a peculiarly eastern Mediterranean fashion so that none of the normal cuts of meat can be recognised. Lamb and beef are the most expensive and pork and chicken the least.

Fish Is expensive. Large fish such as red snapper and grouper are very expensive and the prices of prawns and lobsters are astronomical.

Fruit and vegetables Are reasonably priced and usually fresh. In the smaller centres fruit and vegetables are seasonal. All fresh produce should be washed.

Staples Can be obtained in even the smaller villages. Many items (sugar, rice, legumes, beans etc.) are often sold loose. Packaged items often contain weevils.

Cheese Imported cheeses such as Dutch Edam are widely available and not too costly. Local hard cheeses are good. *Feta*, a soft sheep's cheese, is available everywhere and is good value.

Canned foods Local canned goods are excellent and cheap but there is not a wide variety. Canned tomatoes and fruit are good value. Canned meat is usually imported and is expensive.

Through the Corinth Canal which cuts the Peloponnesus off from mainland Greece.

Coffee and tea Instant coffee is very expensive, about twice the price of that in Britain. Local coffee is ground very fine and tends to clog filters and percolators. Local tea bags make an insipid cup of tea, imported tea bags are more expensive. Some of the loose tea packed locally is cheap and good.

Wines, beers and spirits Bottled wines are numerous and vary from excellent to terrible, local wine can often be bought cheaply from the barrel but taste it first. The ubiquitous *retsina* is an acquired taste. Wine is on the whole cheap. Local beer is quite palatable and cheap. Local spirits, *ouzo* (akin to *Pernod*) and brandy (sweetish) are excellent value especially when bought in bulk. Imported spirits are expensive.

Recommended Greek yoghurt is the best in the world. If you like soft cheese, *feta* is good value. Tinned fruit. Local salami. *Ouzo* and local brandy.

EATING OUT Greece is not a country for the gourmet. But the food is only a part of eating out, it being as much a social occasion, a piece of theatre, as a culinary occasion. Not that the Greeks don't eat well — they do. The food is invariably fresh, simply cooked and appetising; but the choice will often be limited, the food sometimes served cold or lukewarm and the garnishing meagre. In the larger towns and cities a wider choice will be found on the menu than in the smaller islands and villages.

When you first go into a taverna do not be confused by the menu, it will probably have printed on it a large variety of food and drink, but only those items with prices beside them are cooked in that particular taverna. There are two prices on the menu and it is the higher you must pay — it includes service and you always pay for service even if it is poor! A word of advice: do not order all your food at once or your main course, side orders and starters will arrive at the table at the same time. Eating is done slowly and leisurely in Greece and it is quite alright to occupy a table for a whole evening.

A taverna generally prepares its dishes for the day in the morning and these will be cooked in time for the mid-day meal when they will be served hot and for the evening they will be re-heated and luke warm at best. You will find that it is better to eat the oven-cooked dishes such as *moussaka,* stuffed vegetables, *pastitsio,* etc. at mid-day and in the evenings order something grilled or fried. Do not expect even this to be rushed to your table piping hot as Greeks believe hot food to be bad for the stomach — a notion not, incidentally, entirely without medical support.

Although there are numerous categories of taverna ranging from A to D, in my experience this has had little to do with the food offered and everything to do with the decor and furnishings and the toilet facilities. There is virtually no alternative to the Greek menu in most of Greece. Nowadays you get chips with everything and in the more popular tourist resorts a half-hearted international cuisine (epitomised by steak, eggs and chips) is on the menu.

For starters ask for *tzatsiki* (yoghurt with grated cucumber and garlic), aubergine salad and *kalamaris* (fried baby squid). For a main course try kebabs and pork chops grilled over charcoal, *moussaka* (Greek shepherd's pie), *stifado* (beef stew), stuffed vine leaves *(dolmades)*, green peppers or tomatoes. Greek salad (tomatoes, onions, green peppers, cucumber and *feta*) is part of every meal. Sweets are usually taken in a patisserie and not a taverna.

PILOTS AND CHARTS

Admiralty *Mediterranean Pilot* Vol. III (NP47). Covers the Ionian Sea.
Admiralty *Mediterranean Pilot* Vol. IV (NP47). Covers the Aegean.
Admiralty *List of Lights and Fog Signals* Vol. E (NP78)
Greek Waters Pilot. Rod Heikell. Imray. Covers all Greek Waters.
The Ionian to the Anatolian Coast. H. M. Denham. John Murray. Covers the Ionian and Crete.
The Aegean. H. M. Denham. John Murray.
The Admiralty charts are adequate if you are used to them. The Admiralty harbour plans are out of date. The charts of the German Hydrographic Service are good. Greek charts also cover the area but are not widely available.

USEFUL BOOKS

The Blue Guide to Greece. ed. Stuart Rossiter. A must.
The Greek Islands. Lawrence Durrell. Glossy photographs and Durrell's inimitable description of the islands.
The Greek Islands. Ernle Bradford. Collins Companion Guide. Excellent background guide from an author who has sailed around the islands.
Fortresses and Castles of Greece. Vols I and II and *Fortresses and Castles of the Greek Islands.* Alexander Paradissis. Detailed.
The Colossus of Maroussi. Henry Miller. Penguin. A 'must' to read even if you are not going there.
Flowers of Greece and the Aegean. Anthony Huxley and William Taylor. Excellent colour photographs and line drawings aid identification.
Food of Greece. Vilma Chantiles.
Greek Cooking. Robin Howe.

Turkey

Area 780,576 square kilometres (301,380 square miles)

Population 48,000,000

Capital Ankara (2,500,000)

Language Turkish. English, German, and some French spoken along the coastal region

Religion Islam

Time zone G.M.T. + 3

Currency Turkish lira (TL)

Electricity 220V 50Hz AC

Banks Open 0830-1200 and 1330-1800 Monday to Friday. Eurocheques, some credit cards, and travellers' cheques accepted in the cities and tourist centres.

Mail Generally reliable. Packages are all opened by customs and take a considerable time to get to you. You may have to pay duty on some items

Medical Ranges from excellent in the cities to poor in out of the way places. Fees are moderate. Many items can be bought over the counter in pharmacies

Internal travel Some internal flights. Buses offer an excellent and cheap service with the *dolmus* (shared mini-bus) serving more remote areas. Trains are mostly slow and serve few areas

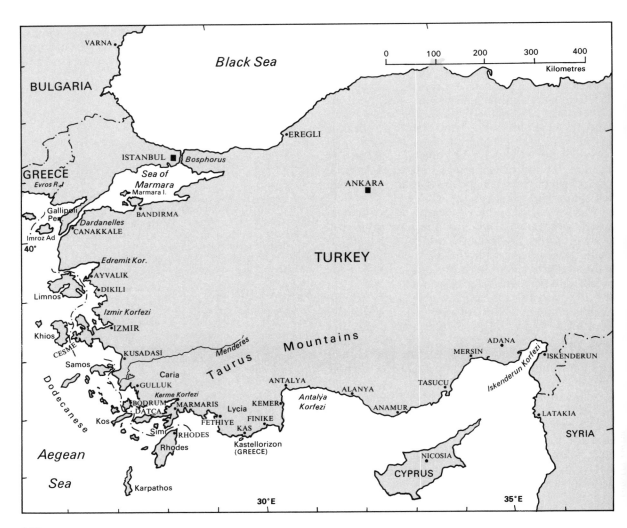

International travel Istanbul and Ankara are the main air ports. There are some international flights (mostly in the summer) to Izmir, Dalaman and Antalya.

Public holidays
January 1 New Year's Day
April 23 Children's Day
May 1 May Day
May 19 Youth Day
May 27 Freedom and Constitution Day
August 30 Victory Day
October 29, 30 Republic Days

GEOGRAPHY

COAST AND ISLANDS Turkey is a large rectangle extending eastwards from the Aegean and Mediterranean Seas to Iran and the Soviet Republic of Armenia and Georgia — a fact mentioned by all writers when they talk of Turkey as the bridge between east and west and between two continents. In the north the Black Sea coast stretches for some 700 miles from the Soviet border to the Bosphorus which with the Sea of Marmara and the Dardanelles divides most of the country from the European continent. The Aegean coast forms the western side of the rectangle, adjacent to Rhodes the coast turns eastward along the Mediterranean coast to Syria.

This length of coast is covered by extremes of climate: from that of the Balkans along the Black Sea (in a bad winter pack ice may extend as far as the northern entrance to the Bosphorus) to the almost North African climate in the south.

Two mountain chains traverse the north and south sides of Turkey hemming in the central Anatolian plateau; in fact most of the coast is bordered by high mountainous terrain, much of it grandly spectacular. Many of the mountains drop sheer into the sea so that there is deep water close to the coast where many otherwise good anchorages are simply too deep for a yacht to anchor in comfortably and even in those with moderate depths it is common practice to take a line ashore to a tree.

Most of the coast is wooded; in the north there are extensive pine forests and wooded areas of chestnut, oak, walnut and hazel (Turkey is the world's biggest exporter of hazel nuts). Along the Aegean seaboard there are also extensive pine forests and large areas of cultivated land close to the coast which have been famed from ancient times for their fertility. A temperate climate makes it a prime market garden and orchard region since ancient times. In the spring the acres of blossom and the green fields dotted with wild flowers are remarkably beautiful. Along the Mediterranean coast there is a different tropical green strip along the otherwise rocky surroundings.

Istanbul. Dolmabaçhe Palace.

CRUISING AREAS The geography determines four well defined cruising areas.

The Black Sea Coast This coast is the least cruised. It is mostly straight with few natural indentations but at intervals there are well protected artificial harbours for the local fishing boats. Those who have cruised this area say it is most attractive and that the locals are friendly and generous.

Sea of Marmara This sea is locked in by the narrow Bosphorus in the northeast and by the Dardanelles in the southwest. It has rich historical associations and of course the great city of Istanbul (Constantinople) sitting astride the Bosphorus. A yacht will have to contend with the currents in the Dardanelles (up to 4 knots in places) and again with the currents of the Bosphorus (up to 4 knots) to get into the Black Sea. There are two marinas at Istanbul near the entrance to the Bosphorus. Parts of the Sea of Marmara, especially the area around the Marmara islands and the Gulf of Erdek, offer a superb cruising ground little visited by yachts.

The Aegean Coast This coast bordering the Aegean Sea stretches from the Evros river that forms the frontier between Greece and Turkey to Marmaris where the coast angles south and east along the southern Mediterranean. The coast south of Izmir is the most popular section and there are five marinas in this area with more planned. There are many well sheltered and beautiful anchorages in the deep gulfs that cut into the coast; the Gulf of Güllük, Gulf of Gokova and Gulf of Hisarönü are popular cruising areas with an increasing number of charter fleets operating in the vicinity.

Bodrum marina.

The Mediterranean Coast Is less indented than that of the Aegean except at the Gulf of Fethiye are anchorages and a few small off-lying islands. There are two marinas and a number of commercial and fishing harbours. The coast east of Antalya is little frequented by yachts.

Along both the Aegean and Mediterranean coasts there are numerous interesting sites of the great cities which existed in the Graeco-Roman period.

CLIMATE AND WEATHER

The climate varies dramatically from north to south. Along the Black Sea coast it is very cold in the winter with a heavy rainfall and snow. Pack ice obstructs the northern part of the Black Sea and may extend down to the Bosphorus in a harsh winter. In the Aegean the summers are hot and the winters mild but it does rain a lot in the north. The further south you go the less rain there is in the winter. South of Fethiye the summers are hot and in August the heat can be oppressive.

WINDS Over most of the region (Sea of Marmara, Aegean and the northern part of the Mediterranean coast) the prevailing wind in the summer is the *meltem*. It follows the coast in the northern Aegean blowing from the north except where it curves into the gulfs and blows from the west. Around Çeşme it blows from the northwest and west into the gulfs. At Marmaris it curves again to blow from the west or west-southwest. In the south (from the gulf of Antalya and east) a day breeze blows from the southwest and occasionally south in the afternoon until evening; in the early morning there is often a northerly.

Like the *meltemi* in the Aegean, the *meltem* along the Turkish coast blows hard in July and August when it can at times reach Force 7. It blows less frequently and with less force in June and September.

LOCAL NAMES FOR THE WINDS
Imbat the name for the *meltem* in the Gulf of Izmir.

The winds are named from the cardinal points of the compass: *Yildiz* (pole star) — north; *Poyraz* — northeast; *Gündoğuşu* — east; *Keşiļleme* — southeast; *Kible* (towards Mecca) — south; *Lodos* — southwest; *Bati (Günbatişi)* — west; *Karayel* — northwest.

GALES   These are rare in the summer. In the winter they blow most frequently from the south and average about two a month and in the spring and autumn gales are usually from the south. In the northern Aegean and the Sea of Marmara gales often blow from the north. In the spring the incidence of gales drops off rapidly after March.

See the Coptic calendar Appendix III for gale predictions.

THUNDERSTORMS   Occur occasionally in the summer and more often in the spring and autumn, they are accompanied by heavy rain and a strong squall, but are over quickly, usually in an hour or less.

TIDES AND CURRENTS   The tidal range at springs does not exceed 0.5 metre and is mostly less than 0.3 metre, it is easily cancelled by a moderate breeze. Strong currents flow down the Bosphorus and the Dardanelles to the Aegean and in the narrow parts of the channel may reach four or five knots. If you are contemplating a trip through the Dardanelles and the Bosphorus, I strongly recommend Admiralty charts nos. 2429 (Dardanelles) and 1198 (Bosphorus) which show the direction and strength of the currents in the channels. In the channel between Samos and Turkey there is an east going current of two or three knots for a short stretch.

WEATHER FORECASTS   In the summer, daily weather forecasts are posted in the Turizm Bank marinas. Otherwise listen to the Greek weather forecasts for the Aegean and Mediterranean. See Greece page 142.

Most coast radio stations broadcast on VHF Ch 67 in Turkish and English at 0900, 1200, 1500, 2100 local time. They are repeated 3 times at 5 minute intervals.

HARBOURS AND ANCHORAGES

WHAT TO EXPECT   There are nine marinas in Turkey with several more under construction or planned for the future. The marinas are at: Fenerbaçhe and Ataköy, (close to Istanbul), Golden Dolphin marina near Çesme, Sigaçik, Kusadasi, Bodrum, Marmaris and Antalya. A large marina is planned for Fethiye. In the Gulf of Gülluk it is planned to build a large marina and holiday village near Güvercinlik. A number of other marinas are planned for the future: at Ayvalik, Datça, Göçek and Kas, though it is likely to be some time before they are completed.

SECURITY   The Turks are honest and it is highly unlikely that anything will be stolen from your boat. However in the cities and tourist resorts normal precautions should be taken.

Ayvalik

WINTERING AFLOAT Kusadasi, Bodrum, Marmaris and Kemer are the favourites for wintering afloat. A number of yachts have reported enjoyable winters in Ayvalik (a bit chilly), Bozburun, Fethiye and Antalya.

PASSAGE PLANNING

GENERAL As the prevailing northerlies become progressively stronger throughout the summer until August, yacht skippers cruising northwards usually do so in the spring when the winds are not as strong and consistent and then head south and east in the summer.

SPECIFIC Yachts on passage to Cyprus from the Aegean generally head there directly taking advantage of the prevailing northerlies and westerlies. From Antalya/Anamur a yacht leaving in the late afternoon will have a good westerly for the passage to Cyprus which will later be replaced by the night breeze thus giving it the chance of a fast passage. Returning from Cyprus a yacht will usually work its way up the Turkish coast to avoid a long tedious beat into the prevailing winds.

CHARTERING The two main charter boat bases are Bodrum and Marmaris but charter boats also operate from Kuşadasi and Fethiye. Charter boats operate almost exclusively in the area between Kuşadasi and Fethiye but as the charter fleets expand it is likely that they will explore further afield.

NAVIGATION AIDS

Buoyage Buoyage is neither developed nor consistent. The Turkish government has accepted in principle the I.A.L.A. System 'A' but no date has been given for its implementation. The old system uses a black conical buoy on the starboard side of the channel and a red can buoy on the port side.

Cineviz Liman. A spectacular anchorage on the Lycian coast.

Lights The coast is well lit around commercial harbours but elsewhere lighting is poor. Turkish lights, even major ones, are not always to be relied upon.

Radiobeacons The beacons on the Greek islands nearby are also useful.

Antalya YT 302 kHz 50M 36°53'N 30°47'.5E
Tekirdag EKI 360 kHz 50M 40°57'.13N 27°25'.57E
Istanbul/Ataturk TOP 370 kHz 50M 41°01'N 28°54'.5E
Yalova YAA 305 kHz 75M 41°35'N 29°22'.3E
Bozburun BOZ 412 kHz 40°31'.3N 28°50'E
Bandirma BDM 450 kHz 75M 40°18'N 27°58'E
Biga BIG 428 kHz 40°16'.5N 27°21'.5E
Izmir CIG 363 kHz 75M 38°31'.5N 27°01'.1E
Izmir/Cumaovasi KAD 330 kHz 70M 38°24'.9N 27°08'.8E
Muğla/Dalaman DAL 346 kHz 36°42'.7N 28°46'.7E
Finike FR 303.4 seq. 3, 4 300M 36°16'.8N 30°09'.5E

Coast radio stations Unless otherwise stated services are 24 hour.
The Turizm Bank marinas and the Golden Dolphin marina listen out on VHF Channels 11, 12, 16. English spoken.
Main operating frequencies are shown in bold type.
All times are GMT.
All stations offer a 24 hour service unless otherwise stated.
The marinas listen out on VHF channels 11, 12, 16. English spoken.

Station	Transmits (kHz or VHF Channel)	Listens (kHz or VHF Channel)	Traffic Lists (Freq. & times)
Istanbul (TAH)	2182, **2670,** VHF Ch. 16, 26, 28	2182	2670 ev. H + 5 and + 35

Camlica (TAA 2) Controlled from Istanbul	VHF Ch. 16, 26, 28		0900-1700
Bandirma (TAA 4)	VHF Ch. 16, 03, 24		
Çanakkale (TAT)	1850, 2182 VHF Ch. 16, 1, 4, 25	2182	
Ayvalik (TAE 2)	VHF Ch. 16, 7, 28		
Izmir (TAN)	1850, 2182, 2760 VHF Ch. 16, 4, 24	2182	
Kuşadasi (TAE 3)	VHF Ch. 16, 3, 26		0800-2400
Bodrum (TAE 5)	VHF Ch. 16, 3, 26		0800-2400
Marmaris (TAE 4)	VHF Ch. 16, 4, 23		0800-2400
Datça (TAE 7)	VHF Ch. 16, 5, 27		
Fethiye (TAE 6)	VHF Ch. 16, 25, 28		
Antalya (TAL)	2182, 2693 VHF Ch. 16, 25, 27	2182	
Alanya (TAC 4)	VHF Ch. 16, 25, 27		
Anamur (TAC 6)	VHF Ch. 16, 23, 26		0800-2400
Mersin (TAM)	2182, 2820 VHF Ch. 16, 24, 28	2182	
Iskenderun (TAI)	2182, 2629, 3648 VHF Ch. 16, 26, 27	2182	
Taşucu (TAC 5)	VHF Ch. 16, 2, 3		0800-2400
Kaş (TAC 2)	VHF Ch. 16, 2, 25		
Finike (TAC 3)	VHF Ch. 16, 23, 27		

RESCUE SERVICES In the bigger harbours patrol boats of the Turkish navy (*Sahil Güvenlik*) are stationed. They are easily recognised by their livery of cream with two diagonal orange stripes on the hull. These boats will answer any distress calls as well as patrolling the coastal waters. Most of the radio operators on board speak English.

FORMALITIES

ENTRY FORMALITIES A yacht entering Turkey must go to a port of entry where the necessary officials for clearing a yacht in are stationed. The officials are normally seen in the following order, although this may vary in some ports: passport police, customs, health, and harbourmaster.

The passport police will stamp you in for a three month period. Customs may want to come aboard your yacht to search it, but this is usually a cursory procedure. The health authority will get you to fill in a form and no documents are required. The harbourmaster will make a moderate charge for light maintenance and harbour dues.

In 1984 a Transit Log was introduced to replace the cumbersome collection of papers previously required. The Transit Log cost US $20 in 1988 but the charge can be reviewed for each year. The Transit Log is valid for one year except in the circumstances outlined below. At your first port of call you are required to list your itinerary in the Transit Log. If you alter your itinerary there is a section in the log that you must fill out. At any subsequent ports of call the customs will want to inspect your log and you may be asked for another installment of light dues. Between ports of call where customs officers are stationed the coastguard (*Sahil Güvenlik*) may check your papers.

In recent years there have been numerous amendments to the laws governing private yachts in Turkey. The most important of these concerns taking on friends or new crew, which is now limited to two periods of ten days or one of twenty in any one year. When you do this a new Transit Log must be purchased and should you exceed this limit you will be treated as a charter boat and subject to a fee. This new law, designed to stop unregistered foreign yachts chartering in Turkey, has unfortunately made it difficult for private yachts to have friends and relatives on board except for the two ten day or twenty day period stipulated. In the future there may be some correction to this overly restrictive ruling on private yachts.

When leaving Turkey permanently you must surrender your Transit Log. Although a yacht can remain in Turkey for two years, renewable to five, you cannot remain longer than three months at any one time. In practice you simply nip across to Greece on your yacht or by ferry for the day and on your return you will automatically be given another three months.

PORTS OF ENTRY Istanbul, Bandirma, Çanakkale, Ayvalik, Dikili, Izmir, Çeşme, Kuşadasi, Bodrum, Marmaris, Fethiye, Kaş, Finike, Kemer, Antalya, Tasucu, Mersin and Iskenderun.

DOCUMENTS The Small Ship's Register Papers or full registration papers are both acceptable. Insurance papers should be carried although they are rarely asked for. A certificate of competency is almost never asked for. A ship's stamp is invaluable and is often asked for on crew lists, etc.

TAXES Apart from a modest charge for light dues the only tax levied on foreign yachts is the cost of the Transit Log. Berthing and service fees are of course made in the marinas.

FACILITIES

EVERYDAY
Water Is potable from most taps but treat water from cisterns and wells with caution even if the locals use it. In many places you will have to carry water by jerry can.
Fuel Is available in the towns and larger villages but you will often have to carry it by jerry cans.
Electricity Available in the marinas. Elsewhere you will have to rely on generating it yourself.

A Sarcophagus at Kale Köy in Southern Turkey.

Gas Local gas is widely available. *Camping gaz* is available in some places.

Paraffin Widely available in the towns and cities, usually from a pump at a petrol station. Methylated spirits is available from grocery and hardware shops.

BOAT REPAIRS

Engines Spares for a few of the major marine engines: B.M.C. which are assembled in Izmir, Volvo, Perkins, Ford and Mercedes but do not rely on getting spares. What they do not have they will make if it is humanly possible as there are competent mechanics and engineers in the towns and cities.

Electrics Competent auto-electricians in the towns and cities. Electronic repair facilities are limited.

Navigation instruments Spares and new equipment are scarce.

Paints and antifouling Yacht quality paint and antifouling is manufactured in Turkey, including polyurethanes and epoxies. Yacht paints are also imported but are expensive. The antifouling and two component paints made in Izmir under the *Transocean* brand are good quality and comparatively cheap.

Hauling There are travel hoists at Kuşadasi, Bodrum, in several of the yards outside Bodrum, and at Kemer. There are other yards that use a cradle and skids. Hauling and storage fees are often expensive and the facilities poor.

Engineering Good engineering shops that will make almost anything can be found in the cities and towns. Costs are generally cheap.

Wood and GRP Woodwork skills are not developed although the end result may look alright. Hardwoods are impossible to find and the softwoods are of poor quality. GRP skills are low.

DUTY FREE SPARES The position at the moment is confused. Spares and boat gear can in theory be imported on a duty free basis to a yacht in transit but in practice it means a lot of bother and delay. You may be asked to put up a bond equal to the value of the item(s) imported which will be repaid in Turkish lire when it has been put onto your yacht. You may also have to pay for the services of a customs officer to accompany the item from the customs store to the yacht. In some cases it has been necessary to oil the whole process with a little baksheesh but I cannot recommend this — it is a canker that spreads all too quickly.

PROVISIONING

GENERAL In all but the smallest villages basic provisions can be found and fresh produce is excellent. Imported goods can be found in the large towns and tourist centres. Luxury goods made in Turkey (including paper towels, toilet paper, long-life milk, hard cheeses, salad dressing, etc.) can be difficult to find away from the tourist centres.

In the larger villages and towns there is a market day once a week when all manner of fresh produce, fruit and vegetables, dried fruit and nuts, poultry, cheese, herbs and spices, staples, are brought from the surrounding countryside for sale. The quality of the produce, especially the fruit and vegetables, would be hard to better in the Mediterranean region. Turkey is known as the market garden of Europe for a good reason.

Shopping hours vary somewhat but generally are 0830-1530 and 1600-1930 Monday-Saturday. Some shops will open on Sundays.

Market day

SPECIFIC

Meat Is reasonably priced and it is always fresh. It is not hung and is butchered in a haphazard fashion so that it is difficult to know what part of the carcass you are getting. Being a Moslem country, pork is not commonly for sale although wild boar is occasionally available.

Fish Is abundant and reasonably priced except for crayfish and prawns which are expensive.

Fruit and vegetables Excellent throughout the year and cheap.

Staples Most basics can be found although some items such as rice tend to be of poor quality.

Cheese Local soft cheeses are cheap and good, hard cheeses (cheddar types) and processed cheeses made in Turkey (mostly by Pinar) are adequate and reasonably priced.

Canned goods Limited mostly to fruit and vegetables.

Coffee and tea Instant coffee is not readily available and is hideously expensive. Local coffee is mediocre and not cheap. Local tea doesn't make a British cuppa but is quite palatable. Drink it Turkish style, strong, black and sweet.

Wines, beer and spirits Local wines are quite palatable and some of the more expensive wines are good. On the whole they are not consistent. Local beer is of the lager type, cheap and eminently drinkable. The local spirit, the aniseed flavoured *raki*, is moderately priced and lethal. Imported spirits, if you can find them, are expensive.

Recommended Dried fruit, nuts, fruit juices, local tea, some wines.

EATING OUT The Turks eat better than anyone else in the eastern Mediterranean. The food in the restaurants is not only tasty and varied but is served with care and attention and it is cheap to eat out.

The cuisine is characterised by grilled or broiled meats and stews of meat and vegetables. Starters are usually cold and often include cold cooked vegetables, (cauliflower, beetroot and spinach being common, steeped in vinaigrette sauce). Vegetable oil (sunflower, cotton) is used for salads and cooking so that food does not have the thick oily taste of the olive oil used elsewhere.

Prices vary from very cheap to reasonable, even those on a tight budget will be able to find a small restaurant to suit their finances. In the more expensive restaurants I have had meals that would not disgrace a moderately priced London restaurant but at less than half the price. The Turks are

beer and *raki* drinkers so you may find the choice of wines limited – otherwise you will eat and drink well for little.

For starters try the cold vegetables, *boreç* (flakey pastry rolls stuffed with cheese and deep fried), yoghurt dishes (with garlic, chopped spinach, aubergine, etc), stuffed vine leaves, bean salads (with chopped vegetables in a vinaigrette sauce), Russian (potato) salad and peppery tomato and garlic purée dips.

For the main course you will most likely be offered charcoal grilled kebabs, steak, chops, liver and kidney. Fish is usually offered grilled and occasionally as kebabs (tuna and swordfish in season). *Doner kebap* consists of slices of lamb roasted on a vertical spit and served on a bed of rice and yoghurt. Stuffed vegetables, commonly tomatoes and greenpeppers, are usually served cold but may be heated up for you. Various stews of lamb or beef with vegetables are usually made for the midday meal but may be served in the evening. Variations on these basic meals are many and in the more sophisticated restaurants you may be lucky enough to encounter delicious dishes such as breadcrumbed steak stuffed with cheese and tomato, Circassian chicken (croquettes with herbs and pounded walnuts), fish salads and fish stews.

A carpet loom.

Desserts are simple but delicious affairs of fresh fruit, sometimes with chopped walnuts and steeped in honey. For pastries you must go to a pastry shop. Coffee is of the Turkish type, strong, thick and sweet, with the grounds in the cup.

In most towns and resorts you will find sandwich shops. The sandwich is half a large loaf of bread stuffed with a variety of fillings (you choose) and flattened on a hot plate so that you can fit it in your mouth. A cheap and filling snack.

CHARTS AND PILOTS

Admiralty *Mediterranean Pilot* Vol. IV (NP48). Covers the Aegean.

Admiralty *Mediterranean Pilot* Vol. V (NP49). Covers the Mediterranean coast of Turkey.

Admiralty *Black Sea Pilot* (NP24). Covers the Dardanelles, Sea of Marmara and Black Sea coasts.

Admiralty *List of Lights and Fog Signals* Vol. E (NP78).

Turkish Waters Pilot. Rod Heikell. Imray. Covers the Sea of Marmara, Aegean coast and Mediterranean coast.

A Pocket Guide to the Southeast Aegean. Rod Heikell and Mike Harper. Imray. A useful guide to Turkey and the Dodecanese.

The Ionian Islands to the Anatolian Coast. H. M. Denham. John Murray. Covers the Turkish coast from Marmaris to the Syrian border.

The Aegean. H. M. Denham. John Murray. Covers the Sea of Marmara and the Aegean coast. Interesting guides, particularly on naval history, although a little dated now.

Charts The Admiralty charts for the area are adequate if sometimes out of date. The Admiralty harbour plans are not worth purchasing. There are good and reasonably priced Turkish charts available from the Turkish hydrographer's office in Çübük, a suburb on the Asiatic side of Istanbul, and at Kuşadasi and Bodrum marinas.

USEFUL BOOKS

Discovering Turkey. Andrew Mango. Batsford. Excellent and readable introduction to the Turks and Turkey.

Collins *Companion Guide to Turkey*. John Freely. Good guide to sites and places.

Turkey Observed. R. P. Lister. Rambling readable account of a journey through Turkey.

Aegean Turkey; Turkey's Southern Shore; Turkey Beyond the Meander; Lycia. George Bean. Benn. The definitive guides to the Graeco-Roman sites.

Memed, My Hawk; Anatolian Tales. Yashar Kemal. Turkey's most celebrated modern novelist.

Turkey: A Short History. R. H. Davidson.

Turkey's Turquoise Coast. Rod Heikell. NET. A general guide to the coastal region between Bodrum and Kekova.

'Carpet mister?'!

Cyprus

Area   3572 square miles

Population   About 500,000 in the south/ 150,000 in the north

Language   Greek in the south/Turkish in the north

Religion   Greek Orthodox in the south/Islam in the north

Time zone   G.M.T. + 3

Currency   Cypriot pound (£) in the south/Turkish lira in the north

Banks   Eurocheques, credit cards and travellers' cheques accepted in the south. Banking facilities are highly developed in the south with offices for Barclays, Co-op, Grindlays and Lombard.

Mail   Reliable. Send it to Larnaca marina in the south

Medical   Good in the south. Poor in the north

Internal travel   Buses and taxis in the north and south. Hire cars in the south

International travel   Flights from many European destinations to Larnaca in the south. Regular hydrofoil and ferry connections with Turkey in the north

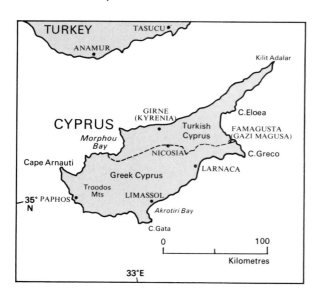

In 1974 Cyprus was partitioned into the unofficial Turkish Federated State of Cyprus (Kibris) in the north and the Republic of Cyprus in the south, the former containing the Turkish population and the south the Greek population. A United Nations peace-keeping force observes the border between northern and southern Cyprus. The partition of Cyprus has effectively made it into two countries and introduced regulations governing passage bet-

ween the north and south and prohibiting landing in certain areas. The following regulations should be studied carefully:

1. A yacht may cross from Turkey to Turkish Cyprus or to Greek Cyprus and vice versa.
2. A yacht cannot proceed from Turkish Cyprus to Greek Cyprus.
3. The government in Greek Cyprus considers any visit by a yacht to Turkish Cyprus to be illegal. It should be pointed out that under the United Nations Resolution 34/30 (1979) and 37/253 (1983) that the United Nations views the Government of Cyprus (i.e. Greek Cyprus) as the legal government of all of Cyprus. If a yacht does visit Turkish Cyprus and then goes to Greek Cyprus, it can incur heavy penalties. Under the laws of the Republic of Cyprus a fine of up to 10,000 Cyprus pounds and/or up to six months imprisonment can be imposed. You have been warned!

A Turkish Cypriot stamp in your passport can mean you will not be allowed into Greece.

The following areas are prohibited for yachts: Turkish Cyprus: In effect the extent of the prohibited areas means that only Girne (Kyrenia) and Famagusta (Gazi Magusa) are available to yachts.

The prohibited areas are as follows:

i. In the vicinity of Famagusta to the border with Greek Cyprus except for the port itself.
ii. The eastern side of the island from Famagusta to Klidhes Island (Kilit Adalar).
iii. From Klidhes Island to 12 miles east of Girne.
iv. From a point 4 miles east of Girne to a point 8 miles east of Girne.
v. In the vicinity of Glykotissa or Snake Island.
vi. From Cape Kormakiti (Koruçam Burnu) to the border in the west.

GEOGRAPHY

ISLAND   Cyprus is the third largest island in the Mediterranean with about 400 miles of coastline; despite its size it has few indentations and no safe natural anchorages, all of the harbours affording good shelter being man-made. The island has two high mountain ranges: the Kyrenia and Karpas mountains (Beşparmak Dağlari) running approximately west to east along the north coast; and the Troodos mountains in the west with Mt Olympus rising to 1922m (6406ft).

CRUISING AREAS   Cyprus is an island that yachtsmen visit rather than one they cruise around. In the north the prohibited areas effectively mean that only Girne (Kyrenia) and Famagusta are available to yachts and of these only Girne warrants a visit. In the south most yachts make for Limassol or Larnaca marina stopping at Paphos en route.

CLIMATE AND WEATHER

The climate is close to the north African type with hot dry summers and mild winters. The summers can be very hot and the humidity in July and August is oppressive. The mild winters make Cyprus a popular place to winter. Snow falls on the mountains in December and lasts until March and skiing there is reported to be good.

WINDS The prevailing summer wind is a westerly which gets up about midday, blows between Force 3-6 (it is strongest in July and August) and dies down at sunset. Away from the coast the wind is west to southwest but closer in, it tends to follow the contours of the coast so that at Larnaca it blows from south-southwest to south. Yachts going west usually leave at night and motor as far as possible until the wind gets up in the morning. From Larnaca a yacht will leave at night for Limassol or Paphos and then depart from there to Greece or Turkey.

In winter winds are divided almost equally between west and east on both the north and south coasts. Gales are frequent from the south or east during the winter (see the Coptic calendar in appendix III) but are rare in the summer.

FOG Sea fog occurs along the south coast in the summer. It appears in the early morning when visibility can be less than a quarter of a mile, but has usually dispersed by midday. This fog does not extend out to sea being usually less than one mile offshore, it is most dense around Limassol (in Akrotiri Bay), Larnaca (in Larnaca Bay) and in Famagusta. It seldom occurs on the north coast.

WEATHER FORECASTS A weather forecast is transmitted on the Armed Forces Radio on 1439 kHz (208m) and 1421 kHz (211m) after the news at 0600, 0700, 0800, 1300, 2000, 2200. It is not a maritime forecast and is generally of little use.

NAVIGATION AIDS

The high mountains of Cyprus can be seen from the Turkish coast on a clear day and there should be no difficulty identifying the island. It is also moderately well lit by night.

On the south coast shoal water extends some distance off in places — the reef off Cape Kiti in the approaches to Larnaca is a renowned yacht trap.

Radiobeacons
Two radiobeacons are useful when approaching the south coast:
Paphos PHA 328 kHz 100M 34°43′.1N 32°28′.6E
Akrotiri AK 363 kHz 120M ⟨34°34′.6N 32°58′.3E
Dhekelia DKA 343 kHz 50M 34°59′N 33°44′E
Larnaca LCA 267 kHz 150M 34°49′.3N 33°33′.3E

Radio
Larnaca marina listens out on HF as follows:
HF Maritime Mobile Net. Call sign: 584MM Operator: Glafkos
0830-0900   7.040 MHz   working.
0900-1000 14.313 MHz

1000-1015 21.380 MHz   listening
1015-1030 28.666 MHz
Everyday except Friday and Sunday. Schedules may change. Times are G.M.T.

FORMALITIES

ENTRY FORMALITIES Entry formalities in northern Cyprus are similar to those in Turkey. The relevant officials will come to your yacht in Girne.

In southern Cyprus you can enter in Paphos, Limassol or Larnaca. Customs and immigration authorities will come to your yacht to carry out the paperwork and stamp you in.

DOCUMENTS The R.Y.A. Small Ship's Register Papers or full registration papers are accepted.

TAXES Marina fees only are payable.

There exists a 1977 law regarding taxing yachts that stay longer than one cumulative year in Cyprus at 3.5% of the value of the yacht. Although it has never been implemented, there remains the possibility it could be applied in the future.

FACILITIES

In general there are few facilities for yachts in the north. In the south, Larnaca marina where there is a waiting list for berths has been a favourite with yachtsmen wintering afloat for some time and consequently service facilities there are good. The new Limassol Sheraton marina some 6 miles E of Limassol will help to relieve the crowding at Larnaca. The following facilities are to be found:

BOAT REPAIRS
Engines Good mechanics in Larnaca and Limassol. Some spares for the major makes of

marine engines can be found. Most spares can be imported by a local agent.

Electrics and electronics Electrical and electronic workshops in Larnaca and Limassol. Most spares for electronic equipment must be imported.

Water At every berth. However water is scarce throughout Cyprus and is only turned on for three days of the week in the summer.

Fuel At the quay.

Electricity At every berth.

Gas *Camping gaz* available. Gas bottles of most types can be refilled.

Paraffin Can be obtained.

Navigation instruments Some spares available but most must be imported.

Paints and antifoulings Imported paints and antifoulings are available but they are expensive. Local paint and antifouling is considerably cheaper.

Hauling A 40 ton travel hoist and hard standing within the marina.

Engineering Most engineering facilities in Larnaca or Limassol.

Wood and GRP Basic wood repairs. GRP boats are built in Limassol.

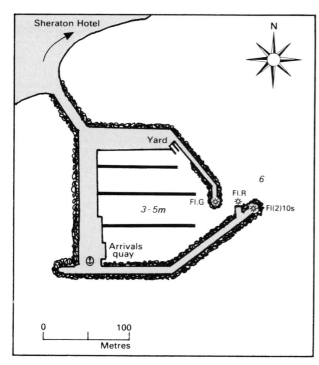

Limassol Sheraton Marina 34°42′N 33°11′E

Note Although Limassol marina has good facilities, it suffers from being some distance from Limassol town itself and hence you cannot pop into the local hardware or grocery shop without a journey into town. At Larnaca the town and facilities are right behind the marina.

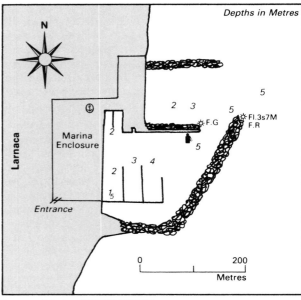

Larnaca Marina 34°55′N 33°38′E

DUTY FREE SPARES Yacht spares can be imported into southern Cyprus on a duty free basis. Generally there are few problems getting them through customs although it will take a little time. This is one of the better places in the eastern Mediterranean to get duty free goods into.

PROVISIONING

GENERAL In northern Cyprus you can find the basics but there is little choice and few imported goods. Fresh produce in the north is excellent and cheap. In southern Cyprus you can find many items not readily available elsewhere in the eastern Mediterranean as the British presence at Akrotiri and Dhekelia means that the local supermarkets are full of all sorts of home goodies: Marmite, HP sauce, Branston pickle, After Eight mints, salad dressings and spreads of all varieties, indeed many familiar things you thought you had left behind. Many charter boats come here especially to stock up for the summer, prices are neither cheap nor overly expensive. Cypriot wines are justly praised and are excellent value.

EATING OUT The local cuisine in northern Cyprus is typically Turkish. In southern Cyprus the cuisine is typically Greek although in the tourist resorts it tends to a bland international cuisine. Cypriot *mezes* are famous and are rather more elaborate affairs than those found elsewhere. You can have a variety of *mezes* at some restaurants and this makes a satisfying meal but by eastern Mediterranean standards, eating out in southern Cyprus is costly.

PILOTS AND CHARTS

Admiralty *Mediterranean Pilot* Vol V. (NP49). Covers Cyprus but the description of the south coast is much out of date owing to the increase in population and building there since 1974.
Admiralty *List of Lights and Fog Signals* Vol. E (NP78).
Turkish Waters Pilot Rod Heikell. Imray. Covers Northern and Southern Cyprus.
The Ionian Islands to the Anatolian Coast. H. M. Denham. John Murray. Includes Cyprus.

USEFUL BOOKS

Bitter Lemons. Lawrence Durrell. Faber. Sympathetic account of Cyprus pre-1974.
Blue Guide to Cyprus. Black.

Syria

Area 185,180 square kilometres (71,498 square miles).

Population 9,600,000

Capital Damascus (1,042,000)

Language Arabic. Some French spoken

Religion Islam

Time zone G.M.T. + 2

Currency Syrian pound (S£) = 100 piastres

Electricity 110V AC

Internal travel Buses run to most destinations and are cheap

International travel International flights to Damascus

With the continuing tensions in the Middle East few yachts visit Syria. A visa must be obtained in advance and this can take a considerable amount of time if it is granted at all. Visas will not be granted to Israelis, Jews, nor to anyone with an Israeli stamp in their passport. Holders of American passports have difficulty getting visas.

The Syrian coast is one long sandy beach except for a short stretch at the northern end. There are no natural harbours and few man made ones. H. M. Denham lists the following harbours and anchorages in *Southern Turkey, the Levant and Cyprus*: Bassite Bay, Latakia, Baniyas, Tartous and Ruad.

Although the coast offers little to the cruising man, the interior has a wealth of ancient monuments and ruins including the remarkable Crusader castle, Krak des Chevaliers. Syria stands at the crossroads of western civilisation, at the point where the West meets the Middle East with Damascus said to be the oldest continuously inhabited city in the world. If you wish to visit the interior then I suggest this is best accomplished by leaving your yacht in Turkey or Cyprus and travelling there by other means although an intrepid few have cruised successfully along the coast.

Lebanon

Area   10,399 square kilometres (4,015 square miles)

Population   2,600,000

Capital   Beirut

Language   Arabic. Some French and English spoken

Religion   Islam and Christian

Time zone   G.M.T. + 2

Currency   Lebanese pound (L£) = 100 piastres

Electricity   220 and 110V AC

Internal travel   Restricted at present

International travel   Flights to Beirut when the airport is open

At the time of writing Lebanon, having been engulfed by bloody civil war and occupied by neighbouring Syria and Israel, is quite simply an unsafe country to visit. Even should you desire to visit Lebanon for some inconceivable reason, visas are not being issued and should you stray into Lebanese waters you will be apprehended by a patrol boat Israeli, or otherwise.

If problems are resolved and restrictions lifted the following harbours are listed by H. M. Denham although it is likely that the war has severely damaged many of them: Tripoli commercial harbour, Byblos, Jounieh marina, Beirut commercial harbour, Sidon anchorage and Tyre.

Recently a yacht visited Jounieh marina eight miles north of Beirut. The first week there is free and not surprisingly there are numerous empty berths. Electricity, water, and fuel are available and there is good shopping nearby in Jounieh. Despite this report I would not advise a visit to Jounieh in the current state of the bloody civil war being waged in nearby Beirut and its environs.

Israel

Area   20,702 square kilometres (7200 square miles).

Population   4,100,000

Capital   Jerusalem (366,300)

Language   Hebrew, Arabic, English. Some French and German spoken.

Religion   Judaism.

Time zone   G.M.T. + 2.

Currency   Shekel.

Electricity   220V AC

Banks   Open 0830-1230 Sunday-Friday also 1600-1800 Sunday, Tuesday. (Remember Saturday is the day of rest.) Eurocheques, credit cards and travellers' cheques accepted.

Mail   Reliable. Send to *Poste restante*/the marina at Tel Aviv P.O.B. 16285 or the yacht club at Haifa.

Medical   Very good. Hospitals in Tel Aviv, Haifa, Jerusalem, Beer Sheva, and Eilat. Private treatment is expensive.

Internal travel   Israel's internal airline, Arkia, links the major cities. There are only limited rail links. Buses to most destinations. Organised coach tours are good value. Hire cars.

International travel   Flights to major European airports from Tel Aviv. Ferries to Cyprus, Piraeus and Genoa.

GEOGRAPHY

THE COAST   The coastline is a long straight strip of low-lying sand and shingle with no indentations forming natural harbours. In recent years a number of marinas have been built along the coast. Most yachts visit perhaps one or two places in Israel, staying in one harbour and taking trips inland to the numerous historical sites.

CLIMATE AND WEATHER

Summers are hot and humid. The winters are warm although temperatures plummet at night.

The predominant winds are westerlies mostly from west-southwest. This sea breeze gets up about midday and blows until dusk.

HARBOURS

Most yachts make for Haifa or Tel Aviv and clear in there. As well as Haifa and Tel Aviv there are small marinas at Acre (Akko) and Jaffa. At Tel Aviv and Jaffa the harbourmaster will send a boat out to guide you in should you need assistance. Details and plans of Tel Aviv, Acre, and Jaffa are included here.

NAVIGATION AIDS

Buoyage   I.A.L.A. System 'A' yet to be agreed upon.

Lights   The coast is adequately lit.

All operate continuously.
Marine radiobeacon
Haifa HA 287.3 kHz 75M 32°49′.69N 34°58′.07E
(Note: HA x3 16.5 sec and then long continuous for 25 sec.)

Air radiobeacons
Haifa HFA 317 kHz 100M 32°43′.5N 35°02′.2E
Ramat David RMD 368 kHz 250M 32°39′.5N 35°02′.2E
Herzlia HRZ 250 kHz 100M 32°10′.5N 34°49′.4E
Tel Aviv LL 331 kHz 100M 32°03′.5N 34°45′.1E
Ben Gurion BGN 380 kHz 100M 32°01′.2N 34°53′.5E
Askelon AKE 245 kHz 250M 31°39′N 34°34′E
Eilat ELT 345 kHz 100M 29°30′.1N 34°55′E

Radio stations

Haifa transmits on 2182, **2649**, 3656 kHz
Police boats listen in on 2182 kHz

VHF transmissions (all 24 hour unless otherwise stated)
Haifa Port Channels 12, 14, 16. Working channels 12, 14. Call sign *Haifa point (Tatzpit Haifa)*
Ashdod Port Channels 14, 16. Working channels 12, 14. Call sign *Ashdod point (Tatzpit Ashdod)*
Tel Aviv Marina Channel 16. Working channel 11. Call sign *Marina Tel Aviv.*
Hadera Port Channel 10, 16. Working channel 10. Call sign *Hadera.*
Acre (Akko) Marina 0800-1800 channel 16. Working channel 11. Call sign *Marina Akko.*
Lido Kinneret Beach 0700-2000 channel 16. Working channel 11. Call sign *Lido Tiberias.*
Ashkelon Tanker Port Channels 12, 13, 16. Working channels 12, 13. Call sign *Delek* (Petrol).
Eilat Port Channels 14, 16. Call sign *Yamit.*

Police boats listen in on channel 16.
The Israeli navy listens in on channel 16.

FORMALITIES

As a yacht approaches Israeli waters it may be met by a fast patrol boat and details will be requested: your country of registration, where you are from, where you are bound, and the names and nationalities of those on board. At night this encounter can be frightening: a powerful searchlight trained on your yacht will often be the first warning of the patrol boat's presence. Upon arrival you will be met by the customs and immigration police. If you intend going to any of the Middle East countries at any time ask the immigration police not to stamp your passport, as many countries do not allow visitors with an Israeli stamp in their passport into the country. You will then be issued with a separate page with an immigration stamp on it.

The Israeli Navy listens in 24 hours a day on VHF channel 16. They can be contacted on this channel to advise of your entry into Israeli territorial waters. Call sign: *Israeli Navy.*

The police patrol boats listen in on 2182 kHz and on VHF Ch 16. On approaching Haifa or Tel Aviv you can call them on this channel.

FACILITIES

Water and fuel can be obtained at Haifa and Tel Aviv. Local gas and *Camping gaz* can be supplied. New boat gear and spares are extremely expensive in Israel, local yachts go to Cyprus or Greece to buy gear. Engineering and mechanical repairs can be carried out and woodwork and GRP work at Tel Aviv.

PROVISIONING

GENERAL   There are large supermarkets in Haifa and Tel Aviv where just about anything can be found. In the past Israel had a horrendous inflation rate, some 1000% in 1984, but it is now reported to be around 20% (1989). In Tel Aviv fruit and vegetables are best bought at the Carmel market and for groceries go well beyond the waterfront shops and the Atarim complex to the more modestly priced shops further into the city.

EATING OUT   There are excellent restaurants everywhere and whether kosher or not, the food is invariably delicious though expensive as, again, inflation means that prices are high for the eastern Mediterranean and you may well end up eating in snack bars if you are on a tight budget. In Haifa and Tel Aviv there is an international array of restaurants, including the cuisine of just about every country in Europe, reflecting the diverse origins of the Israelis. At the snack bar level *felafels* and *shwarmas* are traditional snacks. A *felafel* is pitta bread stuffed with deep fried ground chick peas and salad and pickles with a sauce, the latter sometimes hot. A *shwarma* is much the same but with lamb or turkey substituted for the chick peas.

CHARTS AND PILOTS

Admiralty *Mediterranean Pilot* Vol. V (NP49). Covers Israel.
Admiralty *List of Lights and Fog Signals* Vol.E (NP78).
Southern Turkey, the Levant and Cyprus. H. M. Denham. John Murray. Out of print.
Admiralty charts cover the coast and Haifa adequately.

USEFUL BOOKS

Fodors Guide to Israel. Hodder and Stoughton.
Blue Guide to Israel. Black.

HAIFA

Approach Two power station chimneys are conspicuous and aligning these brings you into the harbour.

Mooring The Carmel Yacht Club at the mouth of the Kishon River has berths for around 70 boats as well as an inner fishing harbour.

Facilities Water and electricity. Fuel can be arranged. Some repair facilities.

General Haifa Port, the commercial port, is not recommended for use by yachts and a visitor should make for the yacht club.

TEL AVIV

Approach The skyscrapers of the city and a tall column are conspicuous from the distance. The approach can be difficult with strong onshore winds and dangerous with an onshore gale. The marina will send a boat out to guide you in if you call up on VHF channel 16. The service is free. A night approach should not be made. The entrance was dredged to 3 metres in 1989 making the final approach and entry into the harbour safer than in the past.

Mooring Secure to the outside jetty or where directed. Good all-round shelter once inside.

Facilities A port of entry. Water and electricity. Fuel on the quay near the entrance. A crane can haul yachts onto hard standing. Good repair facilities. Chandlers. Good shopping for provisions and numerous restaurants nearby.

General Tel Aviv is the logical harbour to head for in Israel, timing your arrival for daylight hours. There are good facilities here for all travel arrangements for independent trips or organised tours inland; to Jerusalem, the Sea of Galilee, the Dead Sea, the Red Sea, or wherever.

JAFFA

Approach Jaffa lies immediately S of Tel Aviv. The old town is easily identified with the belfry of St Peters Church and the lighthouse

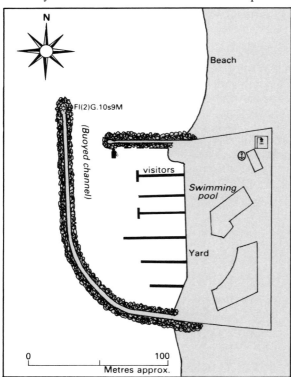

Tel Aviv Marina 32°05′N 34°46′E

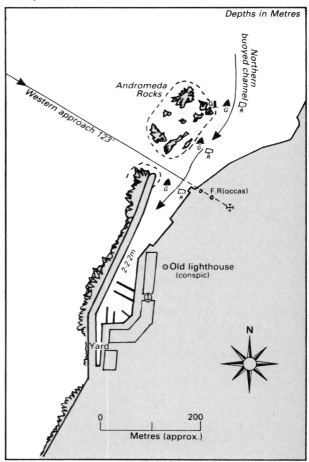

Jaffa Marina 32°03′.3N 34°43′.1E

with red and white bands conspicuous. Care needs to be taken of the Andromeda rocks, a low-lying reef in the entrance to the harbour. Entrance can be made from the N inside Andromeda rocks through a buoyed channel. Alternatively entrance can be made from the W on a bearing of 123° on St Peters Church belfry. Entrance can be difficult in W winds, and with strong onshore winds would be dangerous. Call up the marina office on VHF channel 16 if you have problems and they will send a boat out to guide you in.

Mooring Berth where directed. There are mostly 2.2-2 metre depths inside. The marina is uncomfortable in W-NW winds.

Facilities Water and electricity. Provisions and restaurants nearby in the town.

General The town has an ancient pedigree: it was named after Noah's son Yaphet; from here Jonah set sail for Tarshish in Spain, though the whale prevented him getting there; King Solomon shipped cedar from Lebanon into here; and the Crusaders and Saladin alternately took the city or lost it. The marina is the ancient port, reconstructed after centuries of use. It is still being completed and it is likely there will be improvements in the near future.

AKKO (ACRE)

A small marina to the N of Haifa. With care small to medium sized yachts could call here. At present there are berths for 100 yachts. Water and electricity. Provisions and restaurants nearby. The view and atmosphere at Akko is said to be not unlike a Greek island.

There are plans to lengthen the breakwater in the future which will provide more berths and make the harbour safer.

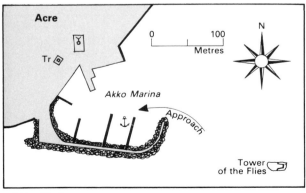

Akko Marina

Egypt

Area   1,000,250 square kilometres (386,200 square miles)

Population   50,000,000

Capital   Cairo 9,000,000

Language   Arabic but English and French are spoken in the cities

Religion   Islam (90%) and Christian (10%), the latter mostly Copts

Time zone   G.M.T. + 2

Currency   Egyptian pound (E£) = 100 piastres

Electricity   220 and 110V AC

Banks   Open 0900-1230 Monday-Thursday and Saturday. 1000-1200 Sunday. Travellers' cheques widely accepted. Credit cards can be used in Cairo and Alexandria

Mail   Generally unreliable. Have your mail sent to the yacht club at Port Said

Medical   Good in Cairo and Alexandria, poor in the country. Treatment can be expensive so make sure you are covered by insurance

Internal travel   Internal flights on Misr Air between Cairo and Luxor and Aswan. Rail travel is cheap and good. Taxis are cheap at the official rates but the meters are always broken. Shared taxis running on set routes are cheap. Buses are invariably overcrowded, often spectacularly so

International travel   Flights to most European destinations from Cairo. Ferries from Alexandria to Cyprus, Piraeus, Ancona, Venice, Naples, Genoa and Marseille

Public holidays
January 1 New Year's Day
February 22 Unity Day
March 8 Revolution Day
May 1 Labour Day
June 18 Republic Day
July 23 Revolution Day
September 1 September Revolution Day
October 6 Armed Forces Day
October 24 Suez Day
December 23 Victory Day
Moveable: First Monday after Coptic, Easter:
Sham-en-Nessim (National Spring Festival)

GEOGRAPHY

THE COAST   The coastline is mostly straight with a bulge where the Nile delta has pushed out into the sea. Most yachts heading for Egypt will be going directly to Port Said to head south down the Suez Canal to the Red Sea, a few will go to Alexandria and an intrepid few have sailed up the Nile, although not without difficulty. Otherwise there is little along the coast to attract yachtsmen although there is much of interest inland.

CLIMATE AND WEATHER

The climate is of the North African type with very hot dry summers and warm dry winters. Rainfall in the winter is low. The summer heat can be oppressive and any wind deposits sand on and in everything.

The prevailing wind is a northerly sea breeze – the direction varying between NW-NE. The *khamsin* can blow off the land with considerable force and reduce visibility drastically. In April the *khamsin* blows regularly and with some violence.

NAVIGATION AIDS

Buoyage   The approaches to Port Said and the canal itself are well marked. The canal is steep-to at the sides but stick to the buoyed channel in the Great Bitter Lakes.

Lights   Both Port Said and Alexandria are well lit but check the characteristics with an up-to-date list of lights.

Air Radiobeacons
El Gora GOR 309 kHz 100M 31°05′N 34°08′E
Port Said PSD 352 kHz 31°17′N 32°14′E
Alexandria AXD 403 kHz 31°11′N 29°57′E
El Daba DBA 415 kHz 31°02′N 28°28′.7E

Radio Stations

Port Said   VHF channels 16 (Harbourmaster), 12 (Pilots), 13 (Inside harbour), 73 (Measurement Office).
Alexandria   VHF channel 16.

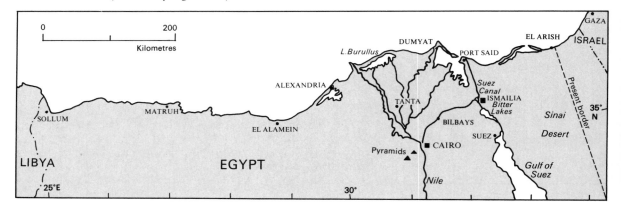

CRUISING IN EGYPT

Sailing in Egypt, either along the Mediterranean or Red Sea coasts, or going through the Suez Canal or up the Nile can be a difficult process. A yacht must clear in at a Port of Entry and then obtain permission to visit other ports. Not all of the Ports of Entry listed by the Egyptian authorities have proved to be actually a Port of Entry in practice. Some harbours and anchorages require special permission before you can visit them and some are prohibited to yachtsmen. The best plan is to try to get some first-hand reports from yachtsmen who have recently been there rather than rely on official information. If you are leaving from Cyprus for Israel and Egypt, you may be able to find someone there who has recently cruised in Egyptian waters to supply up-to-date information.

Yachts heading for the Suez Canal will find things more straightforward though still expect delays and changes to the scheme of things I have outlined below and to the official scale of charges. Yachts intending to go up the Nile will find there are numerous difficulties in obtaining permission, especially for the Security Permit. A great deal of patience and possibly a little backsheesh may help. On the whole the Egyptian authorities are not familiar with 'cruising' as it is known to us and to most other authorities in the Mediterranean.

THE SUEZ CANAL

The canal was opened in 1869. It is 87.5 miles long of which 66.5 miles is canal and the remainder lakes. Procedures for handling the required paperwork for a transit appear to change from year to year, but at the Port Said Yacht Club the staff are most helpful and there is a scrapbook of useful information contributed by those who have tackled the task ahead of you. Many of those who have negotiated the obstacle course to clear through the canal would consider engaging an agent for the second time around. The charges made by an agent seem to vary widely – I've heard figures ranging from £80 to £200. You can do your own paperwork (allow 2-3 days) as follows.

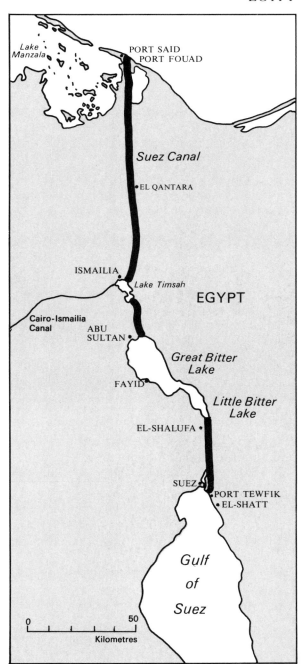

i. Go to the Small Craft Department at the main building of the Canal Authority. The director will prepare letters to: Credit and Commerce Bank; Ports and Lights Authority; the Harbour Police; the Immigration Office; and Misr Insurance Company. You must then visit the following offices.

ii. Customs Authority office to obtain the Customs Clearance Certificate.

iii. Credit and Commerce Bank. Pay the canal transit fees (payable in travellers' cheques or

A *felucca* on the Nile

dollars only) whereupon you will be given a draft for the Canal Authority.

iv. Misr Insurance Company to obtain the insurance policy.

v. Ports and Lights Authority in Palestine Street and the Maritime Inspection Office also in the same street to pay the port and light fees and inspection fee. You then obtain the Harbour Clearance Permit.

vi. Harbour Police station to obtain the Security Clearance Certificate.

vii. Return to the Small Craft Department at the Canal Authority building where the yacht will be inspected and a transit permit issued. You will then be informed at what time the pilot will come aboard for the transit of the canal to Ismailia.

viii. With the boat's papers, transit permit, and passports, go to Immigration to be stamped in.

The official costs are as follows, though I cannot vouch that these will be the actual costs in practice.

Customs dues   E£20
Health certificate   E£5
Departure fees   E£1
Canal customs clearance fees   E£11 (E£28.60 on holidays and weekends)
Transit fees   US$10 per person, US$20 for the yacht
Insurance   E£8 for yachts under 100 tonnes
Ports and Lights dues   E£7 (E£14 after normal working hours, holidays, or weekends)
Pilot dues   US$52
Security Clearance Certificate dues   E£25.30

In addition to the normal entry requirements, if you are going up the Nile the following procedure must be followed:

i. Customs inventory: An inventory of all the boat's equipment will be made by a customs representative and a Customs Clearance Certificate and a Departure Certificate issued.

ii. Security Permit: This must be applied for at the Port of Entry, which will be Alexandria, and as it can take some time to obtain, it should be applied for well in advance.

The pilot who will join you for the transit of the canal will be a fourth grade pilot who will know little about yachts and may in fact know little about the canal. He is really along for the ride while you do the work and will expect a tip once you are through.

RIVER NILE

It is difficult to arrange the permit to navigate on the Nile but with persistence and the help of the Yacht Club of Egypt it can be arranged. The Nubaraya Canal from the western harbour of Alexandria to Cairo has least depths of 1.65m. It is used by the commercial motor barges running between Alexandria and Cairo. The depths in the Rashid entrance to the Nile (at the western end of the delta) are variable with constantly shifting sandbanks. In the Nubaraya Canal and the upper reaches of the Nile you must take down your mast(s) to get under the bridges (about 3m clearance). To make way against the stream (3-4 knots in places) and to get off sandbanks you will need a powerful engine.

Note Passage up the Nile should be made only in the winter months (October to May) as in the summer the depths in the river decrease considerably.

FORMALITIES

A yacht entering Egyptian waters should be flying a 'Q' flag. At Port Said you may be met by a pilot boat which will direct you to the Port Said Yacht Club. If you plan to stay within the confines of the harbour (Port Said is a free port) and simply want to transit the canal then you will not need a visa. If you wish to explore inland then a visa must be obtained and it is best to get it before you enter Egypt although you will not be turned away if you do not have one. If you are going through the canal you will be visited by a representative of the Suez Canal Company who will detail the paperwork necessary and issue you with a handful of forms. In Alexandria you should go to the eastern harbour (not the western commercial harbour) where the Yacht Club of Egypt is a helpful contact. While in Egypt you must change a certain amount of money every month, currently US$150 per person per month, and keep the official receipts to prove you have done so.

PROVISIONING

Stores can be ordered at Port Said but some care must be taken over the description of what you are to get from the chandler as goods stated to be fresh have been reported to turn up in tins! However this is really the only place to provision after Cyprus if you are heading down the Red Sea.

CHARTS AND PILOTS

Admiralty *Mediterranean Pilot* Vol V (NP49). Covers Egypt.
Admiralty *List of Lights and Fog Signals* Vol E (NP78).
Red Sea and Indian Ocean Cruising Guide. Alan Lucas. Imray. Port Said to the Far East and Australia.
Egypt For Yachtsmen. A booklet issued free by the Egyptian Tourist Office. Yachtsmen using the booklet report that the information in it should be treated with caution, but nonetheless some of it will be of use.
Admiralty charts for the coast are adequate and there are large scale plans of the Suez Canal.

USEFUL BOOKS

The Alexandria Quartet. Lawrence Durrell. Faber. Required reading if you are going to Alexandria.
Fodor's Guide to Egypt. Hodder and Stoughton.
Berlitz Guide to Egypt.
Arabia Through the Looking Glass. Jonathan Raban. Fontana. No holds barred look at Egypt and the other Arab countries.
Alexandria: A guide. E. M. Forster.

PORT SAID

Approach The numerous ships anchored off, and the Port Said and Damietta lighthouses identify the port. Proceed down the buoyed channel to the harbour. If you have problems call up the Pilot Station at Port Said on VHF channel 16.

Mooring Berth at the Port Fouad Yacht Club just before the ferries that cross the canal. A club member will help you sort out the entry formalities.

Facilities Water. Fuel can be arranged. Minor repairs possible. Charts from *Marinekart*. Provisions in Port Said. Local bars and restaurants.

General Take the ferry across to Port Said for provisions and eating out.

ALEXANDRIA

Approach A yacht should make for the eastern harbour rather than the western. Rasel-Tin lighthouse and Fort Quaid Bey are conspicuous. Closer in the monument to the unknown soldier and several minarets will be seen.

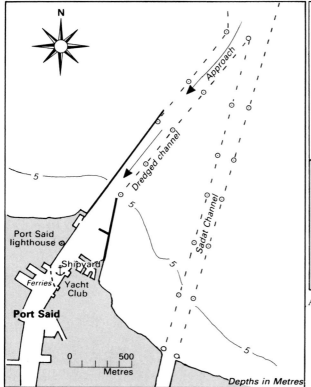

Approaches to Port Said 31°18′N 32°18′E

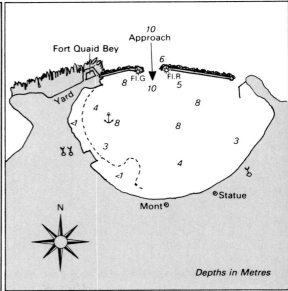

Alexandria Eastern Harbour 31°12′.8N 29°53′.5E

Mooring Anchor in the western side of the harbour. With strong northerlies the harbour is uncomfortable and in gale force northerlies could be dangerous.

Facilities The Yacht Club of Egypt based near Fort Quaid Bey will help with formalities. Water and fuel can be arranged. Provisions and restaurants nearby. Slipways and repair yards in the harbour.

General The Yacht Club of Egypt makes you an honorary member and administers charges for the harbour. They will also assist you to make arrangements for passage up the Nile. The trip from the mouth of the Nile to Cairo is calculated to take around 12 to 14 days by the time you have negotiated the opening bridges and run aground a few times.

Libya

Area   1,759,537 square kilometres (679,400 square miles)

Population   3,400,000

Capital   Tarabulus (Tripoli) and Benghazi (joint capitals)

Language   Arabic. Some Italian and English spoken

Religion   Islam (exclusively)

Time zone   G.M.T. + 2

Currency   dinar (D) = 1000 dirhams

Electricity   125 or 220V AC

Banks   Most credit cards, cheque cards and travellers' cheques accepted

Internal travel   Good cheap bus service to most destinations

International travel   International flights to Tripoli and Benghazi

You should not attempt to enter Libya without a visa, which is very difficult to obtain. The Libyan government does not need tourism to top up its vast oil revenues and indeed goes out of its way to discourage it. One yachtsman who visited Tripoli without a visa was simply put into prison for three weeks and then without explanation given twenty-four hours to leave. Not surprisingly he did — with alacrity.

It is reported that a chain of marinas is to be built at intervals along the Libyan coast. However these are for Libyans exclusively, and not for foreign yachtsmen although perhaps in the future foreigners will be permitted to utilise what will no doubt be lavishly equipped marinas.

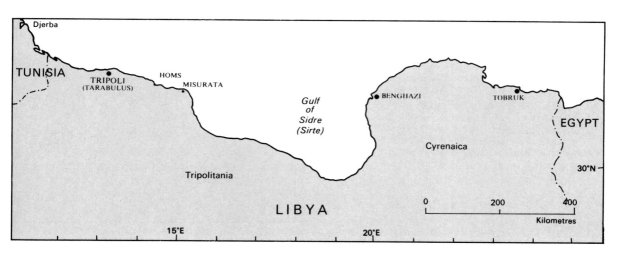

Tunisia

Area   164,000 square kilometres (63,362 square miles)

Population   7,600,000

Capital   Tunis

Language   Arabic. French commonly spoken

Religion   Islam

Time zone   G.M.T. + 1;   D.S.T. (April-September)

Currency   Tunisian Dinar (D) = 1000 millimes

Electricity   220V 50Hz AC

Banks   Open 0800-1100 Monday to Friday in the summer. Open 0800-1100 and 1400-1615 Monday to Thursday, 0800-1100 and 1330-1515 Friday in the winter. Major credit cards, Eurocheques, and travellers' cheques accepted in the cities and tourist centres.

Mail   Generally reliable. *Poste restante* letters are returned to the sender after two weeks so if your arrival date is uncertain have your mail sent to a private address (e.g. a marina).

Medical   Ranges from adequate in the cities to poor in the less populated areas. Fees range from moderate to high.

Internal travel   Some internal flights. Buses and trains are inexpensive but nearly always crowded. *Louages* are shared taxis (six people usually) covering more or less a fixed route at a reasonable price. Hire cars are costly.

International travel   Tunis is the centre for international flights. In the summer there are also international flights to Monastir and Djerba. Ferries run from Marseille, Genoa, Naples and Palermo to Tunis. Hydrofoil service in the summer from Trapani to Kelebia via Pantelleria.

Public Holidays
January 1 and 18
March 20
April 9
May 1
June 1
July 25
August 3 and 13
September 3
October 15
Moveable: Festival of the Sheep, Ramadan (end: 2 days), Prophet's Birthday, Moslem New Year

GEOGRAPHY

COAST AND ISLANDS   The coast of Tunisia extends eastwards from the Algerian border for approximately 160 miles to Cape Bon then turns south for about 330 miles to the border with Libya.

Cape Bon, the northeasternmost extremity of Tunisia is the pivotal point in the narrow Sicilian channel which separates the western from eastern Mediterranean.

The north coast between Tabarka and Cape Bon is flanked by high mountains although there are

extensive coastal flats and some shallows extending seaward. This area is more fertile than that of the eastern seaboard with extensive cultivation along the coast including many market gardens and citrus orchards. The eastern seaboard becomes progressively more low-lying with the great wastes of the Sahara meeting the sea between Chebba and the Libyan border. Shallows extend seawards for some considerable distance in places along this coast. The vegetation decreases the further south you go until the desert is encountered, although there are oases surrounded by date palms which provide welcome ribbons of green amid the sands. The fabulous oasis at Gabes, the last jumping-off spot for the desert, is a little piece of paradise in the Sahara with date palms shading vegetable patches. Meagre grazing grounds along the coast give way to the desert which then stretches clear into Libya.

Tunisian National Tourist Board

Bizerte

CRUISING AREAS The Tunisian National Tourist Board produces a map showing four cruising areas: from Tabarka to Cape Zebib; Cape Zebib to Cape Bon (the Bay of Tunis); Kelibia to Chebba; and Chebba to Zarzis. In practice it is easier to think of two cruising areas: the north coast between Tabarka and Cape Bon on which there is one marina, two harbours with a yacht club, three fishing harbours and some anchorages; and the east coast between Kelibia and Zarzis on which there are two marinas, fourteen harbours and many anchorages.

The two cruising areas differ quite dramatically, the northern coast is mountainous and navigation along it is straightforward with few shallows fringing the coast. The eastern coast is mostly low-lying with shallows S of Monastir extending some distance offshore requiring care and an eye on the depth sounder. A considerable tidal range S of La Chebba adds to navigation problems.

CLIMATE AND WEATHER

The climate is North African with high summer temperatures and mild winters, however winter nights can be chilly. There is little rainfall and invariably it occurs briefly in torrential downpours. The amount decreases from north to south with about 750mm in Tabarka, 420mm in Tunis, 325mm in Sousse and less in the far south.

WINDS The prevailing winds in the summer are northerlies although there are local variations along the coast as follows:

Along the north coast summer winds are mainly from the W to NE with predominant NW winds between Tabarka and Bizerte and N to SE winds in the Gulf of Tunis. In the winter westerlies are the most frequent.

S of Cape Bon the wind regime is markedly different with onshore easterly winds in the summer and offshore winds in winter. In the summer the sea breeze usually starts in the morning from the NE and after veering to the SE dies down towards sunset. In springtime it can reach up to Force 5-6.

In winter the situation is reversed with mostly westerlies.

Sirocco, called *Chihli* in Tunisia, is a hot and dusty Sahara wind which can occur in autumn or spring. It is more noticeable on the E coast and usually of short duration.

Seaweed grows abundantly along the entire E coast of Tunisia, sometimes rendering entrance to the smaller fishing ports impossible. South of Monastir and around the Kerkenah Islands it has a calming effect on the waves and in these areas one can sail in strong winds in unusually calm water.

GALES Are rare in the summer with the exception of the N coast around Bizerte where strong northwesterlies are common all year around and gales occur regularly in winter. On the E coast gales are rare in summer and not frequent in winter but strong easterlies can put up quite a sea at Kelibia due to the long fetch making it impossible to enter the port. In the Gulf of Gabes gales are more frequent than further N around Sousse. In the Sicilian Channel gales from the W can blow with considerable violence and since the waves can travel a long distance it can be exceptionally rough. (A wave height of 10 metres has been recorded.)

THUNDERSTORMS May occur occasionally in the summer but are most frequent in the autumn, they will be recognised as a dark line of cloud moving rapidly. These thunderstorms are usually accompanied by heavy rain and a strong squall and are generally over in·one to three hours.

TIDES AND CURRENTS In the Sicilian Channel there is a constant SE current which averages about 1 knot in the summer. Currents off the Tunisian coast are weaker but of unpredictable direction and they can affect navigation when on passage from Pantelleria or Lampedusa. The tides in the north of Tunisia are negligible and can be ignored for most purposes but south from La Chebba the tidal range starts to become noticeable and in Gabes it reaches a spring range of 1.8 metres. In the shallow waters around the Kerkenah Islands, the range reaches up to 1 metre and one has to take care of strong tidal currents in the channels around the islands and allow sufficient depths when anchoring. Strong onshore winds can increase the range. In the Ajim channel between the Island of Jerba and the mainland tidal currents are even stronger and navigation is dangerous due to the lack of a reliable buoying system.

The *marrobbio* affects Tunisia as well as southern Sicily and the Balearics. This is a form of tidal surge with a period of between 10 and 26 minutes which can raise and lower the water level by 0.6 to 0.9 metres. It occurs during undisturbed weather and there are no real warning signs. Fortunately it is quite rare.

WEATHER FORECASTS French from the following stations (Times are G.M.T.):

Tunis 1820, 2670, 2182 kHz at 0805 and 1705
Sfax 2719, 2200 kHz at 0933 and 1733
La Goulette (local forecast only) 1743, 2182 kHz at 0405 and 1905
Radio Tunis. Chaine International 963 kHz at 0630, 1230 and 1630 G.M.T.

The Italian weather forecasts for southern Sardinia and the Sicilian Channel are also useful as is the weather forecast from Malta.

HARBOURS AND ANCHORAGES

WHAT TO EXPECT There are three marinas in Tunisia: at Sidi Bou Said, El Kantaoui and Monastir. There are two yacht clubs, in Bizerte and La Goulette, a marina/fishing port in Tabarka and work on a new marina in Jerba is starting in 1990. Plans exist for marinas at Ghar El Melh and Hammamet. The other harbours are either fishing or commercial ports. The fishermen are friendly and helpful and will often help you find a berth and tie up. There are numerous anchorages but most of them are only suitable in fair weather.

Tunisian National Tourist Board

At Gabes

SECURITY The Tunisians are by and large honest but normal precautions should be taken, especially in the large cities and popular tourist resorts. The marinas are very safe, but be a little more careful in the fishing ports as most of the time you lie along public quays.

WINTERING AFLOAT The marinas at Sidi Bou Said, El Kantaoui and Monastir are the usual places for yachts wintering afloat. A number of yachts have reported enjoyable winters afloat in Tunisia. The marinas of Monastir and El Kantaoui sometimes offer special incentives to attract winter customers. Malta is a short distance away should you desire the facilities there.

PASSAGE PLANNING

GENERAL There are no obvious routes other than to follow the coast leaving a reasonable margin of time for going north if you are planning to return.

SPECIFIC On passage to or from Tunisia there are three popular routes:
i. From Carloforte on the southwest tip of Sardinia to Tabarka, Bizerte or Sidi Bou Said on the north coast.
ii. From Trapani or Marsala on the southwest coast of Socily to Sidi Bou Said or Kelibia.
iii. From Malta to Kelibia via Pantelleria or from Malta to El Kantaoui or Monastir via Lampedusa.

NAVIGATION AIDS

Buoyage I.A.L.A. System 'A' was officially introduced in 1980-81. Buoyage is good around the commercial ports but unreliable elsewhere. Some care should be taken to get the latest information on buoyage in the southern parts of Tunisia where you will often be navigating from buoy to buoy or following buoyed channels in the extensive shallows off the coast.

Lights The coast is well lit but Tunisian lights, especially harbour entrance lights, do have a reputation for being frequently out of action.

Radiobeacons The radio beacon on Pantelleria (Italian) is useful when on passage to Tunisia from Sicily.

Marine Radiobeacons

West Mediterranean group 313.5 kHz
   Cap Bon BN 200M every 6 min. Seq. 1, 2.
   Ras Caxine (Algeria) CX 200M every 6 min. Seq. 3, 4.
   Porquerolles (France) PQ 200M every 6 min. Seq. 5, 6.

El Attaia KR 308 kHz 100M. Seq. 3, 4.[1].
Cap Blanc BC 310.3 kHz 100M. Seq. 3, 4.[2].
Pantelleria PT 287.3 kHz 90M. Seq. 1, 2[3]
[1]Continuous in fog and ev. H + 02, 08, 32, 38.
[2]Occasionally inoperative.
[3]Continuous in fog and ev. H + 00, 06, 30, 36. Grouped with Cozzo Spadaro and Augusta (See Italy page 95).

Air Radiobeacons

Gabes GAB 267 kHz 33°53′N 10°06′E
Jerba/Zarzes JER 371 kHz 33°52′.5N 10°44′.8E.
Tunis KDN 385.5 kHz 36°49′.4N 10°18′.5E

Coast radio stations
Most commercial ports and marinas keep a listening watch on VHF Channel 16.
Main operating frequencies are shown in bold type.
All times are G.M.T.
All stations offer a 24 hour service unless otherwise stated.

Station	Transmits (kHz or VHF Channel)	Listens (kHz or VHF Channel)	Traffic Lists (Freq. & times)
Sfax (3VS)	2182, 2200, **2719** VHF Ch. 05, 16, 22, 24	2182	2719 at ev. odd, H+ 35 0600-2400 0600-2400
Mahdia (3VM)	**1771,** 2182, 2190 VHF Ch. 16, 27, 28	2182	
Tunis (3VX) (3UT)	**1820,** 2182, 2670 VHF Ch. 16, 1, 10, 12, **18, 21,** 25, 26	2182	1820 at 0120, 0250, 0450, 0615, 0805, 0950, 1205, 1350, 1620, 1750, 2005, 2150, 2350
Bizerte (3VB)	2182 VHF Ch. 16, **23,** 24	2182	0700-1900

FORMALITIES

ENTRY FORMALITIES A yacht entering Tunisia for the first time must go to a port of entry where the requisite officials for clearing in a yacht are stationed. You must remain aboard until you have been stamped into the country. At the port of entry you will have your passports stamped by the frontier police for a three month period, renewable for another three months. E.C. nationals (with the exception of Benelux citizens) do not require a visa. Customs *(Douane)* will want a list of goods liable to duty and will then issue you a *triptique* (often called a *dyptique*) which permits you to cruise in Tunisian waters for the period stated. Normally the period is three months but this is renewable for another three months out of any one year. The harbourmaster ('marine marchand' in commercial ports and CGP officials in fishing ports) will want to know how long you intend staying and details of your yacht so that he can calculate harbour dues. Harbour dues in fishing ports (a small sum) have to be paid per week and unused days can be utilised in subsequent fishing ports. At subsequent harbours you may or may not encounter the following officials who will want to see your *triptique* and will want crew lists: the national guard (either the maritime branch or the land branch), the local police, the harbourmaster and customs. When leaving a har-

bour, advise the national guard of your next destination and pay the harbourmaster. In practice these formalities are not as time consuming as they may sound and are generally carried out in an amiable fashion by the officials concerned. Moreover formalities are becoming more relaxed as yachting develops in Tunisia.

When leaving Tunisia you must surrender your *triptique* to customs and be stamped out of the country by the frontier police. A yacht may cruise in Tunisian waters for any six months out of a year. If you wish to winter your yacht in Tunisia, afloat or on the hard, you must make arrangements with customs to have it put in containment. In practice this usually means giving your *triptique* to customs and getting it back when you plan to leave or resume cruising in Tunisia. You may live aboard the yacht during the period of containment.

Ports of Entry (north to south): Tabarka, Bizerte, Sidi Bou Said, La Goulette, Kelibia, El Kantaoui, Monastir, Sfax, Gabes, Houmt Souk (Djerba), Zarzis.

DOCUMENTS The Small Ship's Register Papers or full registration papers are both acceptable. Insurance documents should be carried and a ship's stamp is useful.

Tunisian National Tourist Board

The port at Tabarka

TAXES Modest harbour dues only. If you stay over the six month period specified in the *triptique* without putting your yacht in containment then Article 8 of a 1980 Decree states that 'Rights are suspended and taxes levied if this occurs.' The amount of the tax is not stated. Marina fees payable where applicable. Yachtsmen who stay in Tunisia for an uninterrupted period of 6 months are liable for a resident tax of TD45 (approximately £60) per person.

FACILITIES

EVERYDAY

Water Generally a sufficient supply of good quality water is available in all the ports but for sensitive stomachs it is useful to boil it. The marinas have water points for each berth and in the other harbours there is always a tap somewhere but you may have to carry jerry cans.

Fuel Is obtainable from pumps in almost every port. Diesel is quite oily and smelly and not of the best quality but unless taken from a pump with dirty tanks it works alright.

Electricity Is available in the marinas and if you carry sufficiently long extension cords and a few tools it can be arranged in many ports.

Gas Is cheap and available in large bottles in every town. *Camping gaz* and European DIN type propane bottles can be refilled. With an open-ended hose on your bottle you can often get a refill from a local bottle.

Paraffin Available as 'Petrol Blue' at many service stations. The quality varies from good to mediocre.

BOAT REPAIRS

Engines Spares cannot be found but competent mechanics can be found in the larger centres and at the marinas.

Electrics Competent electricians can be found in the larger centres only. Electronic repairs are best undertaken in Malta.

Navigation instruments Spares and new equipment cannot be found. Go to Malta or Italy.

Paints and antifoulings Yacht quality paint cannot be found. Locally produced antifouling under Transocean licence is available. The quality is good and price very reasonable. Imported brands of antifouling are not available.

Hauling There are travel hoists in Sidi Bou Said and El Kantaoui and eventually Monastir will have one. Cheap hauling out is possible with 250-tonne travel hoists in the fishing ports of Tabarka, Bizerte, Kelibia, Monastir (new fishing port) and Sfax. Some of these can be used by yachts but usually there is no high-pressure hose and water may not be easily available.

Engineering Good engineering shops that will make almost anything at a reasonable cost can be found in most cities and larger towns.

Wood and GRP Woodwork skills are not developed and it is difficult to find boat carpenters experienced in yacht work. GRP skills are low. A shipyard in La Goulette builds GRP fishing boats.

PROVISIONING

GENERAL Except in the small villages, basic provisions can be obtained everywhere although imported goods are non-existent except in the cities and large tourist centres. In the major towns there are the French Monoprix supermarkets which have a good range of local and imported goods. All the towns and larger villages have excellent markets for local produce, not only fruit and vegetables but meat, fish, herbs and spices, staples and bread as well. It is best to go early to get the best choice. Most of the fruit and vegetables are seasonal and by the end of the summer the choice is limited.

Shopping hours vary somewhat but are generally 0830-1230 and 1300-1530 Tuesday to Saturday. Some shops will close on a Friday and open on Sundays.

The fishing port at Ghar el Melh

Tunisian National Tourist Board

179

SPECIFIC

Meat Is reasonably priced but the quality is not always the best, it is not hung and is often butchered in a strange way. Chicken is good value and is usually bought live, though it will be killed and dressed for you if you ask. Turkey is excellent if you can find it. Being an Islamic country, pork is not for sale, but during the hunting season you may get wild boar in the north.

Fish Fish is abundant, fresh and cheap compared to other Mediterranean countries.

Fruit and vegetables Seasonal. Excellent in the spring and early summer, less choice in late summer.

Staples Most basics can be found but stock up in the Monoprix when you can.

Cheese Imported cheeses are expensive. Local cheese, some of the processed variety and those resembling Camembert and Gervais, are good.

Canned goods Limited variety and not cheap.

Coffee and tea Instant coffee is expensive. French coffee is not overly expensive. Local tea doesn't make a British 'cuppa' but is acceptable — use it for lemon tea.

Wines, beer and spirits Local wines vary from terrible to good. For a Muslim country Tunisia has a surprising selection but none of the wines are cheap due to high taxes. Beer is relatively cheap and drinkable. Imported spirits are expensive. Local spirits, *boukka* made from figs and *thiba* made from dates, are an acquired taste. In general stock up on wines, beer and spirits before coming here.

Recommended Herbs and spices bought loose.

EATING OUT Most of the dishes are Arabic in origin with the ubiquitous cous-cous being virtually a national dish as it is for the rest of the Maghreb. Most of the dishes are hot, flavoured with a pureé of chilli peppers called *harissa*, although some of the tourist restaurants tone down this fiery sauce for palates less accustomed to chillis. There are also French restaurants serving French cuisine. Prices vary from moderately expensive in the more sophisticated restaurants to very cheap in the smaller local restaurants.

You should try cous-cous, which is a granule manufactured from hard durum wheat and looks not unlike semolina. It may be served with a variety of meat or fish sauces and cooked vegetables.

You should try cous-cous, which is a granule manufactured from hard durum wheat and looks not unlike semolina. It may be served with a variety of meat or fish sauces or just with *harissa*.

You may be offered a soup, *sdirr* thickened with cous-cous, or *chorba*, a thick soup. Salads are good value and contain many fresh vegetables and often olives, cooked vegetables, tuna, cheese — whatever is on hand. Meatballs, a species of *moussaka (Tajin)*, and roast lamb are often on the menu. Also the Arabic version of scrambled eggs *(oujja)*, with tomatoes, onions, pimento and *harissa*, a variation is to put a fried egg on top (it is then *chakchouka*).

You should also try *brik*, a thick pancake which can be bought from vendors with a variety of fillings, egg being popular. Sweets and pastries are either French influenced or of the sticky sweet eastern Mediterranean variety.

CHARTS AND PILOTS

Admiralty *Mediterranean Pilot* Vol. 1 (NP 45).
Admiralty *List of Lights and Fog Signals* Vol. E (NP78)
North Africa Pilot. RCC Pilotage Foundation. Imray. Up-to-date yachtsman's pilot covering the Tunisian coast.
A Bridge and Galley Guide to Tunisia. Ann Maurice and Bryan Lockyear. McMillan-Graham. Slightly outdated but interesting sailing guide.
The Admiralty charts for the area are adequate but the charts of the French Hydrographic Service (S.H.O.M.) give the best coverage of the area, although they are not updated as well as Admiralty charts.

USEFUL BOOKS

Fodor's Guide to North Africa. Hodder and Stoughton.
Berlitz Guide to Tunisia.
The Rough Guide to Tunisia. RKP. Good basic guide.

Algeria

Area 2,382,000 square kilometres (919,600 square miles)

Population 24,100,000

Capital Algiers

Language Arabic, but some French and English spoken.

Religion Islam

Time zone G.M.T. D.S.T. + 1

Currency Dinar

Electricity 220V AC

Banks Travellers' cheques or cash are accepted in the banks. Credit cards are not accepted anywhere. Exchange regulations are strict; all foreign currencies must be declared on a special form which is checked on departure and all change transactions are marked on it. In 1989 each foreign visitor to Algeria was required to change DA 1000 (roughly £100 at the official exchange rate) but this was not strictly enforced on yachtsmen. In practise most likely you will be allowed to change what money you need. Although there is a thriving black market it is advised to stay away from it as penalties are severe.

Internal travel Compagnie Nationale Air Algérie flies to all major towns. Trains run to many places and are cheap. Buses run to most destinations but are crowded. Taxis are expensive.

International travel Flights from Algiers to most European destinations.

GEOGRAPHY

THE COAST There is approximately 570 nautical miles of coastline between Morocco on the west and Tunisia on the east. From the west roughly up to Oran the sparsely populated coast is made up of steep hills with several uninhabited islets and the Habibas Islands a short distance offshore. From Oran to Algiers green wooded lower hills slope gently towards the shore and several villages line the coast although not many with a port. From Algiers eastward the coast becomes increasingly mountainous towards the beautiful Bay of Bejaia and this landscape terminates abruptly in Annaba from where the coast becomes low until the Medjerda mountain range which makes up the border with Tunisia.

CLIMATE AND WEATHER

Of the North African type. The summers are hot and dry, the winters are mild with a considerable amount of rain along the coast and in the Atlas mountain range. The predominant summer winds west of Algiers are N and NW and east of Algiers N and NE but winds often follow the coast. The eastern part of the coast can have very stable and strong easterly winds in July and August during daylight hours making a trip in this direction impossible. However, as is common in other parts of the Mediterranean, there are numerous days of no wind at all. In the winter winds are predominantly from SW to NW and on average they are less strong than in spring and summer. Gales are rare in winter except along the eastern part of the coast where northerly gales can be dangerous as the coast is completely exposed from this sector.

WEATHER FORECASTS are transmitted from the following coast radio stations in French:

Annaba (7TB) 1743, 2775 kHz at 0920, 1033, 1720, 1833. Storm warnings on receipt. Area 4.

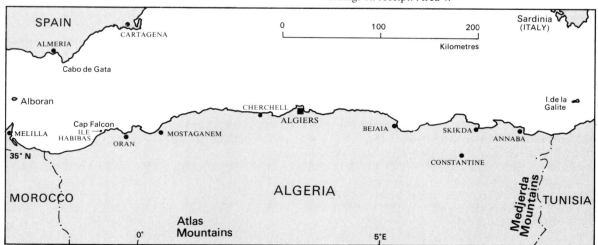

Algiers (7TA) 1792, 2691 kHz at 0903, 1703. Storm warnings on receipt. Areas 1-5.
Oran (7TO) 1735, 2586, 2719 kHz at 0920, 1033, 1720, 1735. Storm warnings on receipt. Area 2.
A forecast is sometimes available from the port captain.

HARBOURS

There are a few anchorages which provide shelter from either the west or east but good shelter is only found in the ports. The commercial ports of Oran, Arzew, Algiers and Annaba are among the largest on the North African coast and as they are not very clean and because authorities are abundant these ports are not particularly interesting. Entry in the port of Algiers is forbidden for yachts. Visiting yachts will find a better welcome in the smaller commercial and fishing ports although they offer few facilities. Distances between the ports allow day hopping but some early departures will be necessary and sufficient time should be reserved to fulfill formalities in each port. Apart from the only marina in Sidi Ferruch (also called Sidi Fredj) there are yacht clubs in the commercial ports of Oran and Annaba. Eight fishing ports, five more commercial/fishing ports and a few fair-weather anchorages complete the Algerian cruising grounds. Even though some of the fishing ports are completely packed the fishermen will often make room for visitors. Keeping in mind that all of the ports are the working place for fishermen and cargo ships the waters are clean and oil pollution is rare.

NAVIGATION AIDS

Buoyage I.A.L.A. System 'A' was introduced in 1980. Buoyage is good around the commercial harbours but is non-existent elsewhere.

Lights The coast and commercial harbours are reasonably well lit but are not always to be relied upon.

Radiobeacons The coast is well supplied with radiobeacons (some temporarily inoperative).

Marine Radiobeacons

West Mediterranean group 313.5 kHz.
 Ras Caxine CX 200M every 6 mins. Seq. 3, 4.
 Porquerolles (France) PQ 200M every 6 mins. Seq. 5, 6.
 C. Bon (Tunisia) BN 200M every 6 mins. Seq. 1, 2.

Grouped on 298.8 kHz.
 Ras el Hamra GD 50M Seq. 1, 2.
 Ras Bougaroun CB 50M Seq. 5, 6.

Ras Matifou MF 296.5 kHz 30M.
Algiers AL 305.7 kHz 20M[1].
Fog only and synchronised for distance finding.

Ras Tenes TS 296.5 kHz 30M. Seq. 3, 4.
Mostaganem MN 305.7 kHz 5M.

South-east Spain group 294.2 kHz
 Ras Aiguille AG 100M. Seq. 1, 2.
 C. de Palos (Spain) PA 50M. Seq. 3, 4.
 C. de la Nao (Spain) NO 50M. Seq. 5, 6.

Air Radiobeacons

Jijel/Taher DJI 340 kHz 50M 36°48'.8N 5°52.'4E
Dellys DEL 370 kHz 50M 36°55'N 3°54'E
Cherchell CHE 397 kHz 50M 36°37'N 2°12'E
Mostaganem MOS 334 kHz 100M 35°54'.5N 0°08'.2E
Annaba ANB 366 kHz 60M 36°50'.4N 07°47'.2E
Oran OLN 265 kHz 200M 35°39'.3N 00°37'.6W
Bejaia BJA 423 kHz 36°42'.3N 05°01'.5E
Zemmouri ZEM 359 kHz 36°48'.1N 03°37'.1E

Coast radio stations Some Algerian coast radio stations maybe temporarily inoperative
 Most commercial ports keep a listening watch on VHF channel 16.
 Main operating frequencies are shown in bold type.
 All times are G.M.T.
 All stations offer a 24 hour service unless otherwise stated.
 Most commercial ports keep a listening watch on VHF channel 16.

Station	Transmits (kHz or VHF Channel)	Listens (kHz or VHF Channel)	Traffic Lists (Freq. & times)
Annaba (7TB)	**1911**, 2182, 2394 VHF Ch. 16, 24, 25, 26, 27, 28	2182	2182 at ev. H+50
Skikda (7TS)	VHF Ch. 16, 26, 18		
Bejaia (7TG)	VHF Ch. 16, 25		
Alger (7TA)	**1792**, 2182, 2691, 2775 VHF Ch. 16, 24, 25, 26, 27, 28	2182	1972 and ev. odd H+03
Oran (7TO)	**1735**, 2182, 2586, 2719 VHF Ch. 16, 24, 25, 26, 27, 28	2182	2182 at ev. even H+35

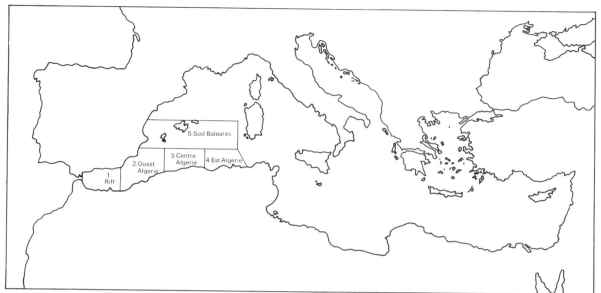

Algerian weather forecast areas.

The commercial port of Bejaïa formerly called Bougie.

Anchorage in the Habibas Islands near Oran.

FORMALITIES

Entering Algeria for the first time it is best to go to one of the larger harbours or Sidi Ferruch, a purpose built marina 15 miles west of Algiers. Customs and immigration police are stationed in all harbours and as likely as not there will be a coastguard detachment as well.

Customs may want to search a yacht but a glimpse inside may suffice as well. Holders of British passports do not need a visa for Algeria but holders of American and Canadian passports do and for Europeans the procedure varies from country to country. It is possible to visit the Algerian ports without a visa but you will have difficulty in obtaining a *Permis d'Escale* in some of the commercial ports which means you cannot leave the harbour area. Upon first entry in Algeria a 'Declaration of Gold and Foreign Currencies' is made up and all subsequent change transactions are marked on it by the bank. When leaving Algeria the currency count on this form may be checked to see if a sufficient amount for your stay has been changed. If weapons are on board these should be declared on the same form. You will be stamped in the country for 2 or 3 months and you clear in and out in each harbour you visit. When first encountered Algerian officials appear surly and ill-mannered, but most yachtsmen have found that after a short acquaintance they are friendly and helpful. In the past yachts on passage to or from Gibraltar and close to the Algerian coast have been asked by patrol boats to accompany them to the nearest port but with Algeria being visited by a small but slowly increasing number of yachts no such incidents have been reported in recent years.

FACILITIES

Basic facilities (water, fuel, ice etc.) can be found in most of the ports. The water quality varies but in general it is best to be careful and as bottled water is not available it is wise to stock up in advance. Good quality diesel is very cheap. There is a 16-tonne travel hoist in Sidi Ferruch. Facilities for yacht repairs do not exist but emergency repairs can usually be cobbled up.

PROVISIONING

Provisioning in Algeria can be difficult. Before oil and gas revenues declined many food products were imported but in recent years even the basics have sometimes become scarce. Bread, milk, meat, chicken and a limited assortment of fruits and vegetables can usually be found but things like cooking oil, butter, cheese and canned products are hard to come by. Many of the ordinary wines are very heavy and not cheap but for just a little more some very good red wines can be found.

EATING OUT On the whole meals are expensive and standards are mediocre to poor. When the French left Algeria restaurants often changed hands so that although a façade may be imposing and interesting the food inside may be a poor imitation of French cuisine.

CHARTS AND PILOTS

Admiralty *Mediterranean Pilot* Vol. 1 (NP45)
Admiralty *List of Lights and Fog Signals* Vol. E (NP78)
North Africa Pilot. RCC Pilotage Foundation. Imray. Covers the Algerian coast.

USEFUL BOOKS

Fodors Guide to North Africa. Hodder and Stoughton.
Traveller's Guide to North Africa. J. C. Publications.

Tunisia. Cap Monastir Marina with Ile Sidi el Rhedamsi in the foreground.

Morocco

Area   450,000 square kilometres (240,160 square miles)

Population   24,800,000

Capital   Rabat

Language   Arabic. French and some Spanish along the north coast.

Religion   Islam

Time zone   G.M.T.

Currency   Dirham (DH) = 100 centimes

Electricity   220V AC

Banks   Open 0830-1500 Monday-Friday. Eurocheques, major credit cards, and travellers' cheques accepted.

Medical   Adequate to poor. Medical fees are moderate to high. It is recommended that you go to Gibraltar for treatment if possible.

Internal travel   Royal Air Maroc serves the major cities with reasonably priced flights. Two classes of buses operate almost all over the country. Fares are cheap and services reliable. The CTM luxury buses are usually not as crowded as the normal buses. Good trains with first and second class operate between the major cities. Petit taxis run local routes for fixed prices and normal taxis are cheap. Hire cars are expensive.

International travel   International flights to Tangier, Rabat, Casablanca. Fez, Oujda, Marrakech and Agadir. Casablanca is the principal international airport. Ferries from Gibraltar to Tangier and Ceuta, from Algeciras to Tangier and Ceuta, from Málaga to Melilla, and occasionally from Toulon to Tangier and Casablanca.

Public holidays
March 3 Independence Day
May 1 Labour Day
July 9 Youth Festival
Moveable: Ras el Am, New Year's Day, Ashoura, Memorial Day, Mouloud, Birth of Mohammed, Aid-es-Seghir, End of Ramadan, Aid-el-Kebir

GEOGRAPHY

COAST   It has been said that Morocco is surrounded by three seas: the Mediterranean, the Atlantic and the Sahara. The Mediterranean coast extends approximately 170 miles from the Spanish enclave Ceuta to the Algerian border. Most of it is flanked by the inaccessible Rif mountains and several strategically located rocks and islets off the coast are still in Spanish hands as well as the enclaves of Ceuta and Melilla.

CLIMATE AND WEATHER

Climate is of the Mediterranean type with hot summers and mild winters. The great Atlas mountain range is covered in snow in the winter.

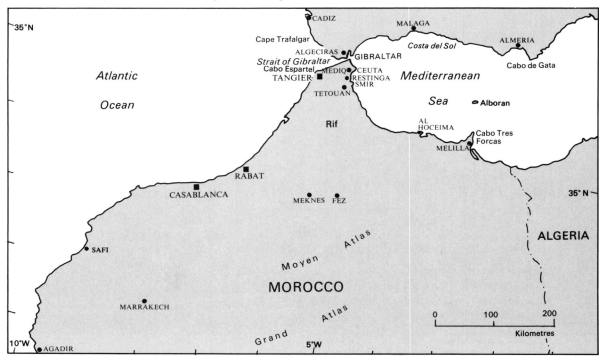

For winds in the Strait of Gibraltar see the notes on page 65. From Tangier it can be difficult to get out of the bay with the prevailing onshore winds, most yachts leave very early in the morning when the wind tends to be lighter. Off the North African coast eastwards of the Strait winds in the summer tend to be from the west-northwest or northeast and occasionally from the southeast. The average wind strength is not high and calm days are common in the summer. In the winter westerly and northwesterly winds are predominant.

Weather forecasts for the Strait of Gibraltar are broadcast from Gibraltar and for the North African coast from Spain. (See the relevant sections on Gibraltar and Spain.)

HARBOURS AND ANCHORAGES

There are four fishing ports, one nearly finished marina at Restinga Smir and the Spanish ports of Ceuta and Melilla which both offer facilities for yachts. Al Hoceima is a busy fishing port with a small quay reserved for visiting yachts, set in one of the prettiest bays along the North African coast. There are a few settled weather anchorages which can be used if authorities are advised. Tangier on the Atlantic coast is becoming a popular stopover for yachts en route to and from Gibraltar and it is a good jumping-off point for the Canary Islands.

NAVIGATION AIDS

Buoyage I.A.L.A System 'A' was introduced in 1980 but buoys are a rare phenomena.

Lights The coast is moderately well lit and the lighthouses work most of the time but port entrance lights cannot be relied upon.

Radiobeacons
Marine Radiobeacons

Cabo Espartel SP 312.6 kHz 200M. Seq. 1, 2.
Ceuta CE 305.7 kHz 6-10M (directional) ev. 3 mins.
Beam centred 158° leading to entrance.
Signed 'N' on 2° sector E of beam 'A' on 2° sector W of beam.
[1]Continuous in fog and for 30 mins at 0600, 0900, 1200, 1800, 2300.

Air Radiobeacons

Nador NDR 384 kHz 35°10′N 2°56′W
Tetuan/Sania Ramel TUN 285 kHz 35°37′N 5°17′W
Tangier TBR 324 kHz 35°44′.7N 05°50′.9W
Melilla MLL 292 kHz 50M 35°18′N 02°57′W

The naval and fishing port of Al Hoceima, formerly Villa Sanjurjo set in the Bay of Al Hoceima.

FORMALITIES

Compared to some other Arabic countries formalities in Morocco are easily dealt with and do not require much time. Officials will always show up soon after arrival if they are not waiting for you on the quay when tying up. The immigration police (or *Gendarmerie* in smaller ports) will check passports which usually are kept in custody along with the ship's papers (usually photocopies are accepted). Visas are only required from Benelux country citizens. Customs operate in Tangier and Al Hoceima only, and when planning a trip inland this should therefore be done from either port or once finished, from the new marina in Restinga Smir. When leaving the boat alone for more than a few hours it can be useful to arrange for a 'guardian' to watch your boat although chances of theft in Morocco are probably less than in Spain. The guardian is a typical feature of the Moroccan ports and a token payment, cigarettes or spirits will usually suffice. No harbour dues are charged for normal stays of a few days.

DRUGS TRAFFICKING

The Rif mountains along the north coast of Morocco are the traditional growing area for marijuana, called *kif* in Morocco. Transportation routes to Europe are multiple and every year shipments are found on board yachts. Most likely one will only become aware of this trade when spending more time than a holiday but new patrol boats have been purchased for coastal surveillance and occasionally they check yachts out at sea. Because of the drug trafficking one should not anchor along the coast unless authorities have been informed in advance. Failing to do so and going ashore in some deserted part of the coast will lead to strong suspicion of drugs trafficking and one will almost certainly be arrested for questioning. Having warned about this particular problem it has to be said that yachts arriving with honest intentions will have nothing to fear when cruising along the Moroccan coast.

FACILITIES

Specialist yacht facilities are virtually non-existent in Morocco, however with a little persistence and the help of a 'guardian' you can make do for simple repairs. For major repairs and maintenance it is best to cross to Gibraltar or Spain.

PROVISIONING

Shopping for provisions is good in the large centres although imported goods are expensive. Every village has a market and there will be a good selection of staples, poultry, cheeses, herbs and spices, etc., as well as fresh fruit and vegetables.

EATING OUT Restaurants in Morocco fall into two categories: the cheaper local restaurants serving kebabs, *boulbaf, kefta,* cous-cous, etc. and the *haute cuisine* of the rich which can be very good at reasonable prices by European standards. Mint tea is the standard drink in Morocco but wines are made here and some of them are reported to be excellent.

CHARTS AND PILOTS

Admiralty *Mediterranean Pilot* Vol. 1 (NP45). Covers the Mediterranean coast of Morocco from Ceuta.
North Africa Pilot. RCC Pilotage Foundation. Imray. Covers the Moroccan coast.

USEFUL BOOKS

The Traveller's Guide to Morocco. Christopher Kinmonth. Jonathon Cape.
Morocco. Neville Barbour. Thames and Hudson.
The Rough Guide to Morocco. RKP. Good guide to out of the way spots.

APPENDIX

I. USEFUL ADDRESSES

TOURIST OFFICES IN LONDON

Gibraltar Gibraltar Tourist Office, 4 Arundel Great Ct., Strand, London WC2.

Spain Spanish National Tourist Office, 58 St James St., London SW1A 1LD. *Tel.* 071 499 0901

France French Government Tourist Office, 178 Piccadilly, London W1V 0AL. *Tel.* 071 493 3171

Italy Italian State Tourist Office, 1 Princes St, London W1R 8AY

Malta Maltese Tourist Office, 16 Kensington Square, London W8

Yugoslavia Yugoslav National Tourist Office, 143 Regent St., London W1.

Greece Greek National Tourist Organisation, 195-7 Regent St., London W1.

Turkey Turkish Tourism Information Office, Egypt House, 168 Piccadilly, London W1V 9DE.

Cyprus (South) Cyprus High Commission, 211 Regent St., London W1

Syria Syrian Consulate, 8 Belgrave Square, London SW1

Lebanon Lebanese Consulate, 15 Palace Garden Mews, London W8.

Israel Israel Government Tourist Office, 18 Great Marlborough St., London W1.

Egypt Egyptian Tourist Office, Egypt House, 168 Piccadilly, London W1V 9DE. *Tel.* 071 493 5282

Libya No diplomatic relations at the time of going to press.

Tunisia Tunisian National Tourist Office, 7a Stafford St., London W1

Algeria Algerian Consulate, 54 Holland Park, London W11

Morocco Moroccan Tourist Office, 174 Regent St., London W1

Albanian Society, 26 Cambridge Rd., Ilford, Essex IG3 8LU.

OTHER USEFUL ADDRESSES

Cruising Association, Ivory House, St Katherine's Dock, London E1 9AT. *Tel.* 071 481 0881

Royal Yachting Association, R.Y.A. House, Romsey Rd., Eastleigh, Hampshire SO5 4YA. *Tel.* (0703) 629 962 *Telex* 47393 BOATIN G *Fax* (0703) 629 924

Ministère de l'Equipement et du Logement, Direction des Ports Maritimes et des Voies Navigables, 2e Bureau, 244 Boulevard St Germain, 75 Paris 7. (For a list of current *chomages* on the waterways)

Touring Club de France Service Nautique, 65 Avenue de la Grande Armée, 75782 Paris, Cedex 16 and at 178 Piccadilly, London W1V 0AL.

Little Ship Club at The Naval Club, 38 Hill St., London W1X 8DP.

Shell International Petroleum Co Ltd, SPS/3113, Shell Centre, London SE1. (For the Shell Credit Scheme)

Port Said Yacht Club, Port Said, Egypt. (Helpful in the Suez Canal transit)

Amateur Radio Licensing Unit, Chatwynd House, Chesterfield, Derby S49 1PF

Gibraltar Licensing Authority, Postal Telegraph and Telephone Office, Second Floor, Main Street, Gibraltar

National Tourist Organisation of Greece, 3 Amerikis St., Athens. *Tel.* 322 3111

BOATMINDERS

Eurovoiles S.A., Route de la Plage 83400, Hyères Port, France. *Tel.* 94 38 60 33 Telex 404737 EDEN

Sibaris Marina, Cantieri Nautici di Sibari, Localita Sibari, Cosenza, Italy. *Tel.* 0981/74271 *Telex* 800072 CABI.

Contract Yacht Services, Petrou Filippa 3a, Levkas, Greece. *Tel.* 0645/24490 *Telex* 0342 108 LETR.

Roger Stafford, 29 Grigoriou E' Street, Kastella, 185 34 Piraeus, Greece. *Tel.* 4136416, 4134469. *Telex.* 241623 STAF GR.

Frank's Yacht Station, Frank Wenzlaff, Odos Costa 2, Porto Kheli, Greece.

II. BEAUFORT WIND SCALE

WIND STRENGTH All wind strengths are described as a force on the Beaufort scale. To get the wind speed in knots from its force, multiply the Force by 5 and then subtract 5 (up to Force 8).

Sea State	Beaufort No.	Description	Velocity in Knots	Velocity in Km/h.	Term	Sea State Code	Height of waves/metres
Like a mirror	0	Calm	<1	<1	Calm glassy	0	0
Ripples	1	Light airs	1-3	1-5	Calm rippled	1	0-0.1
Small wavelets	2	Light breeze	4-6	6-11	Smooth wavelets	2	0.1-0.5
Large wavelets	3	Gentle breeze	7-10	12-19	Slight	3	0.5-1.25
Small waves, breaking	4	Moderate breeze	11-16	20-28	Moderate	4	1.25-2.5
Moderate waves, foam	5	Fresh breeze	17-21	29-38	Rough	5	2.5-4
Large waves, foam and spray	6	Strong breeze	22-27	39-49			
Sea heads up, foam in streaks	7	Near gale	28-33	50-61	Very rough	6	4-6
Higher long waves, foam in streaks	8	Gale	34-40	62-74			
High waves, dense foam, spray impairs visibility	9	Strong gale	41-47	75-88	High	7	6-9
Very high tumbling waves, surface white with foam, visibility affected	10	Storm	48-55	89-102	Very high	8	9-14
Exceptionally high waves, sea covered in foam, visibility affected	11	Violent storm	56-63	103-117	Phenomenal	9	Over 14
Air filled with spray and foam, visibility severely impaired	12	Hurricane	>63	>118			

III. COPTIC CALENDAR

Below is reproduced an extract from a Coptic almanac which shows when strong winds can be expected. The Copts are a Christian sect living in Egypt and Ethiopia, the Christian descendants of the ancient Egyptians who became Monophysites and split from the general church at the Council of Chalcedon in A.D. 451. About 12 per cent of Egypt's population are Copts. I reproduce the extract from the almanac for the reader to use with discretion but I have found the accuracy to be about 60 per cent. Why or how such a chart works I haven't a clue but any aid to forecasting gales, however odd it might appear, is a welcome bonus to the other more commonly accepted methods.

The list of gales shows the date on which it can be expected, the Arabic name, the direction, the translation of the Arabic name (phonetically rendered as near as possible) and the duration of the gale. Deviation is rarely more than 48 hours either way.

Date	Name	Direction	Type (translation)	Duration
27 Sept	*El Saleeb*	W	Cross	3 days
21 Oct	*El Saleebish*	W	Crusade	3 days
+26 Nov	*El Micness*	W	Broom	3 days
+6 Dec	*Kassim*	SW	Gale	7 days
20 Dec	*El Fadrel Saggra*	SW	Small gale	
+11 Jan	*El Fadrel Saggra*	S	Strong gale	3 days
19 Jan	*El Fedra El Kibirain*	W	Feeder	5 days
27 Jan	*El Fedra El Kibirain*	W	Feeder	2 days
+18 Feb	*El Shams El Saggira*	NW	Feeder	5 days
10 Mar	*El Hossom*	SW	Brings the Equinox	8 days
+20 Mar	*El Shams El Kabira*	E	Big sun gale	2 days
25 Mar	*Hawa*	E	A wind	
29 Apr	*Khaseen*	E	Sand wind	2 days
16 Jul	*El Nogia*	E	Black wind	2 days

+ Indicates a severe gale!!

IV. MARINE DISTRIBUTION AND SERVICE AGENCIES (MAIN DISTRIBUTORS)

While every care has been taken collecting these addresses nonetheless caution should be used especially if work is being carried out under warranty. A telephone call or letter to the U.K. distributor to check on warranty agreements is advised by the author as there have been incidents where the parent company has refused to pay a distributor and the unfortunate yachtsman has been landed with the total bill.

NAVIGATION EQUIPMENT

Brookes and Gatehouse Ltd.

SPAIN
Dahlberg, 32 Nicholas de Pax, Palma de Mallorca 1

FRANCE
Grimaud Marine Electronic, 3 Rue de L'lle Longue, Port Grimaud, 83360

ITALY
Champion Marine snc, Via Andrea Doria 17, Milan 20124

MALTA
Fabian Enterprises, 20 Msida Road, Gzira

GREECE
Internaftiki Co. Ltd., 130 Kountouriotou Street, Piraeus 7

TURKEY
SOS Bodrum, Neyzen Tevfik Cad 214, Bodrum. *Tel.* (6141) 2610. *Telex* 52567 SOHA TR.

Lucas Marine Ltd

SPAIN
Lucas Service Espana, S.A., Avenida Fuentemar 23, Poligono Industrial, Coslada, Madrid

FRANCE
Lucas Service France, S.A.R.L., 26 à 32 rue Lavoisier, 92002 Nanterre, BP 210

ITALY
Lucas Ricambi Spa., Viale Brianza 166, 20092 Cinisello Balamo, Milan

MALTA
Mizzi Brothers Limited, 203 Rue Dargens, Msida.

GREECE
Lucas Service Hellas, S.A., 72, Constantinoupoleos Avenue, Athens 308

CYPRUS
P. D. Orphanides, Mercury Divers Company Limited, Head Office Division, P.O. Box 469, Limassol

Seafarer Navigation International Ltd.

All deal with radar equipment except *

GIBRALTAR
Marine Electronics Company Limited, P.O. Box 235, 33 Irish Town. *Tel.* 4417

The Yachtsman, Benady Barton Limited, 4/16 Queensway. *Tel.* 70252/71182

SPAIN
Berry Marine Electronics, P.O. Box 65, San Pedro de Alcantara, Málaga. *Tel.* 52 81 37 49

Electronica Trepat, Calle San Fernando 10-16, Barcelona 31

La Industrial Velera Marsal S.A., Muntadas 8 Y 10, Barcelona 14. *Tel.* 325 50 62

Marco Auxiliar de Comercio Exterior, S.A. (Macoexsa), C/Parque No. 3, Barcelona 2. *Tel.* 318 51 84

Payma S.L., Enrique Larreta, 9, Madrid 16. *Tel.* 733 20 50

Ridamar S.A., Muntaner, 114, Barcelona 36. *Tel.* 254 34 51

*Rudo S.A., C/Anoia, S/n Naves 30 y 31, Poligono Ind Urvasa, Santa Perpetua de la Moguda, Barcelona. *Tel.* 560 1453

Sitesa, S.A., Muntanér 44, Barcelona 11. *Tel.* 254 80 05

Yates & Motores S.A. (Yamosa), Astillero 8 y 10, Barcelona 3. *Tel.* 315 3412

Balearic Islands
Berry Marine Services S.L., Paseo Maritimo, 35, Palma de Mallorca. *Tel.* 71 23 7558

*Centromar S.A., Paseo de Mallorca,15, Palma de Mallorca. *Tel.* 71 23 15 49

FRANCE
Avon S.A., 4 Rue Francois Moisson, 13002 Marseille. *Tel.* 91 90 71 71

GMT ETS Wingfield, Galerie du Port, Rue Lacan, 06600 Antibes. *Tel.* 93 34 23 87

Radio Ocean, 78 Bis, Rue Villiers de L'Isle-Adam, Paris XXe. *Tel.* 358 16 16

S A R L Pierre Gueguen & Cie, 53 Avenue de la Perrière, 56100 Lorient. *Tel.* 97 37 08 66/37 15 57

*Tecnimer, ZI, Du Bois De Leuze, 13310 Saint-Martin De Crau. *Tel.* 90 47 01 10.

ITALY
Finder Spa, P.O. Box 92, Via Giordano Bruño 2/E, 00053 Civitavecchia. *Tel.* 0766 24601

MALTA
Medcomms Limited, 4 Msida Road, Gzira. *Tel.* 35521

GREECE
Cherma Electronics S.A., Electronics Building, 26 Bouboulinas Street, Piraeus. *Tel.* 411 9121/35

Electromarine Company, 143 Leoforos Dimokratias, Keratsini, Piraeus. *Tel.* 46 33 651

Electronava, Kolokotroni, 156, Piraeus 10. *Tel.* 452 6636

Internaftiki Company Limited, 130 Kountouriotou Street, Piraeus 7. *Tel.* 4126 997

Marel Electronics Company S.A., 6 Sotiros Dios Street, Piraeus. *Tel.* 412 3943

Marac Electronics S.A., 455 Dimokratias Ave, Ikonio, Piraeus. *Tel.* 46 26 216/46 17 530

*G Milionis — S Zarganes Inc. 10 Ionos Dragoumi Street, Thessaloniki. *Tel.* 268 140

Naftiki Hellas Limited, P.O. Box 1167, 31 Satovriandou Street, Athens 101. *Tel.* 529 588

Nautex Marine Limited, 16 Mavromichali Street, Hatzikyri-akion, Piraeus TT26. *Tel.* 412 6733

Piraeus Electronics, 50 Har Tricoupi Avenue, Piraeus. *Tel.* 453 1027

Radiohellenic Limited, 81 Atki Miaouli Street, Piraeus. *Tel.* 45 20 000/45 11 879

A Rokka, 19 Kountouriotou Street, Thessaloniki. *Tel.* 513 050

*Sail Company, 11 Akti Moutśopoulou, Piraeus 17. *Tel.* 417 95 45/417 95 46

Telectronics Company Limited, 5 Kalimnou Street, Moschato, Piraeus. *Tel.* 952 1008

Zarganis Kanellakis S.A., Store 5, Tsimiski Street, Thessaloniki.

TURKEY
Intermarin Denizcilik AS, Cumhuriyet Caddesi, No. 295, Harbiye, Istanbul. *Tel.* 48 38 10/40 12 24

*Skantur Otomobil Ticareti, Sehit Muhtar, Cad. 36/A, Taksim, Istanbul. *Tel.* 45 54 10

Target Electronic Systems Company Limited, Tekiner Is Han Kat, 3/305, Nushet, Sokak, No. 11, Kadiköy, Istanbul. *Tel.* 49 16 82

CYPRUS
A P Hadjipieros, 14A Sikinou Street, Zakaki, Limassol. *Tel.* (51) 63905

Mercury Divers Company Limited, P.O. Box 469, 53 Spyrou Araouzou Street, Limassol. *Tel.* (51) 65492

Star Fiber Glass Limited, P.O. Box 1989, 23 Crete Street, Nicosia. Tel. (21) 49444/66121

ISRAEL
Sheba Trading Company Limited, P.O. Box 9170 - Post Code 61 091, 17 Totzeret HaAretz Street, Tel-Aviv. *Tel.* 253 579

ALGERIA
*Pavillon Marine, 12 Rue Larbi Ben M'Hidi, Oran. *Tel.* 33 06 87

Sharp Auto Pilots Ltd.
SPAIN
Sitesa, Muntaner 44, Barcelona 11. *Tel.* 010 34 3 93 2548005 *Telex.* 0061 54218

FRANCE
Grimaud Marine Electronics, 3 Rue de l'Ile Longue, 83360 Port Grimaud. *Tel.* 010 33 94 5628 04 and, 5629 43 *Telex.* 0022 970067

ITALY
Generalmare S.r.l., Via Trieste 8, 16145 Genova. *Tel.* 010 39 369066 and, 303198 *Telex.* 0023 211193

MALTA
Industrial Marine Repairs & Services Ltd., Mariner 1, Hay Wharf, Pieta Creek, Sa Maison. *Tel.* 010 356 629556 *Telex.* 0082 671

TURKEY
Suat Karaosman, Sisli, Elmadag Cad. 57, Istanbul. *Tel.* 010 90 11 482528 and 482170 *Telex.* 0084 22644

CYPRUS
Mercury Divers Co. Ltd., Head Office Division, P.O. Box 469, Limassol. *Tel.* 010 357 51 65492

MARINE ENGINES

BMW

SPAIN
BMW Iberica S.A., División Náutica, Paseo de la Castellana 149, Edificio Gorbea 2, E-Madrid 16. *Tel.* (1) 2 70 23 23 +, *2 70 28 06 + and 2 70 48 07 Telex.* 49341

FRANCE
BMW France, Département Moteurs Marins, 3 Avenue Ampère, B.P. 63, F-78 390 Bois d'Arcy. *Tel.* (3) 0 43 82 00 *Telex.* 698739

ITALY
BMW Italia S.p.A., Motori Marini, Casella Pastale 546, 1-37100 Verona. *Tel.* (045) 7180166 *Telex.* 480255

MALTA
Euch. Zammit & Sons Ltd. 148 Rue D'Argens, Msida. *Tel.* 3 30 01 + 3 30 04 *Telex* 376

YUGOSLAVIA
Tehno Union, Abt. 231 BMW, Vosnjakova 5, YU-61000 Ljubljana. *Tel.* (061) 3 20-8 55 *Telex* 31200

GREECE
Samouhos Bros. S.A., Sygrou Ave. 328-330, Athens. *Tel.* (01) 9 59 45 67 + 9 58 78 70 + 9 51 96 77 + 9 58 80 26 *Telex.* 214276

TURKEY
Mustafa Hikmet Müessesesi, Cagaloglu kled farer caddesi, Güven han kat 1/201, Istanbul. *Tel.* 22 41 98 + 28 56 65 *Telex.* 22915

CYPRUS
Char. Pilakoutas & Sons Ltd, P.O. Box 1168, 7 Larnaca St Nicosia. *Tel.* (021) 7 63 12/3/4 *Telex.* 2245

Hawker Siddeley Marine Ltd. (Petter & Lister)

ITALY
Diesel Commerciale, 16128 Piazza Cavour 85, Genova. *Tel.* 291587 *Telex.* 213864 DICOM 1

Marind Soc. ARL, P.O. Box 1338, 1-34100 Trieste 3. *Tel.* 68-326 *Telex.* 460337 MARS

GREECE
N P Lanitis (Hellas) S.A., 1 Ipirou Street, Athens 103. *Tel.* 8228-947 & 8220-710 *Telex.* 216385 OBO GR

Zafiris Xanthis, 24 Akti Kondyli, Piraeus 24. *Tel.* 4175 457 *Telex.* 212659 INDU GR

CYPRUS
N P Lanitis Co. Ltd., Limassol. *Tel.* 051 66161 *Telex.* 2384 PLANITIS CY

Perkins

GIBRALTAR
J. Lucas Imossi & Sons Ltd., 1/5 Irish Town, P.O. Box 167. *Tel.* 3465 *Telex.* 2221 IMOSSIGK ·

SPAIN
Motor Iberica S.A. (Division Zona 2), Carretera del Aero-Club, Carabanchel Alto, Madrid. *Tel.* 208 52-40, 208 96-40, 208 98-40 *Telex.* 27324 AIE — Office 23593 AIE

FRANCE
Moteurs Perkin S.A., 9-11 Avenue Michelet/Boîte Postale 69, 93402 Saint Ouen/Cedex. *Tel.* 257 14 90 *Telex.* Per Koil 642924

ITALY
Motori Perkins S.P.A., Via Gorizia 15, P.O. Box 12, 22070 Portichetto Luisago (Como). *Tel.* (031) 927364 (10 lines). *Telex.* 380658 PERKIT I

MALTA
International Automobiles, 363 Rue D'Argens, Gzira. *Tel.* 30001/2/3. *Telex.* 450 GASAN MW

YUGOSLAVIA
Motora Rakovica, Industrija Patrijarha Dimitrija 7-13, Rakovica, Belgrade. *Tel.* 562-043 562-322 562-992. *Telex.* 11341 YU IMR

GREECE
Petros Petropoulos S.A., P.O. Box 18, Egaleo, 96 Iera Odos, Athens 301. *Tel.* 3473300. *Telex.* 216189 PIPI GR

TURKEY
Dizel Makina Ltd., Sirketi, Cumhuriyet Caddesi No. 10/c, Sisli, Istanbul. *Tel.* 473675, 460941. *Telex.* 26357 Elig TR

CYPRUS
Char. Pilakoutas & Sons Ltd. P.O. Box 1168, Larnaka Road, Nicosia. *Tel.* 76312/3/4. *Telex.* 2245 Pilaku CY

ISRAEL
N. Feldman & Sons Ltd., 137A Jaffa Rd, P.O. Box 9720, Haifa 31096. *Tel.* 528255. *Telex.* 46679 Felso IL

EGYPT
Egyptian Engineering & Trading Co., (H. Degheidy Company), P.O. Box 2167, 45 Champollion Street, Cairo. *Tel.* 755229, 755887. *Telex.* 93815 DEGED UN.

TUNISIA
ETS Louis Montenay, 49 Avenue De Carthage, Tunis. *Tel.* 240-312/240-324. *Telex.* SECFA 12043 TN

Society Tunisienne de Metallurgie, Rue Immam Al Boussoiri, 2038 Ben Arous, B.P. 18, Tunisia. *Telex.* MECAM 13055 TN

MOROCCO
Dimateq, 83, Boulevard de la Resistance, Casablanca. *Tel.* 30 15 62. *Telex.* Dimateq 26907 M

SAAB

ITALY
Andrea Patania, Via XX Settembre 11, 1-96100 Siracusa (Sicilia)

MALTA
Medway Marine Ltd., 11 Enrico Mizzi Str., Msida. *Tel.* 51 25 55

TURKEY
Skantür Otomobil, Ticareti, Sehit Muthar Cad. 36/A, Taksim, Istanbul. *Tel.* 45 54 10

CYPRUS
Star Fiber Glass Ltd., Box 1989, Nicosia. *Tel.* (66121) 49 44 4

Thornycroft

H. Sheppard & Co. Ltd., Waterport, P.O. Box 130, Gibraltar. *Tel.* 77183. *Telex.* 2324GK

FRANCE
British Leyland France, S.A., Division Vehicules Industriels, Rue Chauvart, B.P. 33 Gonesse. *Tel.* 987 25 24

Saint Line Cruisers, Port Des Poujats, La Collancelle, 58800 Corbigny. *Tel.* (86) 58 37 22

ITALY
British Leyland Italia, S.P.A., Via Paolo di Dono, 00142 Rome. *Tel.* 06 546811

MALTA
Valletta Motor Co., 30/39 Jetties Wharf, Marsa. *Tel.* 22395-30965

GREECE
General Automotive Co. S.A., P.O. Box 5200, Athens. *Tel.* 346-5321

CYPRUS
Star Fibre Glass Ltd., P.O. Box 1989, Nicosia. *Tel.* 66121-49444

EGYPT
Alexandria Supply & Marine Services Office, 71 Bab El Akhdar, 57, Gomrok, Alexandria. *Tel.* 22917

Seagull

SPAIN
British Seagull Espana, Hernan Courtes 38, Santander.

FRANCE
France Motors S.A., Z.1. Haut Galy, B.P. 127, 93600 Aulnay-Sous-Bois

ITALY
Eugenio Silvani s.a.s., Via Oropa 3, 21032 Milano.

GREECE
The British Seagull (Hellas) Co., 33 Leof Kalliroes, Athens 410

TUNISIA
Sotumo, 2 Rue Danton, Tunis, Tunisia

MOROCCO
Ets Damestoy, 26 Bvd. Mohamed El Hansili, Casablanca.

Volvo Penta

GIBRALTAR
H. Sheppard & Co. Ltd., Waterport, P.O. Box 130, Gibraltar. *Tel.* 77183 *Telex.* 2324 GK.

SPAIN
Volvo Concesionarios, S.A., Paseo De la Castellana 130, Madrid 16. *Tel.* 262 22 07. *Telex.* 23296 VOLCO E

FRANCE
Volvo Penta France, S.A., 1 Chemin de la Nouvelle France, Boite Postale 45, F-78130 Les Mureaux. *Tel.* 474 72 01. *Telex.* 695221

ITALY
Volvo Penta Italia, s.p.a., Via Copernico 20, 1-20090 Trezzano Sulnaviglio, Milano. *Tel.* 02 4458641/2/3/4/5. *Telex.* PENTA I 340650

MALTA
John Ripard and Son Ltd., 22 Lascaris Wharf, Valetta. *Tel.* 24862. *Telex.* 252

YUGOSLAVIA
JTP — RO Tankerkomerc, Gazenica bb, 57000 Zadar. *Tel.* 24-255. *Telex.* 27164

GREECE
Saracakis Brothers S.A., 71 Leoforos Athinon, P.O. Box 5200, Athens 301. *Tel.* 346 5321, 346 7011. *Telex.* 215420

TURKEY
ERK Mühendislik, Sanayi ve Ticaret Ltd Sti, Yildiz Caddesi Akdogan SOK No. 27, PK 535 Karaköy, Istanbul. *Tel.* 612434. *Telex.* 22999

CYPRUS
Marina Marine Enterprises Co Ltd., P.O. Box 1378, Limassol. *Tel.* 51 55405. *Telex.* 3497 MARINA CY

ISRAEL
Mayer's Cars & Trucks Co. Ltd., 23 Carlebach Street, P.O. Box 16164. Tel-Aviv. *Tel.* 289191. *Telex.* 342230

EGYPT
Orascom, Onsi Sawiris & Co., 160, 26th July St. Aguza, P.O. Box 296, Cairo. *Tel.* 650658, 818262. *Telex.* 92768 ORSCM UN

TUNISIA
Maghreb Nautisme S.A., Zone Industrielle-Ben Arous. Tunis. *Tel.* 298176. *Telex.* 13265 NAUMAG

ALGERIA
Volvo Bureau de Liaison, 13 Avenue Tarting, Kouba Alger. *Tel.* 582022

MOROCCO
Star Auto, 88 Boulevard Lalla Yacoute, Casablanca. *Tel.* 224161. *Telex.* SAIDA 21850

Watermota

FRANCE
E.H.M. S.A., 45 Rue Charles Nodier, 93310 Le Pre-St-Gervais. Paris. *Tel.* 845 03 94

ITALY
Autonautica Sprot srl., 00197 Roma, Piazza Santiago del Cile. *Tel.* 39 6874931

GREECE
Andreas & Lefteris Mniestris, Akti Moutsopoulou 50, Piraeus. *Tel.* 41 17 336

TURKEY
Sinan Ozer, Neyzen Tevfik Cad. 148, P.O. Box 155, Bodrum. *Tel.* 388

Mustafa Aras, Birlik Ticaret, Carsi Iskele Meydani 14. Bodrum. *Tel.* 344

Yanmar

SPAIN
Santa Eulalia S.A., Paseo de Gracia 60, Barcelona-7. *Tel.* 215 4216. *Telex.* 53138

FRANCE
Fenwick (Dept. Moteur), B.P. (P.O. Box 155, 111-113 Rue Du Docteur Bauer 93404 Saint-Ouen. *Tel.* 252 8285. *Telex.* 660390 FENMAR

ITALY
Stern Drive s.a.s., 20154 Milano-Via Losanna, 1. *Tel.* 02 312627, 02 3189145. *Telex.* c/o Italmarine Motori Euoriboredo Evintude 331134 Italmai

YUGOSLAVIA
Rodokomerc, our Inozastupstva 1 Konsignacije, 4000 Rijecta, Beogradski trg 3. *Tel.* 051 25 453, 051 33 533, 051 25 391. *Telex.* 24245 YU BRODOK

GREECE
Hadjikyriakos (Hellas) Ltd., P.O. Box 327, Piaeus, 67, Akti Miaouli, Piraeus. *Tel.* 4510918, 4130381. *Telex.* 213050 YMAR GR

TURKEY
Ranklin Ticaret Kontuari, Bdullah Hilmi Sismanoglu, Gilipazari Meclisi B Mebusan, Cad No. 487/2, Karaköy, Istanbul. *Tel.* 45 32 14. *Telex.* 24359 CENO TR

CYPRUS
Hadjikyriakos & Sons Ltd., PO Box 1587, Nicosia, Prodromos St 121, Nicosia. *Tel.* 42358. *Telex.* 2273 HADJIK CY

EGYPT
Futainasr Trading Co., 28(A), Talaat Harb Street, Cairo, P.O. Box 59. *Tel.* 974972. *Tel.* 2581 FUTNSR UN.

MOROCCO
J. J. Corsin S.A., 24 Rue Saint Savin, Casablanca. *Tel.* 241694, 244350, 244141, 245151. *Telex.* 21967M CORSINSA, MOROCCO

Univers Motors, Bd de la Corniche, Ain Diab, Casablanca. *Tel.* 25 81 15, 25 82 27. *Telex.* SOMVA 21718M

INFLATABLES
Tinker Inflatables, manufacturers of the *Tinker Tramp, Traveller,* and *Tinkeress,* and the survival packs for these, can arrange delivery to most parts of the Mediterranean. Contact:
Tinker Inflatables, J. M. Henshaw (Marine) Ltd, Verrington Lodge, Wincanton, Somerset, England, BA9 8BN. *Tel.* (0963) 33237 *Telex* 46123 LONGNC G.

V. USEFUL BOOKS

The following is a small selection of books relating to the Mediterranean that you may find useful. At the end of the sections on the countries there is a list of useful books for that country and these are not listed here.

HISTORY

The Mediterranean and the Mediterranean World in the Age of Philip II. Two volumes. Fernand Braudel. Fontana.

The Penguin Atlas of Ancient History and The Penguin Atlas of Medieval History Colin McEvedy.

The First Merchant Venturers William Culican. Thames and Hudson.

Sailing to Byzantium Osbert Lancaster. Murray.

Man and the Sea. Philip Banbury. Adlard Coles.

Eothen A. W. Kinglake. Century.

The World of Odysseus M. I. Finley. Pelican.

Mankind and Mother Earth Arnold Toynbee.

The Ancient Mariners Lionel Casson. Gollancz.

Long Ships and Round Ships John Morrison. H.M.S.O.

The Mediterranean: Portrait of a Sea Ernle Bradford.

In Search of the Trojan War Michael Wood. BBC publications

Beyond the Grand Tour. Hugh Tregaskis. Ascent.

GENERAL

Harvest of Journeys Hammond Innes. Fontana.

Fool's Paradise Brian Moynahan. Pan.

Ulysses Found Ernle Bradford. Sphere.

A Money-wise Guide to the Mediterranean Michael von Haag. Travelaid.

Lugworm Homeward Bound Ken Duxbury. Pelham.

The Plundered Past Karl E Meyer. Penguin.

The Traveller's Handbook ed. Ingrid Cranfield. Futura.

On the Shores of the Mediterranean Eric Newby. Harvill.

Larousse Encyclopaedia of Mythology London

Corsair Country. Xan Fielding. Secker & Warburg. O.P.

Marriner in the Mediterranean. John Marriner. Adlard Coles. O.P.

Black Sea and Blue River. John Marriner. Rupert Hart Davis. O.P.

The Innocents Abroad. Mark Twain. Signet.

Mediterranean Sailing. Rod Heikell. Nautical.

Isabel and the Sea. George Millar. Century.

FLORA

Flowers of the Mediterranean Anthony Huxley and Oleg Polunin.

The Oxford Concise Flowers of Europe Oleg Polunin.

The Natural History of the Mediterranean. Tegwyn Harris. Pelham.

MARINE LIFE

Hamlyn Guide to the Flora and Fauna of the Mediterranean Sea. A. C. Campbell.

Hamlyn Guide to the Seashore and Shallow Seas of Britain and Europe A. C. Campbell.

The Yachtsman's Naturalist M. Drummond and P. Rodhouse. Angus and Robertson.

Dangerous Marine Animals Bruce Halstead.

FOOD

Food in History Reay Tannahill. Paladin.

Mediterranean Seafood Alan Davidson. Penguin.

A Book of Mediterranean Food Elizabeth David. Penguin.

A Book of Middle Eastern Food C. Roden. Penguin.

ADMIRALTY PUBLICATIONS

The following British Admiralty publications are relevant. They are available from Admiralty Chart agents and Imray, Laurie, Norie & Wilson Ltd, Wych House, The Broadway, St. Ives, Huntingdon, England. *Tel.* St. Ives (0480) 62114. *Fax* (0480) 496 109

Charts. The complete index is in the *Catalogue of Admiralty Charts and other hydrographic publications* (NP131). Issued annually.

List of Lights and Fog Signals.
Vol. E (NP 78). Mediterranean and Black Sea.

Sailing Directions — Mediterranean Pilot
Vol. 1 (NP45). Covers West Mediterranean to the heel of Italy excluding France, Corsica, Sardinia and West Italy.
Vol. II (NP 46). Covers France, Corsica, Sardinia and West Italy.
Vol. III (NP 47). Covers the Adriatic and Ionian Seas.
Vol. IV (NP 48). Covers the Aegean Sea.
Vol. V. (NP 49). Covers Libya, Egypt, Middle East and Southern Turkey.

Radio Publications
Vol. I (NP 281 (1)) Coast radio stations.
Vol. II (NP 282) Radio navigation aids. Radiobeacons.
Vol. III (NP 283) Radio Weather Services.
Vol. IV (NP 284) List of Meteorological observation stations.
Vol. V (NP 285) Radio Navigation warnings.

VI. SOME FLIGHT DISTANCES

London (Heathrow) to:

Ankara	1765 (miles)
Athens	1500
Beirut	2162
Belgrade	1065
Cairo	2188
Lisbon	972
Madrid	774
Malta	1305
Milan	609
Naples	1011
Nice	647
Palma	833
Rome	907

VII. ARABIC NUMERALS

1	١	10	١٠
2	٢	20	٢٠
3	٣	30	٣٠
4	٤	40	٤٠
5	٥	50	٥٠
6	٦	100	١٠٠
7	٧	200	٢٠٠
8	٨	1000	١٠٠٠
9	٩		

VIII. INTERNATIONAL SEARCH AND RESCUE SIGNS

Require map and compass	□
Require fuel and oil	∟
All is well	∟∟
Require medical attention	—
Require medical supplies	=
Cannot proceed	X
Require food and water	F
Require an engineer	W
Yes	Y
No	N
Do not understand	⊐∟
Require light and radio	- -
Proceeding in this direction	↑
Indicate direction to be taken	K
Require clothing	≡
Shall try to continue	<1

IX. INTERNATIONAL TELEPHONE DIRECT DIALLING CODES

Principal country codes:

Algeria	213
Australia	61
Austria	43
Canada	1
Cyprus	357
Egypt	20
France	33
West Germany	49
Gibraltar	350
Greece	30
Israel	972
Italy	39
Lebanon	961
Libya	218
Malta	356
Monaco	3393
Morocco	212
Portugal	351
Spain	34
Tunisia	216
Turkey	90
United Kingdom	44
United States of America	1
Yugoslavia	38

Principal telephone access codes for direct dialling:

Austria	050
France	19
Greece	00
Italy	00
Monaco	19
Portugal	07
Spain	07
Turkey	99
United Kingdom	010
Yugoslavia	99

X. CONVERSION TABLES

	metres–feet			centimetres–inches				metres–fathoms–feet	
m	*ft/m*	*ft*	*cm*	*in/cm*	*in*	*m*	*fathoms*	*ft*
0·3	1	3·3	2·5	1	0·4	0·9	0·5	3
0·6	2	6·6	5·1	2	0·8	1·8	1	6
0·9	3	9·8	7·6	3	1·2	3·7	2	12
1·2	4	13·1	10·2	4	1·6	5·5	3	18
1·5	5	16·4	12·7	5	2·0	7·3	4	24
1·8	6	19·7	15·2	6	2·4	9·1	5	30
2·1	7	23·0	17·8	7	2·8	11·0	6	36
2·4	8	26·2	20·3	8	3·1	12·8	7	42
2·7	9	29·5	22·9	9	3·5	14·6	8	48
3·0	10	32·8	25·4	10	3·9	16·5	9	54
6·1	20	65·6	50·8	20	7·9	18·3	10	60
9·1	30	98·4	76·2	30	11·8	36·6	20	120
12·2	40	131·2	101·6	40	15·7	54·9	30	180
15·2	50	164·0	127·0	50	19·7	73·2	40	240
30·5	100	328·1	254·0	100	39·4	91·4	50	300

	kilometres–statute miles			kilograms–pounds			litres–gallons	
km	*M/km*	*M*	*kg*	*lb/kg*	*lb*	*l*	*gal/l*	*gal*
1·6	1	0·6	0·5	1	2·2	4·5	1	0·2
3·2	2	1·2	0·9	2	4·4	9·1	2	0·4
4·8	3	1·9	1·4	3	6·6	13·6	3	0·7
6·4	4	2·5	1·8	4	8·8	18·2	4	0·9
8·0	5	3·1	2·3	5	11·0	22·7	5	1·1
9·7	6	3·7	2·7	6	13·2	27·3	6	1·3
11·3	7	4·3	3·2	7	15·4	31·8	7	1·5
12·9	8	5·0	3·6	8	17·6	36·4	8	1·8
14·5	9	5·6	4·1	9	19·8	40·9	9	2·0
16·1	10	6·2	4·5	10	22·0	45·5	10	2·2
32·2	20	12·4	9·1	20	44·1	90·9	20	4·4
48·3	30	18·6	13·6	30	66·1	136·4	30	6·6
64·4	40	24·9	18·1	40	88·2	181·8	40	8·8
80·5	50	31·1	22·7	50	110·2	227·3	50	11·0
120·7	75	46·6	34·0	75	165·3	341·0	75	16·5
160·9	100	62·1	45·4	100	220·5	454·6	100	22·0
402·3	250	155·3	113·4	250	551·2	1136·5	250	55·0
804·7	500	310·7	226·8	500	1102·3	2273·0	500	110·0
1609·3	1000	621·4	453·6	1000	2204·6	4546·1	1000	220·0

INDEX